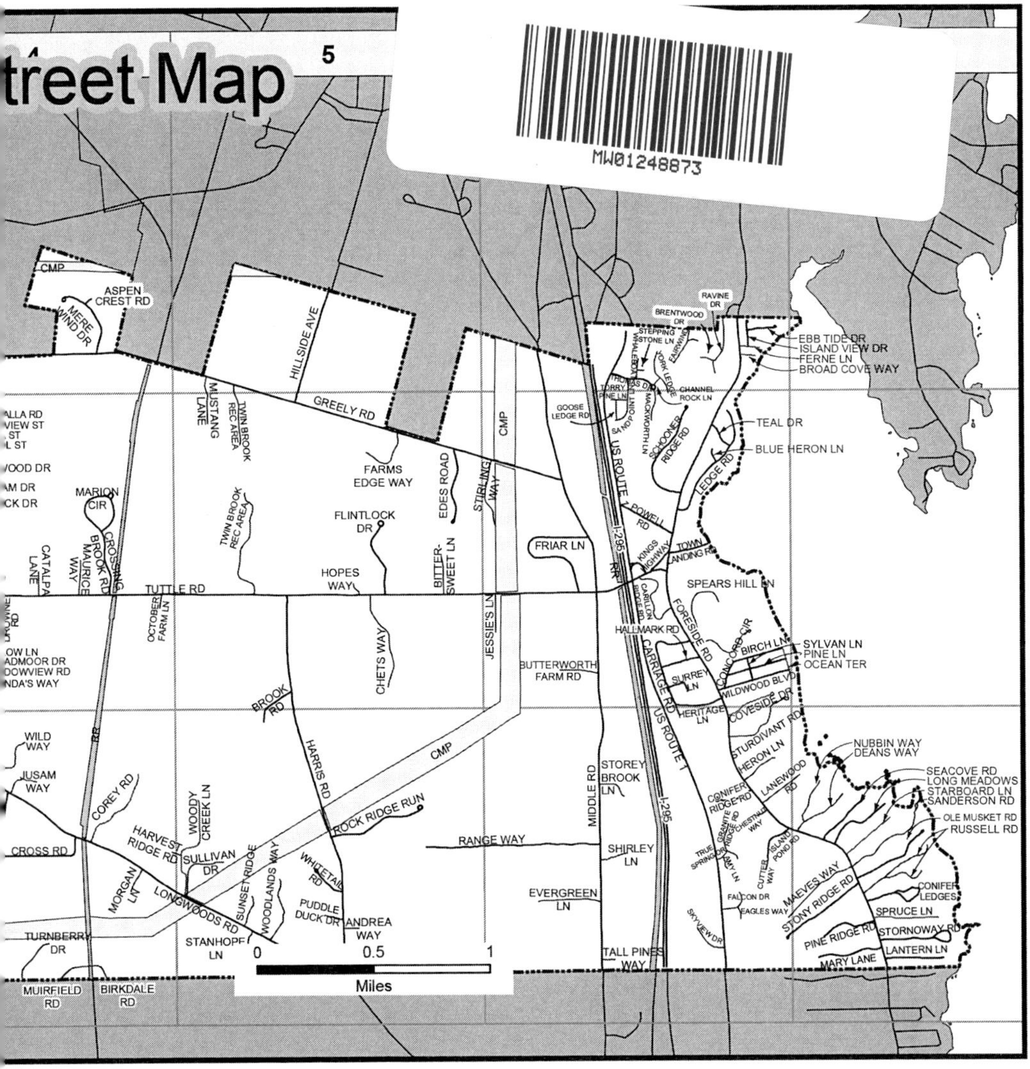

treet Map 5

MW01248873

CMP
ASPEN CREST RD
MERE WIND DR
HILLSIDE AVE
MUSTANG LANE
TWIN BROOK REC AREA
GREELY RD
FARMS EDGE WAY
EDES ROAD
STIRLING WAY
CMP
GOOSE LEDGE RD
TORRY PINE LN
US ROUTE 1
MACKWORTH LN
SCHOONER RIDGE RD
CHANNEL ROCK LN
YORK LEDGE
STEPPING STONE LN
BRENTWOOD DR
RAVINE DR
FAIRWAY
EBB TIDE DR
ISLAND VIEW DR
FERNE LN
BROAD COVE WAY
TEAL DR
BLUE HERON LN
LEDGE RD
POWELL RD
TOWN LANDING RD
KINGS HIGHWAY
FRIAR LN
SPEARS HILL LN
I-295
RR
MARION CIR
FLINTLOCK DR
TWIN BROOK REC AREA
BITTER-SWEET LN
HOPES WAY
CATALPA LANE
MAURICE WAY
BROOK RD
CROSSING
TUTTLE RD
OCTOBER FARM LN
JESSIE'S LN
CHETS WAY
CARILLON RIDGE RD
HALLMARK RD
FORESIDE RD
CONCORD CIR
BIRCH LN
SYLVAN LN
PINE LN
OCEAN TER
BUTTERWORTH FARM RD
SURREY LN
CARRIAGE RD
WILDWOOD BLVD
COVESIDE DR
HERITAGE LN
US ROUTE 1
STURDIVANT RD
BROOK RD
HARRIS RD
CMP
WILD WAY
JUSAM WAY
COREY RD
WOODY CREEK LN
HARVEST RIDGE RD
SULLIVAN DR
ROCK RIDGE RUN
RANGE WAY
STOREY BROOK LN
MIDDLE RD
HERON LN
LANEWOOD RD
CONIFER RIDGE RD
NUBBIN WAY
DEANS WAY
SEACOVE RD
LONG MEADOWS
STARBOARD LN
SANDERSON RD
OLE MUSKET RD
RUSSELL RD
CROSS RD
MORGAN LN
LONGWOODS RD
SUNSET RIDGE
WOODLANDS WAY
WHITETAIL RD
PUDDLE DUCK DR
ANDREA WAY
SHIRLEY LN
TRUE SPRING DR
GRANITE RIDGE RD
CHESTNUT WAY
ISLAND POND RD
CUTTER WAY
FALCON DR
EAGLES WAY
MAEVES WAY
STONY RIDGE RD
CONIFER LEDGES
SPRUCE LN
STORNOWAY RD
EVERGREEN LN
SKYVIEW DR
PINE RIDGE RD
LANTERN LN
MARY LANE
TURNBERRY DR
STANHOPE LN
TALL PINES WAY
MUIRFIELD RD
BIRKDALE RD
0 0.5 1
Miles

MORGAN LN: C4
MUIRFIELD RD: C4
MULBERRY LN: B3
MUSTANG WAY: A5, B5
MYSTICAL WAY: C1
N
NATIVE LN: C2
NEBA WAY: B1
NEWELL RIDGE RD: A3, B3
NUBBIN WAY: C7
O
OAK RIDGE RD: A3
OAK ST: B4
OCEAN TER: B6
OCTOBER FARM LN: B4
OLD COLONY LN: C1
OLD FARM RD: C2
OLD GRAY RD: B1, C1
OLE MUSKET RD: C7
OLIVIA LN: A3
ORCHARD RD: A1, B1

P
PARTRIDGE DR: B3
PHILIP ST: A3, B3
PINE LN: B6
PINE RIDGE RD: C7
PINEWOOD DR: B3, B4
PLEASANT VALLEY RD: A1, A2
POINTER WAY: C1
POND SHORE DR: B1, B2
PORCUPINE RIDGE WAY: B3
POWELL RD: B6
PRESTON WAY: C1
PRINCE ST: B4
PUDDLE DUCK DR: C5
R
RACEHORSE DR: B2
RANGE RD: C2, C3, C4
RANGE WAY: C5, C6
RANGERS WAY: C3
RAVINE DR: A6
RIDGE DR: C2
RIVER WAY: B1
ROCK RIDGE RUN: C5
ROSA WAY: B2
ROSE DR: A1
ROUTE 100: B1, C1, C2
RUSSELL RD: C7
S
SAND POINT LN: A6, B6
SANDERSON RD: C7
SANTIAGO WAY: C2
SAWYER LN: B3
SCHOOL ACCESS RD: B3, B4
SCHOONER RIDGE RD: B6
SCHUSTER RD: C2
SEACOVE RD: C7
SERENITY WAY: A1
SHADY RUN LN: A3, A4
SHAW FARM RD: C2, C3
SHIRLEY LN: C6
SKILLIN RD: B1, C1
SKYVIEW DR: C6
SNOW FARM WAY: A1
SNYDER WAY: C4
SOPHIE'S WAY: A2
SPARHAWK LN: B3
SPEARS HILL LN: B6
SPRING RD: C1
SPRUCE LN: C7
STANHOPE LN: C5
STARBOARD LN: C7
STEPPING STONE LN: A6
STIRLING WAY: B6
STOCKHOLM DR: B3, B4
STONEWALL DR: B1
STONY RIDE RD: C6, C7
STOREY BROOK LN: C6
STORNOWAY RD: C7
STRATTON WOODS LN: C1
STRAWBERRY RIDGE LN: C3, C4
STURBRIDGE LN: A2
STURDIVANT RD: B6, C6
SULLIVAN DR: C5
SUNNYFIELD LN: B3
SUNSET RIDGE: C5
SURREY LN: B6
SYLVAN LN: B6
T
TALL PINES WAY: C6
TAMMY LN: B1
TEAL DR: B6
THOMAS DR: A6
THOMES WAY: A1
THURSTON RD: B2
TIMBER LN: A2
TINKER LN: C1
TORRY PINE LN: B6
TOWN LANDING RD: B6
TRUE SPRING DR: C6
TURKEY LN: C4
TURNBERRY DR: C4
TUTTLE RD: B3, B4, B5, B6
TWIN BROOK REC AREA: B5
U/V
UNION RD: B1, C1
UPPER METHODIST RD: C1
US ROUTE 1: A6, B6, C6
VAL HALLA RD: A4, B4
VALLEY RD: A2, B2
VILLAGE WAY: B3
W/Y
WELLSTONE DR: A1
WESTBRANCH RD: B1
WESTMORE AVE: C1
WHALEBOAT LN: A6
WHISPERING PINES WAY: B2
WHITETAIL RD: C5
WHITNEY RD: A1
WILD APPLE LN: B2
WILD WAY: C4
WILDFLOWER WAY: B4
WILDWOOD BLVD: B6
WILLOW LN: B4
WILSON RD: C2
WINDSOR LN: B3
WINDY HOLLOW: A1
WINN RD: C4
WINTERBERRY CT: B4
WOOD CIR: A3
WOODLANDS WAY: C5
WOODSIDE DR: B3, B4
WOODY CREEK LN: C5
WYMAN WAY: B4
YORK LEDGE DR: A6, B6

Map Created by:

207.846.2355
www.spatialalternatives.com
June 2010

Cumberland, Maine in Four Centuries

Cumberland, Maine
in Four Centuries

Compiled and edited by
Phyllis Sturdivant Sweetser

Revised in 2017 by the
Cumberland Historical Society

Islandport Press
P.O. Box 10
Yarmouth, Maine 04096

www.islandportpress.com

ISBN: 978-1-944762-34-6
Library of Congress Control Number: 2017937678

First edition published 1976

Book design by Michelle Lunt / Islandport Press
Cover Design by Teresa Lagrange / Islandport Press

Front and back cover photographs from the collections of Cumberland Historical Society, *New York Times* of November 1931, Phyllis Sweetser, Herman Sweetser and Daniel Dow.

Dedication

This book is for all people who love Cumberland and is dedicated to the memory of Herman Pittee Sweetser (1887–1974), a native son, who found his greatest happiness in service to his hometown.

Courtesy of Cumberland Historical Society

Herman Pittee Sweetser.

Acknowledgments

The Sweetser family is pleased that this second printing is made possible by the Cumberland Historical Society and the Town of Cumberland. Phyllis Sweetser would be gratified by the continuation of the efforts made by her and other members of the original group who produced the 1976 edition.

Courtesy of Cumberland Historical Society

Phyllis Ruth Sturdivant Sweetser.

Table of Contents

Foreword 2016

In 1976, the first *Cumberland in Four Centuries* was printed, thanks to the devotion and hard work of Phyllis Ruth Sturdivant Sweetser. She was spurred on to this project by her friend, Barbara Berkovich, and the Town of Cumberland to celebrate the town's 155th birthday. Because the Town of Cumberland in 1976 was quite different than the Town of Cumberland in 2016, the book needed to be updated. The Town of Cumberland has grown in many different ways, starting with population. In 1976, there were over 2,000 residents. There are now over 7,800. In 1976 we still had the selectmen form of government; the Town of Cumberland is now operated by the town manager and town council. With the blessing of the Sweetser family, and the help of some of the original assistants of the first book, that has happened. Some of those originals are Barbara Berkovich, who helped with the initial development, and Dan Dow, whose creative photographic skills are displayed in both editions.

Mrs. Sweetser put her heart and soul into that publication, making it the most comprehensive and complete document in town history. This new publication is merely an extension and update of the original book, not a reconstruction. The index was updated and enhanced, making it easier for serious historians and casual readers alike to locate information quickly.

The help with facts and figures donated by several citizens of the town has been greatly appreciated. The suport and patience of town manager Bill Shane and the town council is also greatly appreciated. Our final tip of the hat goes to each member of the Sweetser family for their encouragement for this project. This amendment has truly been a work of the people, by the people, for the people.

We are excited about this new edition, and feel confident that the energy and hard work committed to it will be well received by those who read it. The original book was, for Phyllis Sturdivant Sweetser, a labor of love. It has been, for us, the same. We sincerely hope that she would look upon this effort with approval.

Carolyn F. Small
President, Cumberland Historical Society

Foreword

The work of compiling the history of Cumberland, for the town's project in the bicentennial celebration of our country, has been a long-time project. Much careful research, thoughtful planning, and hard work by many people have gone into it. It has been a delightful experience to work with so many helpful and knowledgeable citizens. We hope that due credit is given to each one, as having written or contributed to the various chapters. We have done our best to find all names of men and women in War Service, but records are very inadequate. We hope no one has been left out.

Our heartfelt thanks to business manager Barbara Berkovich, advisor Elizabeth Sweetser Baxter, proofreader and helper Linwood Crandall, photographer Daniel Dow, typists Helena McGouldrick, Judith Potter, and Fay Brown Bolduc, to Rebecca Hilton and Margaret Wyman for making the index—all of whom spent many painstaking hours on the project.

Special thanks to Bruce Hazelton, president of the Cumberland Historical Society, for his valued assistance. And last but not least, thanks to the Town Council and Town Manager, Jared Clark, for approving the project and bringing it to a happy conclusion.

Phyllis Sturdivant Sweetser
Cumberland Center, Maine, 1976

Chapter One

The Early History of the Area Which Later Became the Town of Cumberland

By Harlan H. Sweetser

The pre-history of Cumberland, Maine, before it became a town, is essentially the history of a portion of ancient North Yarmouth, for it was an integral part of that town for over 140 years. Previous to that only scattered white individuals had inhabited the area, and any organized governing body was lacking.

The development of the area which is now Cumberland was dependent on the development of North Yarmouth, and the following account is an attempt to compile some of the happenings that took place in the area that eventually became Cumberland, and at the same time, to carry along some of the contemporary history of ancient North Yarmouth and that of Massachusetts, of which the Province of Maine was then a part. There were doubtless many other events worthy of note that took place in the early days, regarding which we have scanty or no knowledge.

Ancient North Yarmouth comprised what are now the towns of Cumberland, Yarmouth, North Yarmouth, Pownal, Freeport, a small part of Brunswick, and Harpswell.

The islands included were Great Chebeague, part of Little Chebeague, Hope, Sturdivant, part of Jewells, Crotch, later Cliff and now belonging to Portland, and other very small islands—Bangs, Basket, Bates, Cow, Crow, Goose Nest, Ministerial, Rogues, Sand, Stave, Stockmans, Upper Green, and West Brown.

Information and references used in the following narrative have been taken from Rowe's *History of Ancient North Yarmouth and Yarmouth, Maine* (1937), Rowe's *Shipbuilding Days in Casco Bay* (1924), John Abbot's *The History of Maine* (1892), Marion J. Smith's *A History of Maine* (1949), Mary Sweetser's *History of the Town of Cumberland, Maine* (1921), Goold's *Portland in the Past* (1886), Shepley's *Historical Notes*, Corey's *History of Malden*, the Rev. Amasa Loring's articles in *Old Times*, W. W. Clayton's *History of Cumberland County, Maine* (1880), the York County records, and those of Cumberland County.

Approximately 180 years before the town of Cumberland was incorporated in 1821, the first white settler came to the coast of what is now Cumberland Foreside. At that time the territory that later became Cumberland was part of a larger area stretching along the coast of what then was called Aucocisco Bay. The land was known by the Indian name of Westcustogo, and was a part of the grant given by the Council of Plymouth to Sir Ferdinando Gorges. Later it became a part of the Massachusetts Bay Colony, and the area was incorporated under the name of North Yarmouth.

Aucocisco Bay, which we now know as Casco Bay, was visited by Champlain in 1605 and by Captain Rawleigh Gilbert of the ill-fated Popham Colony in 1607, and doubtless by other early explorers. The first delineation of the shoreline along the Foreside was probably made by Captain John Smith in 1614, when he made a map of the Bay. There is no evidence of permanent Indian villages being located in the area which is now Cumberland, but in the early days temporary Indian occupancy evidently occurred where Schooner Rock subdivision is located today, and at Duck Cove near the end of Longmeadow Road, and at Wildwood.

Sometime before 1640, John Phillips, a Welshman, who was only a squatter without legal right, built a small stone house on what is now Schooner Rock subdivision, near the Old Cumberland Town Landing.

He sold this house and around 300 acres of land to George Felt of Malden in 1640. While this title was worthless in the eyes of the law, Felt strengthened his title later by repurchasing it from Richard Vince, the agent of Sir Ferdinando Gorges. At first, Felt was probably an Indian trader and stayed at Westcustogo for only part of the year, but he can be considered the first permanent white settler in the area of Cumberland. His family remained in Malden until about 1664, when they all came to the area in Maine and carried on a trading business and farming until driven away by the first Indian War. Felt sold 100 of his acres in 1680 to Walter Gendall, and conveyed title of remainder to his son Moses and grandson George in 1684.

John Plaice settled northeasterly of George Felt, but it is probable that his house was over the line in what is now Yarmouth. William Royal was the first permanent settler of Westcustogo in 1639, in the section known as Lower Falls in what is now the Town of Yarmouth. At the beginning of King Philip's War in 1675, there were probably around twenty families comprising sixty or more individuals that were living in the area called Westcustogo, and a sawmill was under construction at the lower falls on what is now Royall's River[1] in the Town of Yarmouth.

The Indians attacked the settlements of Westcustogo in August of 1676, killing several of the settlers, while the others fled for refuge either to Jewells Island or House Island. George Felt, the grandson of the Foreside pioneer, took his family to House Island, and he was killed by the Indians on nearby Peaks Island. Several of the families living to the eastward of Royall's River took refuge on Jewells Island, which is now a part of Cumberland.

On September 2, while the men were harvesting the corn on one of the neighboring islands, the Indians attacked the Garrison House on Jewells Island while the women were washing clothes in the cove now called the Punch Bowl. One of the young boys in the house fired two guns, killing two Indians and giving the alarm. The men returned to the island with all speed and engaged the Indians, but they lost seven of their number and several of the women and children were captured. The Indians then withdrew and one of the settlers started to paddle to

---

[1] Authorities differ on the spelling of Royal's River.

Richmond's Island for help, but came in contact with a vessel from Massachusetts which then went to the island and took the remainder of the garrison back along the coast to a place of safety. The Indian attacks became more frequent and the settlements to the West were abandoned as far as Wells. It was not until April of 1678 that the Peace of Casco was concluded.

In March of 1678, the Massachusetts Bay Colony came into possession of the Province of Maine by purchase from the heirs of Sir Ferdinando Gorges. In 1679, the Indians were quiet, and the settlers returned and rebuilt their ruined homes.

The claim of Sir Ferdinando Gorges dated from 1622, when King James granted to him and to Captain John Mason the Province of Maine, described as being "the Maine land on the seacoast, lying between the Merrimac River and the Sagadohoc, extending to the heads of these rivers."

In 1662, the Massachusetts Bay Colony, which had established its claim eastward to the sources of the Merrimac, sent a couple of vessels along the coast to determine the point on the shoreline that had the same longitude as a point on Lake Winnipesaukee. The sea captains who were sent to accomplish this found a white rock on the shore of Casco Bay where the line crossed, and the Massachusetts Bay Colony claimed its easterly boundary to this point. This easterly boundary of Massachusetts with the Province of Maine lasted until 1678, when the Massachusetts Bay Colony purchased the Province of Maine from the heirs of Sir Ferdinando Gorges. In 1679, Captain Mason's claim was established, and it later became the State of New Hampshire.

In August of 1680, the newly appointed provincial president, Thomas Danforth, of what was now called the District of Maine, came with his assistants and around sixty soldiers to Fort Loyal, in what is now Portland. They came to settle and also confirm the Massachusetts government's authority in the newly acquired territory.

On September 22, 1680, the Commission considered the matter of a previous grant of a portion of Westcustogo by one of the Gorges heirs to Joseph Phippen, who represented the proprietors of the settlement before the first Indian War.

Danforth and the commissioners confirmed the former grant and added to the new township the lands lying between it and the Falmouth line. This new area included the present town of Cumberland. The Commission further ordered that the new plantation should be called North Yarmouth.

Previously, the General Court had appointed four trustees to manage the affairs of the new town. They were Bartholomew Gedney, a native of Salem; Joseph Scottaw, who lived in Scarborough; Capt. Sylvanus Davis, who then lived in Falmouth; and Capt. Walter Gendall, who had lived in Spurwink, now a part of Cape Elizabeth. He had married Joan Guy, whose father lived in what is now South Portland. Gendall had been an artisan and an Indian trader, and during the recent Indian uprising he had commanded the garrison at Spurwink. He was captured by the Indians at Richmond's Island while loading a vessel with goods to take to a place of safety, but he was ransomed together with many other captives.

With the Peace of Casco, which began in 1678, Gendall returned to Falmouth, and in March of 1680 he was deputy from Falmouth to the General Assembly at York, and had the confidence of his fellow citizens. In that same month he was granted 100 acres at what is now Falmouth Foreside. It began at the "White Rock"[2] on the present Falmouth-Cumberland town line and extended southwesterly to a point beyond the present Falmouth town landing. In June of 1680, he purchased 100 acres from George Felt at present Cumberland Foreside. This probably began somewhat southwesterly from Cumberland Town Landing and extended southwesterly to beyond Wildwood. In July, he bought one-half of Chebeague Island. Also in July, 1681, Gendall bargained with Bartholomew Gedney for the mill privilege at the lower falls on the Royall's River in what is now Yarmouth, together with adjacent land. He gave a mortgage for this, as he did not have sufficient money to pay for it. The day after this transaction took place the following entry was made in the new town records: "Mr. Walter Gendall having by allowance of the committee built a house and begun a plantation within the township of North Yarmouth aforesaid, near to the Falmouth bounds, Mr. Anthony Brackett and Mr. George Pearson are appointed to lay out a farm for him not exceeding 200 acres." This probably comprised the area between the purchase he made from George Felt and the Falmouth town line. The

[2] See next chapter.

house he built was probably near the shore, about 1,000 feet northeasterly from present Sea Cove Road at Cumberland Foreside, on the former Blanchard property.

Gendall rebuilt the mill at the falls in Yarmouth, which had been burned in the Indian uprising, and sawed out 100,000 board feet of lumber a year. He had four acres of cleared land on either side of the river, where he raised crops to feed the many men who worked for him and the eight to ten yoke of oxen that were used in the lumbering operations. He also had the plantation and habitation at present Cumberland Foreside, where he kept some livestock and raised field crops. He was second in command at the garrison at Fort Loyal in what is Portland today, and was trustee of the town of Scarborough and Falmouth, as well as North Yarmouth. He also was entrusted with management of the Indian trade in the whole eastern section of the District, and at the probable age of forty-seven, he was a very busy man indeed, with all of his public as well as private interests. He had the confidence of his fellow townsmen, together with that of all the people in that section of the District.

For nearly ten years there had been no serious trouble with the Indians in this vicinity, but early in 1688 friction developed in the Saco area, and some Indians were taken as hostages. This angered the Indians throughout the whole region, and they began seizing settlers wherever they could in reprisal. The settlers became apprehensive and many left their homes and went to the garrison houses for protection.

Gendall was ordered by the authorities to strengthen the garrison house of John Royal with a stockade on the easterly bank of Royall's River in present Yarmouth, and also to build a new garrison house on the west bank. Gendall used his crew at the sawmill to do this. During this time there was some local trouble with the Indians, and Gendall asked for and got a few soldiers to guard his men while they worked on the garrison, but the soldiers proved to be of questionable usefulness.

On the morning of September 19, 1688, two Indians and a captured Englishman came up the river in a canoe to parley with Gendall, who was at that time near the shore on the easterly side of the river, near the Royal garrison. After a few words were exchanged, Gendall realized that it was not a peaceful visit. When the Indians persisted in landing, Gendall called on the soldiers at the fort to fire on the canoe, and it then retreated.

Soon about fifty more Indians in canoes came up the river and landed on the west bank. They proceeded overland to where Gendall's crew was working on the new garrison, on the west side of the river, downstream from the present sardine factory. There they picked a quarrel with the workmen and soon the fight became general. The soldiers from Boston turned out to be of little help to the workmen, for they fled to the river when the fighting became heavy and tried to cross to the Royal garrison on the east side. This put them out of the conflict, and the settlers, who were greatly outnumbered, were left to fight the Indians alone.

The battle lasted all day. The settlers used the riverbank as a cover to fight from, but toward evening it became evident that they were running out of ammunition. Gendall was determined to save his men and, taking plenty of powder and ball, he ordered his Negro servant to paddle him across the river. He, himself, stood in the light boat so that the Indians might recognize him. This he did in spite of the remonstrance of his wife and friends. Before the boat reached the opposite shore both he and his servant received mortal wounds, but he had strength enough to throw the bag of ammunition to his men before he fell, saying "I have lost my life in your service." The extra ammunition turned the tide of the battle, and when it came night the Indians withdrew. Five settlers were killed in the battle, and the Indians killed the four captives that they had taken.

Gendall's death was mourned by the whole District. He apparently left no children. His widow remained for another year on the farm at the Foreside, until she was driven away by further Indian incursions, in 1689. She later married a man from Marshfield, Massachusetts.

The Indians and French completely destroyed Fort Loyal, in what is now Portland, in May of 1690, and it is said that they used Royall's River and its vicinity around the lower falls as a base of operations to attack Fort Loyal with their large fleet of canoes. North Yarmouth and its vicinity now lay desolate for twenty-five years. It is probable that around thirty-six families were compelled to flee from North Yarmouth at this time.

Around 1715, settlers began to return to the Casco Bay area again. The mill at the lower falls on the Royall's River, in what is now Yarmouth, was rebuilt for a second time by Nathaniel Weare of

Hampton, New Hampshire. He had purchased the mill privilege from the heirs of Gedney, in 1697, since Gendall's claim had reverted to the latter. The mill was burned again in 1719, and Peter Weare, Nathaniel's son, came to North Yarmouth and rebuilt the mill the third time. He married the great-granddaughter of George Felt, the first settler in what is now Cumberland. Peter Weare carried on the business until he was drowned in the river, in 1743.

Friction and skirmishes between the English settlers and the Indians had continued all the time throughout New England, and the settlers that returned to North Yarmouth were soon involved. Three garrison houses were constructed for defense—two in what is now Yarmouth, and one in present Cumberland. This latter was the William Scales garrison, probably located on what is now the Phillips Payson property. The names of the settlers who went to the Scales garrison in time of danger were Joseph Felt, grandson of George, the first settler, and James Nichols, his cousin; Francis Wyman who came from Woburn, James Buxton who came from Salem, and Mathew Scales, who, with his brother, came from Rowley. All of these families lived at Cumberland Foreside between 1715 and 1723.

Both the Scales brothers and Joseph Felt were killed in Indian attacks around 1723, and Mrs. Felt was taken captive and carried to Quebec by the Indians, remaining there five years before being ransomed by her son-in-law, Peter Weare. There were around twenty families living in ancient North Yarmouth at that time.

There was much confusion among the original proprietors, their descendants, and assigns, regarding their claims in the old plantation, and on May 30, 1722, a petition, signed by representatives of both the resident and nonresident proprietors, was presented to the General Court, asking that the same privileges of settlement that had been given the former plantation form of government in 1680, be confirmed to them, in order to regulate and facilitate the settlement of the town. They also requested that a committee of five, whose homes were in or around Boston, might be appointed to control the resettlement and manage the affairs of the town. In addition, they asked that a copy of the early town records be available to the new board of trustees.

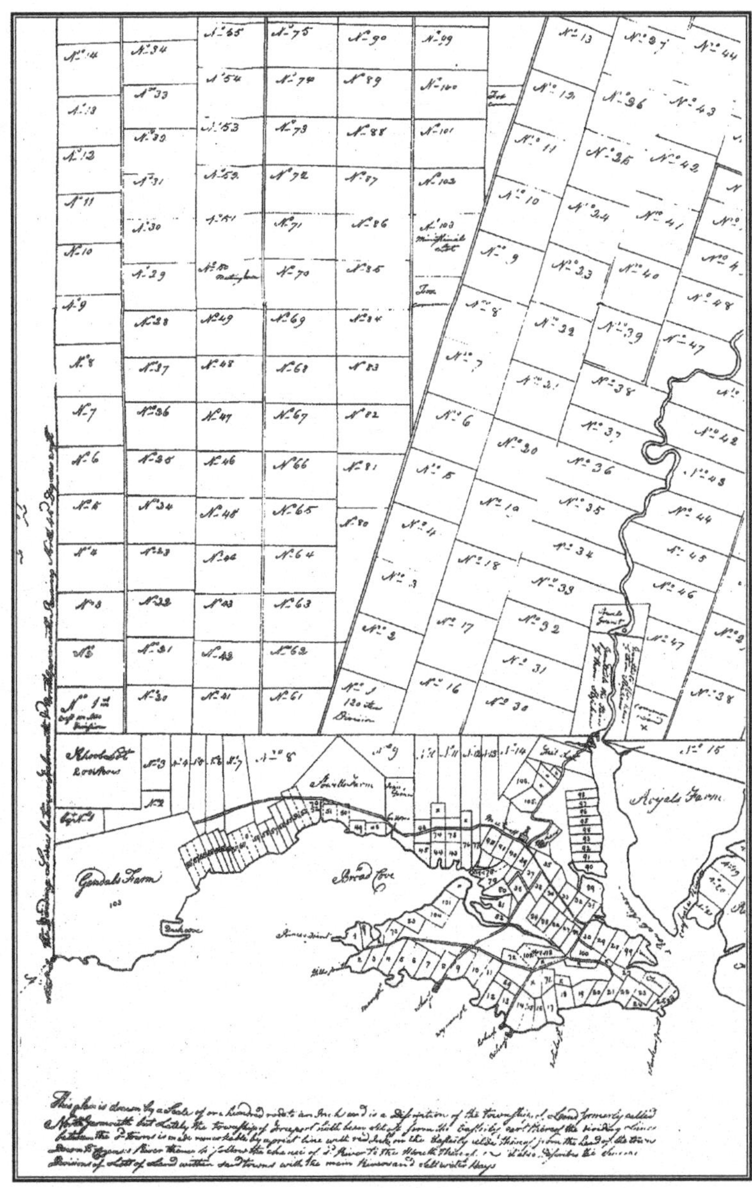

From the collection of the Maine Historical Society

Proprietors' Map of Ancient North Yarmouth, 1733.

On June 28, 1722, the order granting the petition passed both houses, was signed by the governor, and a committee was appointed. It consisted of William Tailer, Elisha Cook, William Dudley, John Smith, and John Powell. Tailer had served as lieutanent governor of Massachusetts, Dudley was a member of the Council, Cook was a member of the Council for the District of Maine, Smith was a brother of Rev. Thomas Smith of the first parish in what is now Portland, and Powell was the brother-in-law of Lieutenant Governor Dummer. All were men of ability and integrity.

John Powell was born in Charleston, Massachusetts, March 7, 1669, of Welsh parents. He had married Anne Dummer, the daughter of Jeremiah Dummer, the silversmith. Her brother was lieutenant governor William Dummer, and for a time John Powell was the governor's private secretary. He was also a successful merchant. Ann Dummer had another brother, Jeremiah, who was agent at the court of Queen Anne. Their uncle, Richard Dummer, had procured title to the area from present Flying Point in Freeport to the present Brunswick-Freeport town line. Thus, John Powell was acquainted with the territory with which the resettlement committee had to deal. The first meeting of the committee was at John Powell's house in Boston, in 1723.

In 1727, the boundary line between Falmouth and North Yarmouth (now Cumberland) was reestablished. Tobias Oakman, a man of seventy, testified that as a young man he had worked for Walter Gendall, and was present and assisted in carrying the chain when the line was first surveyed fifty-five or fifty-six years earlier. He stated that it was then agreed to start at the "White Rock" and proceed in a true northwest direction into the woods. He also pointed out several trees marked when the original line had been established in 1671 and 1672.

After the committee had examined all the original claims, and the North Yarmouth–Falmouth boundary line question had been settled, the resurvey of the lots in the township was completed. The committee then met in 1727, at the inn of James Parker in North Yarmouth, and made a division of 100 home lots. Ten of these ten-acre lots bordered on the lower west bank of Royall's River; then they extended along the shore to Parker's Point, southwesterly to Prince's Point, and continued along the shore of Broad Cove to a point nearly to the location of Sea Cove Road in present Cumberland Foreside. They also extended along both sides of a portion of Gilman Street in Yarmouth. Thirty-six of these were allocated to the original proprietors or their representatives, and sixty-four were drawn by lot for new settlers.

The further division of the remainder of the township into 100-acre lots was complicated by the so-called Gedney Claim, the history of which follows:

On January 19, 1673, a land speculator, Thomas Stephens, from the Kennebec region, obtained a deed from five of the Indian sagamores to a large tract of land, extending two miles on either side of Royall's River, from the first falls to the head of the river. This comprised the greater part of the present town of Yarmouth, and extended southwesterly to what is now Greely Road in Cumberland. It was the cause of the bend in Greely Road a short distance northwesterly of where the Maine Central Railway now crosses the latter. Stephens sold this tract of land on October 12, 1674, to Henry Sayward of York and Bartholomew Gedney of Salem. Sayward built a sawmill and a gristmill, which were burned by the Indians in 1675. Sayward died in 1678.

Gendall bargained for the mill rights and rebuilt the mill in 1681. It was again destroyed by the Indians shortly after Gendall was killed by them in 1688, and the property reverted to Gedney. Gedney died in 1697, and his heirs sold one-third of the large tract of land to Nathaniel Weare of Hampton, New Hampshire. About 1715, a mill was built again, which was also burned in 1719 and rebuilt by Peter Weare, the son of Nathaniel.

Much litigation regarding the validity of the Gedney Claim had taken place as the heirs and assigns had tried to uphold their title to property which had its origin in an Indian deed. The resettlement committee from Boston, finding that it could not come to an equitable understanding regarding the Gedney Claim, decided to allot the greater part of the disputed area and leave the question of title to the court. In time the court disallowed all claims of the Gedney heirs and assigns.

The resettlement committee also found it difficult to deal with the many local problems that came up with the reestablishment of the town, and the division of the timberlands, to its inhabitants. They felt it desirable that one member of the committee should have firsthand information regarding these problems by becoming a resident of the town. John

Powell agreed to serve in this capacity, and entered his name to be drawn as a resident owner of one of the home lots. In the drawing of May 18, 1727, he drew home lot Numbers 49 and 70, and built a fine house for those times on lot 49. This house was located just about where the westerly entrance, known as Ledge Road, goes into Schooner Rocks subdivision in Cumberland Foreside today.

John Powell, at the age of sixty-one, became the resident member of the resettlement committee, with plenipotentiary powers, and he carried on in this capacity until the town was reincorporated in 1733, and the committee was discharged from its duties. His wife Anne apparently never came to North Yarmouth.

Powell eventually acquired several other of the home lots on the Foreside and owned all the property between the present Cumberland Town Landing and the present Cumberland-Yarmouth line.

He erected a sawmill and gristmill, using overshot wheels, at Felts Falls on the brook that ran through his lot. Today it does not seem that sufficient water to run a mill ever flowed in the brook, but it evidently was different 250 years ago, and an examination of subsequent deeds to land bordering the brook (formerly Greely) disclose that there were fairly extensive flowage rights at one time.

John Powell's residence in North Yarmouth added greatly to the prestige and stability of the new town. It took great self-sacrifice on his part, at his age, to give up living in his fine house in Boston and come to this new settlement with all its privations and dangers, and to guard it until it could carry on by itself as a municipality. Falmouth, now Portland, tried to induce him to settle there, but he stayed with North Yarmouth the rest of his life. He was an enterprising businessman and carried on several business activities besides investing extensively in wild land. At one time he controlled 100-acre lot Number 70, at present Cumberland Center.

After the allocation of the home lots the resettlement committee was concerned with the division of the timberlands away from the coast. When the boundary line between Falmouth and the new town had been agreed upon by both towns, range lines, one-half mile apart, were carried back parallel to the Falmouth line. They started from a baseline back of the home lots, and were applied to the territory each side of the Gedney Claim. These

Photo courtesy of Helen Dunn Maxim

House built by John Sweetser, 1740. It stands at 158 Middle Road.

parallel strips were divided into 100 lots, each containing 100 acres on the southwesterly side of the Gedney Claim, the 200 lots each containing 100 acres in the northeasterly side of the claim.

Later, another drawing took place by the 100 proprietors, on August 7, 1733. Each was allocated, besides his previously drawn home lot, a 100-acre lot on the southwesterly part of the town, a 120-acre lot in what had comprised the Gedney Claim, and two 100-acre lots in the northeasterly part of the town. Also each was allotted four acres of salt marsh.

The back line of North Yarmouth was made at right angles to its sides in 1735, thus adding a triangle which was eleven miles along the back line on its northwesterly side and two and one-half miles long on its northeasterly side. This area was divided into thirteen lots of 450 acres, and thirteen lots of 280 acres. These lots were called "squadrons." One squadron was allocated to each nine home lots.

When Cumberland became a town it occupied the greater part of the 100-acre lots in the southwesterly division and those squadrons in the apex of the triangle that was added in 1735.

The first town meeting after the resettlement was held May 10, 1733, and the town officers were chosen. Jacob Mitchell, Joseph Chandler, and Francis Wyman were elected as selectmen. Of this first board of selectmen of the new town of North Yarmouth, Francis Wyman lived in the area that later became the Town of Cumberland. On April 6, 1733, the resettlement committee had been discharged from its duties, and North Yarmouth was granted in full the powers enjoyed by other towns.

Many new families came into the town at this time, and while there was some sporadic Indian trouble, the population of the town grew, and probably by 1738 there were around 400 people living in the township. An epidemic of "throat distemper" went through the colonies, and between 1736 and 1738 over 50 people, mostly young persons, died in North Yarmouth.

Among the families that came to North Yarmouth at this time was that of John Sweetser, in 1732 or 1733. He came from the same section of Charleston, Massachusetts (later set off as Malden, Massachusetts), that George Felt, the pioneer settler at Cumberland Foreside, had come from. At first he lived in the vicinity of the first church near the pioneer cemetery. Later he obtained original lot Number 41, as numbered in the layout of ancient North Yarmouth, and in 1740 built the house now at 158 Middle Road, near the intersection of Middle and Tuttle Roads. He had a family of twelve children.

On October 1, 1742, John Powell died at the age of seventy-three. He had been more closely connected with the settlement of the town than any other early resident, and his guidance had enabled the resettlement to be consummated with a minimum of friction.

France and England were at war again in 1744, and the settlers prepared to defend themselves, as best they could, from the French and Indian attacks that they knew would come.

The stronghold of Louisburg, on Cape Breton Island, gave France a base from which a fleet could operate against the whole of the eastern coastline, and New England was particularly apprehensive. Governor Shirley of Massachusetts, backed by the merchants and fishermen, proposed to the assembly that an attempt be made to take the fortress. It passed by only one vote, and only Connecticut, Rhode Island, and New Hampshire supported Massachusetts in the undertaking. Louisburg was the most strongly fortified point in the western hemisphere, and was called the Gibraltar of America. It is said that the plan for its destruction "was drawn up by a lawyer and executed by a merchant, at the head of a body of husbandmen and mechanics."

The undertaking had the support of the people in most of coastal New England, and recruits were ready to enlist. Since there were no official muster rolls, it is difficult to say how many went from North Yarmouth, but at least six, and probably more, enlisted. One of these was Jonathan Sweetser, the son of John Sweetser. He was killed in the battle for the fortress. The settlers prevailed and the fortress surrendered on June 17, 1745.

Another man from North Yarmouth who was with the Louisburg expedition was Rev. Ammi Ruhamah Cutter, who was born in Cambridge, Massachusetts, and had graduated from Harvard. He was the minister of the first church in North Yarmouth from 1729 to 1735, when his views, liberal for those days, brought about his dismissal. He was captain of a company in the Louisburg expedition, and had charge of the military depot at Canso. After the capture of Louisburg he was detailed to remain as surgeon, but died of dysentery in March of 1746. His remains were brought back to North Yarmouth by Corporal Benjamin Morgaridge of Kittery.

Corporal Morgaridge settled in what is now Cumberland Foreside. He married Sarah, the daughter of Solomon Mitchell, and they lived near the Falmouth line between what is now the Foreside Road and Route 1, on what would be an extension of Stoney Ridge Road. He helped the town greatly during the resumption of the Indian wars, which took place at this time.

The eldest son of Rev. Ammi Ruhamah Cutter, who was named for him, became the famous Dr. Ammi Ruhamah Cutter of Portsmouth, and was surgeon general of the Continental Army during the Revolution. As late as 1774 he owned 100-acre lot Number 71 in the west division of North Yarmouth. This began at what is now Cumberland Center, and extended on the northeasterly side of present Blanchard Road for 1,650 feet. In 1774 he received compensation from the town of North Yarmouth, due to the relocation of present Blanchard Road.

Nine garrison houses were in use in North Yarmouth by mid-1745, and two of them were located in what is now Cumberland Foreside. The Nathaniel Blanchard garrison was located on the northwesterly side of the Foreside Road, between the houses of Milton Kimball and Mrs. Janet Palmer. It had a strong stockade with watch boxes. The house, which had been built by John Powell, and was then occupied by Colonel Jeremiah Powell, his son, was also a garrison house. On the sixteenth of June, Nathaniel Blanchard, the son of the settler, had a narrow escape from ambush by Indians on the road near his father's garrison house, and at the same time from the same ambush, Joseph Sweat, who was riding horseback, was killed and scalped. Several others were killed in what is now Freeport. Early in August, Philip Greely was killed by a party of thirty or more Indians who were concealed to ambush the Weare garrison, just northeasterly of Royall's River in what is now Yarmouth. Greely's dog had smelled the Indians while Greely was walking in the road, and the Indians, realizing they were discovered, shot Greely. His death alarmed and probably saved the garrison. He was the grandfather of Eliphalet Greely, benefactor of Greely Institute.

From this time to the fall of Quebec in 1759, North Yarmouth, like all other towns, was subject to Indian raids. Many people were killed, and women and children were carried into captivity. More depredations took place in what is now Yarmouth and Freeport than in present Cumberland, but most of the time a scouting party of ten men patrolled the area between the Presumpscot River and Royall's River. They had their rendezvous at Colonel Jeremiah Powell's garrison.

The last Indian attack on North Yarmouth came in 1757, and that occurred in what are now Freeport and Harpswell, where several people were killed and others taken into captivity. There were quite a few men from North Yarmouth who served in the expeditions against Canada, and most of the others were engaged, at one time or another, in guarding the community or serving in the military farther east.

When the news of the fall of Quebec, which had taken place on September 13, 1759, reached North Yarmouth on October 14, there was great rejoicing, and October 25 was set aside as a day of public thanksgiving. The trouble with the Indians and French had extended over a period of seventy-five years. It was some time after the close of the war before some of the children, who had been carried into captivity in Canada, were located and returned to their former homes.

Jeremiah Powell was twenty-two years of age when his father died in 1742, and from then on he occupied his father's place at present Cumberland Foreside and took part in the affairs of the town of North Yarmouth. Two years later he was commissioned by Governor Shirley to be a justice of the peace for York County, which was then the only county in the District of Maine. The next year he was elected to represent North Yarmouth in the Colonial Assembly, which office he held for sixteen years.

When Cumberland County was formed from a portion of York County in 1760, Jeremiah Powell was named a justice to the Court of Common Pleas. In 1763, he was named chief justice, which position he held for eighteen years. He had previously been appointed a lieutenant colonel. In 1766, he became a member of the Provincial Council. In 1768, he married Sarah Bromfield, twelve years his junior, whose sister Mary had married his brother William. The couple had no children, but they lived in an elegant and affluent style for that period, and had Negro servants who no doubt were slaves.

The census taken for the Lords of Trade in 1764 showed that North Yarmouth was the third-largest town in Cumberland County, with 1,079 white inhabitants and 18 Negroes, and with 188 families and 154 houses.

With the end of the French and Indian Wars, settlers began to move back from the coast, to locations in the western and northern parts of the town, where they developed new water powers and established homes, which they could not do while there were constant threats of Indian raids. Because of its active coastal trade with Boston and other towns, North Yarmouth early felt the growing unrest brought about by the passage of the stamp tax and other revenue acts imposed by Great Britain.

In 1768, following the refusal of the governor to call the legislature into session, the selectmen of Boston invited the towns of Massachusetts to send delegates to a convention to discuss the situation. Ninety-six towns responded, including North Yarmouth. The convention was held in Faneuil Hall in Boston. Following this, more letters were sent out by the selectmen of Boston, as the situation progressed from bad to worse, and after the Boston Tea Party, December 16, 1773, each town was urged to express its opinion regarding public measures that should be taken.

A committee of seven was chosen in North Yarmouth, to draft their reply. They consisted of Jeremiah Powell, Jonas Mason, David Mitchell, Jonathan Loring, Solomon Loring, John Lewis, and Jonathan Mitchell. The reply was a spirited and lengthy document, setting forth their opinions in eleven tenets, couched in no uncertain terms.

On September 21, 1774, a convention of delegates from the towns of Cumberland County met at what is now Portland "to consider what measures should be adopted for the general interests of the County," and Jeremiah Powell, one of the constitutional councilors of the Province, met with them. Jeremiah Powell had been offered a place on Governor Gage's Council. The Crown hoped that he would thus be on the Royalist side, but he refused the office, although his brother John did side with the Royalist cause, and left Boston in 1776, never to return.

The town of North Yarmouth was divided into three military divisions. The first extended from the Falmouth line to about where the present sewage treatment plant is in Yarmouth. This included the whole of present Cumberland. The second division extended northeasterly to a point near the present Freeport town line, and the third extended to the Brunswick town line. A company of Minutemen was formed in the town. After the Battles of Concord and Lexington, the shore was patrolled each night, to guard against surprise, and to secure the livestock from being taken when the British sent out boats from their fleet to obtain food supplies. Two of the swivel guns used during the Indian Wars were mounted on the ledge near the church, and another at Gray's Wharf, near the present Cumberland Town Landing. They were to be fired in any emergency and all men who heard the alarm were to assemble at the meetinghouse. Jeremiah Powell was a member of the Council of Safety.

On April 23, 1775, the Provincial Congress of Massachusetts voted to raise 13,600 men to defend the State. Cumberland County's share was 549 officers and men, and North Yarmouth raised a company of 49 men, all within a few days' time. The Cumberland County contingent marched to Cambridge the first week in July, one company at a time. These soldiers did guard duty on the outskirts of Boston, and took part in skirmishes with the British regulars until the latter part of the year, when the Continental Congress authorized the organization of a regular army. The Continental Army came into being January 1, 1776. Some of the men from North Yarmouth returned home when the company was discharged, but many reenlisted in the new army and continued as Continental Soldiers.

The bombardment and burning of Falmouth, now Portland, by Captain Henry Mowatt, on October 18, 1775, caused great alarm in North Yarmouth. Deserters from the British fleet reported that Mowatt had orders to plunder and destroy everything east of Boston. An earthwork was built on Prince's Point where a gun was mounted, to guard against enemy vessels entering Royall's River.

A few men from North Yarmouth were involved in the ill-fated expedition to Quebec under Benedict Arnold, since it was made up of men drafted from the soldiers taking part in the siege of Boston. More North Yarmouth men took part in the bombardment of Boston, which resulted in its evacuation on March 17, 1776. The Declaration of Independence came on July 4, 1776. At this time price fixing was put into effect by the selectmen of North Yarmouth and the Committee of Safety. Things went badly for all the colonists until Washington crossed the Delaware and achieved the victory at Trenton.

North Yarmouth men fought at Ticonderoga, Bemis Heights, and Saratoga. Some of them were at Valley Forge, and later at Monmouth. There was a company of sixty-five North Yarmouth men in the disastrous Bagaduce expedition on the Penobscot in 1779, where they were defeated by Captain Mowatt, the man who burned Falmouth (now Portland) in 1775.

The winter of 1779–80 was a difficult time for coastal Maine. The Penobscot disaster, and the fact that only coastal shipping, under very dangerous conditions, could be undertaken, together with the scarcity of all provisions, made it a period long to be remembered. The sloop *Rhoda*, commanded by Captain Gray, had made a coastal trip in the fall of 1779 to one of the harbors to the westward for supplies and returned to Cumberland Foreside, anchoring near Anderson's Rock. The crew left the vessel for the night with two boys on board to keep ship. When the crew returned the next morning, the *Rhoda* had disappeared. The crew and some of the inhabitants armed themselves as best they could, and taking an old sloop that was anchored near the present Cumberland Town Landing, they started out of the harbor to see what had become of their vessel. When they had passed outside of Chebeague Island, they saw the two boys in the small boat of the *Rhoda*. The boys told them that they had been seized about eleven o'clock the night before by a boat from an English cruiser; the cable had been slipped and the sloop taken. They had been set adrift outside the harbor, and knew nothing of where the *Rhoda* was being taken. However, they had overheard someone speak of Monhegan, and the party felt it might be well to go there. They came into the harbor at night and found the *Rhoda* anchored. Feigning ignorance of the anchorage area, the old sloop, with the people from North Yarmouth, ran into the *Rhoda*, which was boarded and captured by its owners. Both sloops got under way at once and started home. The next morning they came up with a large English schooner, loaded with lumber, and they captured her. The three vessels passed through Broad Cove on the way to Falmouth (now Portland). The supplies and prize money enabled the people to have a more comfortable winter than they would have otherwise.

From July of 1775 to October of 1780, there was no governor of Massachusetts, and the affairs of the state were taken care of by the Council. In 1779, an assembly of delegates drafted a state constitution. After several tries this was adopted by North Yarmouth at a special town meeting on May 22, 1779. The first election under the new constitution was held in September, and when the Senate of Massachusetts convened for the first time, Jeremiah Powell was chosen as its president. His wise counsel and service to the town, county, and state, covering the latter part of the French and Indian Wars, the following reconstruction period, and the problems that arose during the Revolutionary War, were of great value to the country as a whole during a very trying period.

The news of Cornwallis's surrender at Yorktown on October 19, 1781, did not reach North Yarmouth until eight days later, on a Saturday. Sunday was a day of thanksgiving, and Monday a day of public rejoicing. December 19 was set aside as a day of public thanksgiving throughout the whole of Massachusetts.

In 1787, the General Court authorized the formation of an assembly composed of delegates from each town, equal to the number of its representatives. The assembly met to consider the adoption of the Constitution of the United States. North Yarmouth had two representatives, David Mitchell and Samuel Merrill, who both voted in the affirmative. Jeremiah Powell, who had done so much for the town and state, died on September 6, 1787, at the age of sixty-six.

North Yarmouth developed very rapidly after the close of the Revolutionary War, including the section which is now the town of Cumberland. The church at Cumberland Center was established in 1794 as the North Western Religious Society of North Yarmouth. There was considerable land speculation, and also immigration from the more densely populated areas of Massachusetts to the District of Maine. The northwestern part of the town was cleared and settled, and there was a thriving business in lumber.

The great demand for shipping, to transport the lumber and other products, brought about the opening of shipyards all along the coast. Many vessels were constructed in Harpswell, Freeport, Yarmouth, and Cumberland. This was the beginning of the great boom in shipbuilding, which had its climax after Maine became a separate state. The demand from outside for ships built in the District of Maine began in 1815, at the close of the War of 1812, and continued for around forty years.

David Spear bought the land where he built his house at Cumberland Foreside in 1809 at the foot of Spear Hill on Route 88, on the northwesterly side. Spear started his shipyard across the road at Cumberland Town Landing, where other small vessels had been built previously. Beginning at the close of the War of 1812, he and his son, David Spear Jr., who succeeded him, carried on the business for some fifty years. During this time at least fifty vessels, and probably more, were built, ranging in tonnage from 250 to over 1,000 tons. Among them was the famous bark, *Grapeshot*.

Several small vessels were also built by individuals, some distance inland from the coast, and hauled to tidewater during the winter. These were vessels of around seventy tons, and required eighty yoke of oxen to transport them (see Chapter 4, "Shipyards").

From the end of the Revolutionary War to the War of 1812, shipmasters trading with the West Indies ran considerable danger of being confiscated by the French or the English, as well as of capture by pirates. At

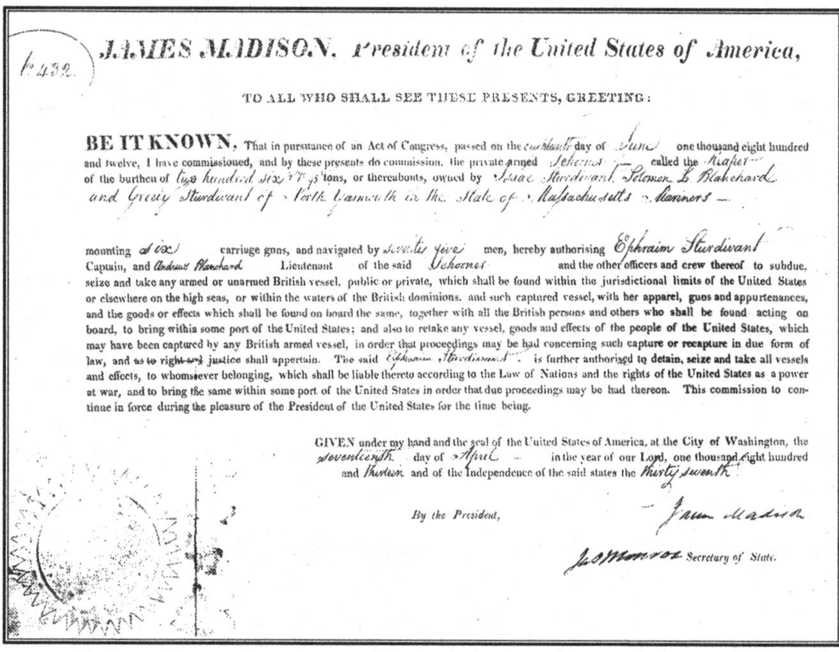

No. 432.

JAMES MADISON, President of the United States of America,

TO ALL WHO SHALL SEE THESE PRESENTS, GREETING:

BE IT KNOWN, That in pursuance of an Act of Congress, passed on the eighteenth day of June one thousand eight hundred and twelve, I have commissioned, and by these presents do commission, the private armed Schooner called the Rapier of the burthen of two hundred sixty [illegible] tons, or thereabouts, owned by Isaac Sturdivant, Solomon L. Blanchard and Greely Sturdivant of North Yarmouth in the State of Massachusetts Mariners — mounting six carriage guns, and navigated by seventy five men, hereby authorising Ephraim Sturdivant Captain, and Andrew Blanchard Lieutenant of the said Schooner and the other officers and crew thereof to subdue, seize and take any armed or unarmed British vessel, public or private, which shall be found within the jurisdictional limits of the United States or elsewhere on the high seas, or within the waters of the British dominions, and such captured vessel, with her apparel, guns and appurtenances, and the goods or effects which shall be found on board the same, together with all the British persons and others who shall be found acting on board, to bring within some port of the United States; and also to retake any vessel, goods and effects of the people of the United States, which may have been captured by any British armed vessel, in order that proceedings may be had concerning such capture or recapture in due form of law, and ~~as to right and~~ justice shall appertain. The said Ephraim Sturdivant is further authorised to detain, seize and take all vessels and effects, to whomsoever belonging, which shall be liable thereto according to the Law of Nations and the rights of the United States as a power at war, and to bring the same within some port of the United States in order that due proceedings may be had thereon. This commission to continue in force during the pleasure of the President of the United States for the time being.

GIVEN under my hand and the seal of the United States of America, at the City of Washington, the seventeenth day of April in the year of our Lord, one thousand eight hundred and thirteen and of the Independence of the said states the thirty seventh.

By the President, James Madison

Jas Monroe *Secretary of State.*

From the collection of Phyllis Sturdivant Sweetser

Letter of marque, 1813, signed by President Madison for Captain Ephraim Sturdivant.

least nine North Yarmouth vessels, and probably more, were taken by the French. The Embargo Act of 1807, which forbade trade between the United States and foreign countries, was passed in an endeavor to force England and France to stop molesting our shipping. It failed to accomplish its purpose, however, and the opposition from New England forced its repeal. The Non-Intercourse Act with England and France was then passed, but it also failed to solve the problem, and in June of 1812, the United States declared war on England, "to secure the freedom of the seas." There was not much war activity in the vicinity, except the engagement between the *Boxer* and *Enterprise* off the mouth of the Kennebec River, until 1814, when the British seized Eastport and

Castine. They then went up the Penobscot, took Hampden and Bangor, and burned the shipping there.

A large British fleet sailed from Castine and blockaded Casco Bay, where the inhabitants feared the same fate met by the people on the Penobscot. The governor of Massachusetts ordered all the militia of Oxford and Cumberland counties, between six and seven thousand men, to assemble at Fort Barrows in Portland, where they stayed for fourteen days.

The British fleet did not attempt to come in to the harbor but sent in some small boats in the night. Men were stationed at Parker's Point, at the entrance to Royall's River; and at the earthworks at Prince's Point, which had been used during the Revolutionary War, they mounted a gun which fired and frustrated one attempt to steal a sloop from the river.

Dennis Doughty, who lived at Cumberland Foreside, secreted a deserter from the British fleet in his blind attic one night, covering the entrance with hay. The house was searched soon after by a detail from the British vessel, but the man, who was an impressed American seaman, was not found. The next night Doughty took him over to the old Sanborn Road to his brother, who lived in the western part of the town, where he was safe.

At this time several letters of marque were granted to residents of North Yarmouth, who owned small, fast, maneuverable vessels that could be used as privateers. At least two were issued to Captain Ephraim Sturdivant at Cumberland Foreside. Three were issued to Captain Joseph Sturdivant, the brother of Ephraim. There were probably others as well.

There is more to be said regarding the homestead of John and Jeremiah Powell, which was located in present Cumberland Foreside. When Jeremiah Powell died in 1787, his widow sold the property to William Martin, who had been a publisher in London. He held the property until 1805, and part of that time his daughter Penelope, who had just graduated from a school in London, conducted a school for young ladies in the former Powell Mansion. Later she continued the school in what is now Portland. It was one of the first of its kind in the western world.

William Martin sold the Powell estate to Alexander Barr in 1805. Alexander and his brother Robert were Scotsmen, who had served their apprenticeship in the machine shop of Richard Arkwright, the inventor and developer of the spinning frame in Derbyshire, England. They prob-

Sketch by Lena Foster, 1975, copied from a hooked rug made by Leona Jones about 1900 and loaned by Sara Jones Bucknam

The old plaster mill at Felt's Brook.

ably came to this country at about the close of the Revolutionary War, and for a time Alexander resided in Falmouth, now Portland, where he married a Miss Mehitable Peabody of Gorham, in 1786. But in that year the Barr brothers were employed in the machine shop of Hugh Orr, in Bridgewater, Massachusetts.

The carding machine and the power loom had been invented by Hargreaves and Peele, respectively, and developed in England at the same time that Arkwright brought out the spinning frame. Thus England had the monopoly in power spinning and weaving, and intended to keep it. In 1774, Parliament prohibited the export of all carding, spinning, and weaving machinery, also plans and parts thereof. After the Revolutionary War all travelers leaving England were closely scrutinized to make sure that these prohibitions were followed, and persons having intimate knowledge of textile machinery were not allowed to emigrate.

We do not know how the Barr brothers got to this country, but they probably came under assumed names. While they were employed in the machine shop at Bridgewater, Massachusetts, their employer, Hugh Orr, became convinced that they had the skill and knowledge to duplicate textile machinery in this country. Orr went to the Massachusetts Legislature and asked that a committee be chosen to interview the Barr brothers regarding this venture. The committee was appointed and reported favorably, whereupon the legislature raised a sum of money to aid the Barr brothers in constructing the machinery here. The machines were made, and they operated satisfactorily. Anyone wishing to copy them was free to do so, and power spinning became possible in the New World. Other mechanics, who came later, were able to reproduce the improvements that had developed in England. It is said that Alexander Barr made the first carding machines used in what is now the State of Maine.

Barr converted one of the mills that Powell had built on Felt's Brook to grind gypsum for plaster of Paris, but he spent much of his time as an agriculturist. He took an active part in the affairs of the town, and his name appears in the county records as a petitioner regarding some roads. He attended the old First Church, in what is now Yarmouth, and sat in pew number 57, which the Powells had occupied. He died in his eightieth year, and was honored and respected by his townsmen. The Barrs had several children, but none of the children had offspring.

Through the years, as the town of North Yarmouth grew, homes were built and a "way out" had to be provided for the settlers. At first there were only bridle paths. After the home lots along the shore were laid out and allocated in 1727, a bridle path was established on the best terrain back of the lots. This connected with Gilman Street in present Yarmouth, and probably followed the general direction of one used by Felt, Gendall, and others when the town of North Yarmouth was incorporated in 1680 and there were only a few settlers. It was used again at the time of the third resettlement. This bridle path eventually became the Foreside Road. As the Foreside Road it was authorized by the town of North Yarmouth in 1740, and the first description of the layout of the section through present Cumberland was in 1752.

Photograph by Daniel Dow, 1975

Marker set up in 1761 shows that Top Knot Farm, 100 Middle Road, is 135 miles from Boston.

The capture of Quebec by the English in 1759 put an end to the French colonies in eastern North America and the threat of Indian raids on the settlements. All action against this area during the wars had been the naval expeditions. Now the Crown felt it would be wise to have a land route, leading toward the former French colonies to the east.

Accordingly the "King's Highway," really a military road, was laid out from Boston to Machias. It was the first "through" or county road that passed through newly formed "Cumberland County," and the date of the court proceeding was 1761. Markers were placed with the aid of Benjamin Franklin's invention, the odometer, which measured distances. Each time the wheeled device hit a mile, a stone was erected and marked with a B and the number of miles from that point to Boston. Four milestones numbered in consecutive order remain along the highway in Cumberland and Yarmouth. B 135 is at 100 Middle Road at old Top Knot Farm—formerly a Sturdivant house. B 136 is on Route 88 a little northeast of the short road to Cumberland Town Landing. B 137 is in Yarmouth at the top of York's Hill, and B 138 is on Pleasant Street. The highway entered Cumberland on the present Middle Road, after passing through Falmouth and towns to the west. It continued to the intersection with the present Tuttle Road, then turned southeasterly, down Tuttle Road, to the intersection with the short piece of road still designated as the "King's Highway." Then it turned northeasterly, on the present Foreside Road, through the Falls section of Yarmouth. From there it went along present East Main Street to Freeport, by way of "Pott's Landing,"

Courtesy of Daniel Dow

Marker where King's Highway meets Route 88 is 136 miles from Boston.

Freeport Corner, the "Mast Landing," and Pleasant Street to the Brunswick Line and points east.

With the threat of Indian raids over, settlers in North Yarmouth began to push back from the coast, and the three range or town roads in what is present Cumberland were gradually opened up (see Appendix I).

There had been some discussion regarding the separation of the District of Maine from Massachusetts, as early as 1786, and several votes were taken on the question from time to time. North Yarmouth had opposed the separation at first, since it had a seaport, and as long as it was a part of Massachusetts the clearance of customs at Boston was not necessary. In 1819, a law was passed that allowed coasting trade along the Atlantic seaboard without resorting to customs, and when the last vote on separating from Massachusetts was taken, the sentiment was more evenly divided. In the town of North Yarmouth 194 voted against it and 178 were in favor. However, the separation took place.

A constitutional convention was called, and met in Portland on October 17, 1819, and the delegates from North Yarmouth were Ephraim Sturdivant, William Buxton, Calvin Stockbridge, and Jeremiah Buxton. On December 6, the town of North Yarmouth accepted the state constitution by a vote of 115 to 54.

In 1818 an article to separate the Town of Cumberland from North Yarmouth was put in the warrant for the annual town meeting, but it was dismissed. In 1820 a petition favoring separation, signed by 176 men, was presented to the new legislature, and although the remainder of North Yarmouth protested strongly, an Act of Incorporation was granted by the legislature of 1821, and it was approved by the governor. The boundary between the new town of Cumberland and the parent town of North Yarmouth was a complicated one. It followed various lot lines that had been established when North Yarmouth was originally laid out.

This made the new town approximately eight miles long and three miles wide, but a provision was inserted in the Act of Incorporation which granted to all persons whose land bordered on the new dividing line the privilege of electing, within ninety days, which town they would choose to be in. This caused much trouble at the time, and resulted in a very irregular dividing line, with problems continuing up to the present time.

1821

State of Maine

In the year of our Lord, one thousand eight hundred And twenty one.

An Act to divide the Town of Northyarmouth and incorporate the Westerly part thereof into a town by the name of Cumberland.

Sec. 1. Be it enacted by the Senate and House of Representatives in Legislature assembled, That all that part of the Town North yarmouth, in the County of Cumberland lying Southwestwardly of the following line viz. begining at the sea shore on the dividing line between the farms of Alexander Barr and Reuben Loring thence North westerly to the easterly corner of the one hundred and twenty acre lot numbered one in the one hundred and twenty acre division on the west side of Royals River; thence north twenty six degrees west to the North corner of lot numbered five; thence south sixty four deg[rees] west on the dividing line between the lots numbered five an[d] six to the south corner of land now owned by Joseph Barstow in lot numbered six; thence north twenty six degrees west, across said lot; thence south sixty four degrees west between lots numbered six and seven to the dividing line between the one hundred and the one hundred and twenty acre division, on the west side of Roy[a]ls River; thence north twenty six degrees west on said line to the southerly side line of the two hundred and eighty acre squadron numb[ered] one; thence south fifty four degrees west to the easterly corner of the four hundred and fifty acre squadron numbered two so called; thence north west to Gray line; with all the flats lying westerly of a line drawn south twelve degrees east from the bou[nd] first mentioned, together with all the islands heretofore belonging to the said town of Northyarmouth except Cousins island, Little Johns island, Lanes island and the two islands called Great Mo[ses and] Little Moses islands, with the Inhabitants thereon be and the same are hereby incorporated into a separate town by the name of Cumber[land]; and vested with all the powers privileges and immunities, and subject to all the duties and requisitions of other corporated towns, Agreeably to the Constitution and laws of this State.

Town Records, Book 1, page 1

Incorporation of Cumberland, 1821.

Chapter Two

The White Rock and the Boundaries of Cumberland

By Robert G. Blanchard

In discussing this boundary point called "the White Rock" and the boundaries of Cumberland, we need to go back in history to the time when this state was known as the Province of Maine, a large, loosely defined tract of land granted by the King of England to Sir Ferdinando Gorges. There were few settlers in the region, with most of the people concentrated in settlements along the coast. About this time Thomas Stevens purchased from the Indians a tract of land two miles on either side of Royall's River and extending from the coast to the head of the river. He later sold this to Henry Saywood of York and Bartholomew Gedney of Salem. Although the claim to this land was eventually declared worthless, it had considerable effect on the layout of the town lines.

In 1653, Massachusetts, claiming title to the land west of ancient North Yarmouth, sent two ship captains to determine where the boundary line between Massachusetts and the Province of Maine would intersect the coastline. These two captains, after taking a number of observations for longitude, determined that a large white rock on the shore should mark the boundary. So for over 300 years this white rock has served as a boundary mark, first between Massachusetts and Maine, later between

Photograph by Daniel Dow, 1975

The White Rock—Sturdivant Island in background.

Falmouth and ancient North Yarmouth, and since 1820, between Falmouth and Cumberland.

After the serious troubles with the Indians had abated in 1725, the Committee for North Yarmouth—which had been appointed by the General Court of Massachusetts, and which was called the Boston Committee—became more active. The members of this committee lived in or near Boston but had general supervision over the town of ancient North Yarmouth. Because of Indian troubles most of the old proprietors and their families had moved away from ancient North Yarmouth, and their homesteads had been vacant for many years. Now that a treaty of peace with the Penobscot Indians had been signed at Boston, these early settlers began moving back to their North Yarmouth holdings. The land claims of these early settlers first had to be taken care of by the Boston Committee, and so two surveyors, Jeremiah Moulton and Benjamin Flagg, with their helpers, Jonas Rice, John Stevens, and Phineas Jones, were engaged to run over the boundary lines of the town and to lay out 100 homestead lots of approximately ten acres, each to be divided among the early settlers who were now returning to their former homes, and many other prospective proprietors who had applied for homestead land.

In attempting to run the line between North Yarmouth and Falmouth, these surveyors were opposed by the selectmen of Falmouth, who claimed that the line was not being run on the right course. There was no question as to the starting point at the shore, as the "White Rock," so called, had long been so recognized. But the direction of the first course, which was eight miles long and extended to the "upper reaches" of the Piscataqua River, was in dispute. So the surveyors gave up their attempt to run this boundary line and turned their attention to laying out the 100 homestead lots as ordered by the Boston Committee. Starting with lot Number 1 at the end of Prince's Point and working northeasterly along the shore to Parker's Point, and thence inland along what is now Gilman Street to Route 88, and thence along Broad Cove to beyond what is now Tuttle Road, they laid out 50 lots, and quit work.

When the Boston Committee learned that only 50 lots had been laid out, they were disappointed, and ordered the surveyors to immediately resume work and complete the 100 lots as ordered. The arrangement of these homestead lots as can be seen on the map was such that they formed a compact area that could be capably defended in case of trouble.

The Boston Committee arrived in North Yarmouth on May 10, 1727, bringing with them Tobias Oakman, an elderly man who had served as a chainman with Walter Gendall in 1672, when a boundary line had first been run from the "White Rock" at the shore. The first order of business for the Boston Committee was a meeting with the Falmouth selectmen, at which Tobias Oakman testified as to the original direction and location of Falmouth–North Yarmouth boundary line. Agreement was soon reached that this line should run due northwest from the "White Rock" at the shore. And so this "White Rock" again serves to designate and permanently fix the boundary.

On May 18, 1727, the Boston Committee, represented by Tailor, Cooke, Smith, and Powell, met at Capt. James Parker's Inn to carry out the work of drawing and assigning the homestead lots. Thirty-six of the lots had already been assigned to the early settlers, giving each of them a lot on or as near to their former holdings as was possible. Three other lots were assigned for use of the minister, the church, and a school.

The remaining 64 lots were to be assigned in the manner of a lottery. The numbers of these lots were written on folded slips of paper and placed in a hat. In another hat were placed in like manner the names of the 64 people who were to participate in the drawing. A number of a lot and a name were drawn from both hats simultaneously, thus deciding without prejudice the future homestead of each proprietor.

To prevent speculation and to ensure permanent settlement, no title deeds were to be given until certain conditions had been met, such as becoming a permanent resident of the town, building a dwelling house, and cultivating part of his lot. Also, if these conditions were not met, the new proprietor would be further punished by forfeiting his rights to the so-called "after divisions," of the extensive timber tracts and wild land which formed the largest and perhaps the most valuable part of the town extending back from the shore eight miles. This land was to be divided among the holders of the 100 homestead lots as soon as this vacant land could be surveyed and plotted.

The Boston Committee, not being able to take care of the many details of management for the town, appointed a committee of five men to take charge of such things as laying out roads, divisions of marshlands, and the care of the undivided timber lots. Samuel Seabury, James Parker, Jacob Mitchell, Gershom Rice, and Phineas Jones comprised this committee. Timber pirates from Boston started to infest the region, cutting the finest trees for masts and staves and hauling them to Boston by boat. At one time there were nineteen timber-cutting crews on Chebeague Island, pilfering the best timber for their Boston clients. Because of the relatively few proprietors who had settled on their homestead lots, it was difficult to prevent the pilfering of this valuable timber. Even three years after the drawing of the homestead lots, there were but 41 houses and 12 frames in the town.

Because of land disputes, the plotting and laying out of the so-called "after divisions" of the timberlands and wild lands was much delayed. However, by 1733 the back lands had been plotted and set off into lots as follows: east and west of Royall's River, 103 lots of 120 acres each had been laid out, 56 on the western and 41 on the eastern side of Royall's River. The westerly edge of this tract, known as the "120 acre division either east or west of Royall's River," was approximately marked by the Greely Road.

Two other sets of 103 lots each containing 100 acres were laid out to the east of the Royall's River lots in territory that is now in the towns of Freeport and Pownal.

And still a third set of 103 lots each containing 100 acres was laid out to the west of the Royall's River lots, extending southwest to the Falmouth line.

As can readily be seen, these lots varied greatly in value and desirability, and to obviate as far as possible any inequality, a committee consisting of Stephen Larrabee, Francis Wyman, and Barnabus Seabury was appointed to combine them, good, bad, and indifferent, so that each proprietor should have an equitable deal, when the final assignments should be made.

All of these lots were drawn at the same time, August 7, 1733. Each proprietor thus had, besides his 10-acre homestead lot, a lot of 120 acres in the vicinity of Royall's River; two lots of 100 acres each in the northeast part of the town (now Pownal and Freeport); another lot of 100 acres in the southwest part of the town between Greely Road and the Falmouth line; and 4 acres of salt marsh or its equivalent, making a total of 434 acres for each proprietor.

In deference to a previous claim, the Committee had reserved 100 acres on each side of Royall's River extending about three-quarters of a mile upstream from the lower falls to the heirs of Bartholomew Gedney.

Also, claims held under Gorges or other established claims were honored and recognized by the Committee. These included the land on Harpswell Neck, Royall's farm of 300 acres lying between Royall's and Cousins Rivers, two farms on the eastern shore of Cousins River, and 200 acres on Flying Point and Little Flying Point.

On February 22, 1733, the Committee made a detailed report to the General Court of Massachusetts and proposed that the Committee be dismissed and that the town be granted all the powers and privileges of other towns. This report was accepted on April 6, 1733, and an order was passed authorizing Samuel Seabury, a justice of the peace, to call a meeting of the inhabitants, to choose selectmen, constables, and other town officers. In accordance with the order which he had received, Samuel Seabury issued his warrant, and on May 14, 1733, the inhabitants of the town gathered in the meetinghouse to organize and to elect the necessary town offices. And so from this date, May 14, 1733, begins a new regime for North Yarmouth, and now we will discuss the formation of the Town of Cumberland.

The incorporation of Cumberland as a separate town was approved on March 28, 1821, by William King, the first governor of Maine. The new town as set off from old North Yarmouth is shown in Town Records Book 1, page 1 (see page 29). To walk around the boundaries of the mainland part of the town would entail a walk of about 27 1/2 miles. Beginning at the White Rock we would walk northwest about 8 miles along the Falmouth line to the Windham line, then northeasterly along the Windham and Gray lines a little over 3 miles to the present westerly line of North Yarmouth; thence, we would have a walk of some 11 miles zigzagging along farm boundaries in four places along Greely Road, until finally we reach the shore of Broad Cove and a stone monument near the upper end of the cove.

From this point, a 3 1/2-mile walk along the shore road would take us back to our starting point, the "White Rock." In walking this boundary line, which is 27 1/2 miles long, we would have come across 49 stone monuments marking the angle points and corners of the town line, and helping to maintain the lines between Cumberland and its good neighbors Falmouth, Windham, Gray, North Yarmouth, and Yarmouth, forever fixed and well defined.

In closing, I will quote an official of the US Geodetic Survey who was in charge of mapping in the State of Maine, as well as in many other states. Mr. Frank Patten told me "that the Town of Cumberland was the best monumented town he had ever mapped."

Let us try to keep it that way.

Bibliography

Maine Historical Society Library.

Original map of North Yarmouth as formally laid out by the proprietors of said town, 1681–1735. Scale: 100 rods to the inch.

Rowe, W. H., *History of Ancient North Yarmouth*, Portland, 1937.

US Geological Survey Maps.

Chapter Three

The Poland's Corner Neighborhood

By Marion L. Chandler

The part of Cumberland that in the 1800s was called Poland's Corner was located, in modern terms, at the crossing of Tuttle and Middle Roads, a quarter-mile inland from Route 88, and about 100 yards from the overpass which spans Route 95 and the Canadian National Railroad tracks. A description written in its own time reads as follows: "Poland Corners, eight miles from Portland, on Lot 61, in the east of the town is a scattered hamlet of some twenty dwellings, centering around the site of Charles Poland's old store . . . and the Cumberland station of the Grand Trunk Railway."[1] Its most noticeable natural characteristic was Weeks' Hill (later called Store Hill), which went from the top of the cut in the rocks now to be seen on the upper side of the corner, down to the railroad tracks under the overpass. The Corner was named for the Poland family that owned the property around it. The surrounding neighborhood extended within walking distance in four directions (see map and Note 10).

Even before roads were built to form a corner, the house said to be the oldest still standing in Cumberland was in the making. "John Sweetser and his brother Benjamin . . . sometime before 1733 settled in what is now Cumberland, near Poland's Corner."[2] In 1740, two years after a

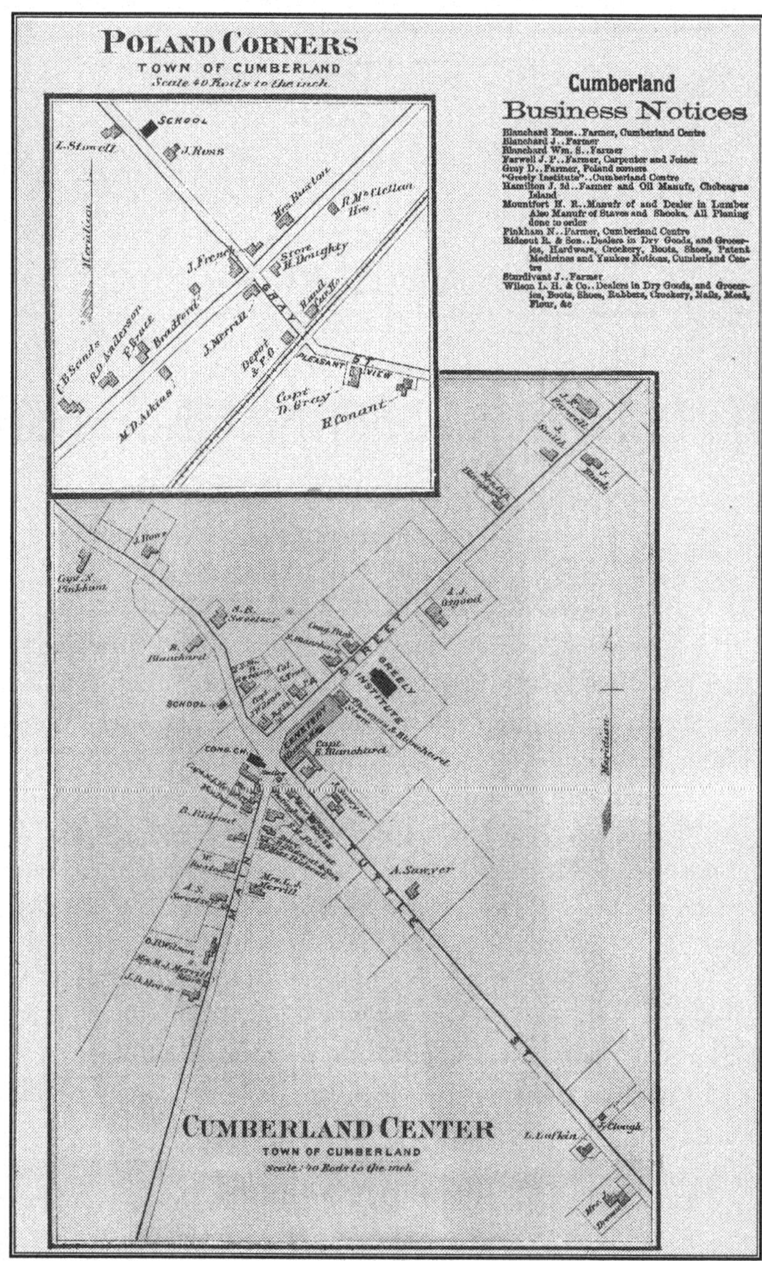

Atlas of Cumberland County, Maine, Beers and Company, 1871

Poland Corner and Cumberland Center.

bounty on wolves had been declared in the area, John built the house that still stands at 158 Middle Road.

No doubt he traveled the half-mile to Broad Cove to make use of the sawmill and plaster mill on Felt's Brook that John Powell had built near his own substantial residence. It may be that when Indians lurked in the town five years after the building of the Sweetser house, its inhabitants took refuge at the garrisoned Powell house then owned by Colonel Jeremiah, John Powell's son. The Powell place was the first house of consequence to be built in what is now Cumberland. For years the foundation depression and the well, eighteen feet deep and lined with fieldstones, could be seen near the present Ledge Road entrance to Schooner Rocks.

This shore acreage had been the scene of even earlier activity, traces of which were found by the family of William P. Russell, who bought the land during shipbuilding days and farmed it for three generations. Before building their house at 240 Foreside Road, near the home of William and Aphia Greely (232 Foreside Road), the family lived across the road on the Powell site. Their plows turned up the foundation stones of an early blockhouse, built on a bluff on the south side of the gully that now marks the Yarmouth end of Schooner Rocks. The old road providing public access to the shore also followed this gully. From this location the blockhouse commanded a view of the coast in all directions and was sheltered from the north wind. It is said that Indians burned the building by shooting flaming arrows from the gully. About 500 feet south of this gully, some distance from the shore, were four circles of hard, dark earth about twenty feet in diameter on which vegetation never flourished. When the land was used for hay or corn, the stunted growth of these circles made them plainly visible. It was thought that these were the sites of Indian lodges and cook fires. Also, timbers and stones from an early settler's cabin were unearthed to the right of the outlet of Felt's Brook.[3]

Indians, humble settlers, and men of means and influence—all had found Broad Cove a desirable place to live before any roads led away from the shore. By 1735, Greely Road was heading inland from the Powell property, along what is now Powell Road. Houses were later built that in time would be part of the Poland's Corner neighborhood. Two, known as the Moxcey houses, are still intact. The older one, 208 Middle Road, had its driveway on the Greely Road. The other is at 18 Greely

Road. Footpaths to bypass the hill went through the woods to Tuttle Road from this neighborhood. By 1761 the King's Highway, coming from Portland, went by the Sweetser house and turned sharply toward the shore. This turn was the beginning of the Corner. At the shore, the Highway bore left at 224 Foreside Road, and continued by the Powell estate on its way to Brunswick. In time, the road now called Tuttle, which had progressed inland as the 100-acre lots were settled, went over the hill to run more or less parallel to Greely Road. The house at 115 Tuttle Road was moved there from its original location on the old Range Road.[4] In 1805 the construction of the Yarmouth end of Middle Road completed the formation of the four corners, which through the 1800s to the 1920s was the site of a thriving neighborhood center.

This was a natural place for such a center to evolve. The people of this coastal area first used the Powell establishment as a focal point. Later they followed the shore to the center of old North Yarmouth. When the division of the town moved the center of Cumberland farther inland, the Corner became the nucleus of a growing community whose native population had been increased by people attracted by the shipyard, and also by the arrival of Swedish and Danish emigrants eager to become landowners. Facilities that gradually developed included a post office, store, school, railroad station, and church. These were all within easy distance of Cumberland Town Landing, Spear's shipyard, and later, the electric car line.

There were also several small enterprises, such as the print shop in the Gray home, and McClellan's blacksmith shop on the site of 179 Middle Road, where Joseph Blanchard lived later. When Gardiner Sturdivant worked as a drover and owned the William Buxton place (172 Middle Road), he had a slaughterhouse across the road from his home, next to the later location of the Dunn barn. Dr. Caldwell ran his Sulphur Springs Sanitarium and health resort in the vicinity of 147 Middle Road. Miss Maria Buxton, daughter of William and Mary Buxton, directed a private school for young ladies in her parents' home at 100 Middle Road before the Buxtons and the Sturdivants exchanged properties. Farmers brought their milk and other produce to the railroad station for the Portland market. Hay, a crop well suited to the coastal soil, was shipped to Boston from the wharf. Occasionally, traveling sawmills were set up at the Corner.

Courtesy of Helen Dunn Maxim

Grand Trunk Station at Poland's Corner before 1923.

The first public service to be established was the postal system. Mail that came from Portland by stage along the King's Highway was distributed at the Corner. The Maine Register of 1822 lists William Buxton as postmaster. At that time the mail stage left Portland each day at four a.m., and single letters could be sent for six cents from a distance not exceeding thirty miles. Mr. Buxton, who worked in the shipyard as a caulker, continued as postmaster through 1842. His house at 172 Middle Road is the only original building that remains at the intersection. Jacob Merrill, who lived across the corner from the Buxton house, was postmaster in 1852.

By 1848 the Atlantic & St. Lawrence Railroad opened from Portland to Yarmouth on the track later used by both the Grand Trunk and the Canadian National. The Cumberland depot was built on the Portland side of Gray Street, as the lower end of Tuttle Road was then called, and the post office was housed there. This station was later destroyed by fire and rebuilt. The first station agent was David Gray, who was postmaster from 1853 to 1870. Captain Gray, who also served as harbormaster with David Spear, lived across the tracks beside the Richard Conant residence (14 Tuttle Road) in a house now moved to the top of Spear's Hill on Route 88. The post office remained at the station into 1895, during the time that John N. Dunn was postmaster and Grand Trunk station agent. During these years many passenger trains from each direction made daily stops at the station. The train to and from Montreal went through every day. Freight traffic was considerable and required a siding and a spur track. Grain, flour, and other supplies for the store on the corner were unloaded there.

After Mr. Dunn's retirement, Fred Wood was at the station for a short time. The next agent was Edgar F. Corliss, who lived in the J. Merrill house until it burned and the family moved to the house across from the church, where his daughter, Grace Brown, was organist for a quarter of a century. John Bunting, stationmaster until 1913, rented the W. Buxton house from the Dunns. The station was destroyed by fire and closed in 1923 when George O'Connor was agent. For a time it was used as a way station.[5]

The post office changed location from the depot to the store in 1896. There it remained until its removal from this end of town in 1919. The following store owners served as postmaster: F. R. Trickey 1895–1904; Alfred W. Doughty 1904–1918.

For ninety years a store did business at Poland's Corner. The first one was opened in 1840 by Charles Poland (1795–1867), who, with his wife Eunice Harris and nine children, occupied a home under the hill on the upper Portland side of the corners. This house was known as the Jerry Buxton house in 1825. Joseph French was the owner in 1871, and sold it to his nephew, J. N. Dunn, whose family owned it until it was demolished in the 1920s. The basement kitchen of this house was dug into the side of the hill, and it was there Mr. Poland started his store. An article in the warrant of the 1847 town meeting read as follows: "To see what measures the town will take if any to lower the hill near Poland's store." This was dismissed, but another attempt in 1850 read: "To see if the town will furnish a man and powder to blow down the hill near Charles Poland's store." Fifty dollars was raised for this purpose.

Courtesy of Helen Dunn Maxim

Charles Poland House, c. 1900.

A separate store building was erected on the lower Yarmouth side of the corners, which in 1871 was operated by Hollis Doughty (85 Tuttle Road). He was succeeded by John E. Dunn, who with his father, John N. Dunn, acquired the property on three sides of the corners. About 1876, J. E. Dunn built a new store across the road from the old one near the William Buxton house, where he resided, and owned the business for some twenty years. The new store was literally on the corner. By pulling to the side of Middle Road, wagons could drive up to the long porch platform and be loaded from the grain room. Customers hitched their horses to the porch posts and went in the main door to buy at the oak counter, or to warm themselves by the stove. Children stopped to look through the glass of the penny candy case by the door. In winter, snow piled under the hill around the store. The town snowplow, made of wood and drawn by two teams of horses, sometimes had to be preceded by a crew of shovelers to break the drifts. Then young people on their bobsleds could coast from the top of the hill to the railroad tracks.

Mr. Dunn sold the store to E. H. Trickey, the next proprietor. He employed Frank H. Jones and Alfred W. Doughty, who later ran it as partners. By 1900 Mr. Doughty (105 Tuttle Road) was the sole owner.

During these years deliveries were made by wagon throughout the neighborhood and in season to summer residents of the Foreside. The store also served the four locally owned summer cottages on the Cumberland Town Landing Road. (These were built up the hill from Simeon Jones's clam shack on land leased from the Dalton farm and were removed when the property changed hands.)

The 1911 Town Report records another attempt to subdue the Store Hill: "Voted to raise the sum of three hundred dollars for cutting down the hill and widening the road on Tuttle Road near the store of A. W. Doughty." It was this cut that fifteen years later slowed the effort to move Mr. Doughty's grain storage building from its location near the railroad tracks to the church grounds for a community house. The building was too wide for the cut and had to be lifted over the rocks by pulleys. It now stands behind the church and is called Doughty Memorial Hall. In 1924 Arthur Flint took over the management of the store and ran the business until it closed in 1930. The main building was later moved to 146 West Elm Street in Yarmouth for a residence.

The schoolhouse of District Number 2 was moved by oxen to the Poland's Corner vicinity from the corner of Tuttle and Harris Roads. It

Courtesy of Helen Dunn Maxim

View of Poland's Corner, c. 1918.

was placed across the road from the gambrel-roofed Luther Stowell house that Seth, son of John Sweetser, had built in duplication of his father's house. The school building was moved in 1854. First called the Weeks' Hill School, it became known as the Tuttle Road School until it was closed in 1950 and became a dwelling, 59 Tuttle Road, diagonally across from the Methodist Church. This was a typical one-room school with a boys' and a girls' entry leading into the main room. Facilities included a box stove in the back of the room and a water bucket on a bench by the door. Behind the building was an outhouse and a woodshed, until modern conveniences were added in the 1920s. A picture taken around 1890 shows May Morrill (Brackett) as the teacher, with twenty-five children representing the following local families: Jones, Doughty, Russell, Peterson, Anderson, Larsen, Gram, Gerow, Sturdivant, Duran, and Strout. Early graduates from the eighth grade could drive by horse and buggy to Greely Institute or, after 1898, ride the electric car along Route 88 to North Yarmouth Academy or the Portland schools. After the school bus program was adopted, older pupils were transported to the Center, and this school was finally used for the primary grades.[6] Two residents of the Corner area acted as superintendent of the Cumberland schools: Miss Maria G. Buxton and Mr. Oscar R. Sturdivant.

Methodist circuit preachers from Portland began work in Falmouth and Cumberland in the early 1800s. In 1831, through the efforts of Rev. Joshua Taylor, a Methodist church to serve both communities was built on the town line at the Foreside.[7] Two of the influential members from Cumberland were sea captains. Captain John Merrill, who built the house at 130 Tuttle Road, later used by his son Asa, attended the church with his wife Sally between voyages. Captain Ephraim Sturdivant (149 Foreside Road) had commanded the schooner *Reaper* as a privateer in the War of 1812. One Sunday the minister gave a blistering sermon on Universalism. Captain Sturdivant, sitting in his pew on the Cumberland side of the church, heard it through. Then he arose and threw open a window, remarking audibly to his wife, "It's beginning to smell mighty strong of brimstone in here!"

These men and branches of their family are buried behind the church (now the Foreside Community Church) in the graveyard that overlooks the sea. The Poland family is there also. Other names on the Cumberland side of the yard are Bruce, Buxton, Harris, Stowell, Greely, Duran, Anderson, Starling, St. Clair, Hitchings, and Brackett.

Because of the distance of the Foreside church from Poland's Corner, supplementary church meetings led by Rev. Elisha Duran, a licensed local preacher, and Sunday School classes with Mr. Edward S. W. Jones as superintendent, were held at the Tuttle Road schoolhouse.

Previous to any organized religious activity, cottage prayer meetings of a nondenominational nature had taken place regularly at the home of Mr. and Mrs. Ira Greely. Mr. Greely used to fish during the winter months after the summer's work was done. One fall when he was walking up the gangplank of a vessel at Spear's Wharf headed for the Grand Banks, he felt the detaining hand of the Lord on his shoulder and heard a voice saying, "Ira, don't go." Without hesitation he turned around, shouldered his sea bag, and walked home. The vessel sailed and was never heard from again. When asked about this experience he would always answer, "I don't know, I suppose I was saved to be better." The Greelys lived near the site of what is now 106 Tuttle Road. To make extra seating for the prayer meeting, rails from the fence that bordered the road were brought into the house and placed between kitchen chairs. Across the road lived Simeon Jones, whose four sons would later settle in that area.

The nondenominational spirit of these early meetings prevailed when it was decided to build the Tuttle Road Chapel in 1882. Residents, regardless of sect, felt that a place of worship was needed in the immediate community, and worked together to provide it. A contractor was hired, and local men experienced in the shipyard did the carpenter work. Joseph Harris (115 Tuttle Road), William Greely, and Alfred Russell hewed out the timbers. Construction was done by Dennis Doughty (179 Tuttle Road) and son George, Asa Russell (97 Greely Road) and brother William, Robert Anderson Sr., and Simeon Jones. Hollis St. Clair (227 Foreside Road) contributed the proceeds from a field of hay to the cause. Also supporting the project were Hollis Doughty, John N. Dunn, Seward Fields (122 Middle Road), James Moxcey, Woodbury Titcomb, Reuben Sawyer, Reuben Brackett, Hans P. Peterson (136 Middle Road), Addison Sturdivant (135 Tuttle Road), and the Strout family, who lived in the J. Ross house across from the church.

The completed meeting-house was a sturdy, one-room structure which Methodist records described as follows: "During the years 1882–1883, through the active exertion of the pastor (Cumberland-Falmouth), Rev. E. W. Hutchinson, a neat and substantial chapel was built in the neighborhood of the post office in Cumberland, at a cost of $1,500; dedicated free from debt. The house is neatly finished and furnished, and is a great advantage to the society."[8]

Courtesy of Tuttle Road Methodist Church

First minister Rev. Eliazar Hutchinson.

After some discussion it was decided that the church should be Methodist and remain part of the Foreside charge, served by the same minister with joint trustees. At the time the new chapel was built, the four trustees from Cumberland were Asa Merrill, John R. Duran, Edward S. W. Jones (19 Brook Road), and Joseph Harris. These men pledged themselves responsible for the land transaction, and the quit-claim was recorded on April 8, 1882.

The Cumberland United Methodist Church, informally known as the Tuttle Road Church, was built on a piece of land 132 feet square on property that went with the old John Sweetser house. Jonathan Bradford was renting the house from the Isaac Sturdivant heirs at the time. This is the reason it is sometimes called the Bradford House. Mr. and Mrs. John E. Dunn (Sarah Sturdivant) were the next owners of the house (remodeled in 1903) and land. They presented to the church trustees the deed of certification for the church land as a gift. A path led from their back door to the churchyard and was used for many years to avoid climbing the Store Hill. Additional land was later given to enlarge the churchyard by their daughter, Helen Dunn Maxim.

> In 1886 Rev. W. P. Merrill wrote in his annual report: "I began a series of revival meetings in Cumberland . . . thirty-five expressed a desire to be saved and asked for the prayers of God's people . . . Our next great need seemed to be shelter for horses, the people living at a distance being unable to come in winter. This enterprise resulted in the erection of eleven first-class horse sheds, affording shelter to twenty-two horses in winter . . . I thank God for this success and for the uniform kindness, constant sympathy and hearty cooperation of this people."[9]

The Ladies Aid Society was organized December 15, 1890. The first president was Annie W. Brackett Hitchings, wife of Samuel K. Hitchings, principal of Greely Institute. Their first church suppers were served in the larger homes, like the one at 86 Tuttle Road. Hay racks or logging sleds coming from each direction picked up customers along the way. Sometimes as many as seventy-five people were served a menu of baked beans, johnnycake, and pie for twenty-five cents a plate. Church socials were also held in the homes. Sabbath School picnics took place annually in the grove on Russell's shore or on the beach at Sandy Point. Occasionally people rode together in hay wagons for a day's outing at Goose Pond (Forest Lake), carrying their rowboat with them. The first cottage on the Pond was built by Mr. and Mrs. H. P. Briel (30 Harris Road), who were members of the church.

In 1915 the Church became a separate charge with its own governing body, and has remained independent throughout its affiliations with Methodist churches of Yarmouth, Portland, and South Portland. Trustees at that time were E. S. W. Jones, O. R. Sturdivant, Frank H. Jones, Hollis Doughty, Aubrey W. Maxim, and Alfred W. Doughty. Mrs. Alvin S. Doughty (86 Tuttle Road) was president of the Ladies Aid. A. W. Doughty was also superintendent of the Sunday School. In his later years, Mr. Doughty (1873–1964) was made an honorary trustee in recognition of his lifetime of service.

The women's organization, currently called United Methodist Women, has ever been responsible for improvements and additions to the church buildings. Doughty Memorial Hall was moved to the grounds in 1924, when Mrs. Charles H. Jones (89 Tuttle Road) was president. In 1947, under President Ragnhild Olson, a kitchen annex was added to facilitate preparing the Swedish meatball suppers that she and Mrs. Anton L. Larson had started for church support. In 1952 a classroom was added to the back of the church while Mrs. Ernest Jones was president. An addition to the hall was built in 1967 with Mrs. Paul N. Gregor as chairman.

In 1974, the church had a membership of 105, and a church school enrollment of 65. Trustees included Dr. William E. Wyatt, C. Walter Olsen, Peter H. Burr, Philip A. Chase, Maurice Small, Russell F. Stevens, George A. Sweetland, and Mr. and Mrs. Burton W. Noyes. Other officials included: Treasurer, John R. Sumpter Jr.; Finance, Mrs. Russell F. Stevens;

Courtesy of Tuttle Road United Methodist Church

Tuttle Road Methodist Church.

Choir Director, Mrs. Virgil P. Wing; Church School Superintendent, Mrs. Vernon B. Russell; President of U.M.W., Mrs. Philip A. Chase. Following the tradition of its founders, the church continues to function as a community organization where people of all ages and conditions worship, work, and play together. Its area of service is ever expanding, and its influence now reaches far beyond what was once called Poland's Corner.

Just as Poland's Corner developed to fill the needs of its citizens, so it passed when advances in transportation made these services unnecessary. The church remains as the last active institution to give a feeling of neighborhood to an area once so self-sufficient. Of the eighteen buildings shown on the 1871 map of the Corner, the following are in their original location: the Cumberland schoolhouse and the homes of J. Ross, W. Buxton, Bradford, or Sweetser, C. B. Sands (136 Middle Road), and R. Conant.[10] With the building of the overpass, even the hill succumbed to progress, and long before that the very name of Poland's Corner had ceased to exist except as it is remembered for its contribution to the growth of early Cumberland.

Endnotes

1. *History of Cumberland Co., Maine*, Philadelphia: Everts and Peck, 1880, p. 266.
2. Rowe, William W., *Ancient North Yarmouth and Yarmouth*, Portland: Southworth Anthoensen Press, 1937, p. 80.
3. Russell, Roy E., *A Conversation*, 1964.
4. Sweetser, Harlan H., *A Conversation*, 1973.
5. Maxim, Helen Dunn., *A Conversation*, 1974.
6. Beach, Jessie L., Teacher 1924–1943, *A Conversation*, 1974.
7. Mitchell, Russell, and Strout, *Cumberland and North Yarmouth Register*, H. E. Mitchell Publishing Co., 1904, p. 40.
8. *History of Methodism in Maine 1793–1886*, by Allen & Pilsbury, 1887, p. 298.
9. Church Records, Foreside Community Church.
10. Atlas of Cumberland County, New York: F. W. Beers & Co., 1871, p. 51.

Doughty, Alfred W., Reminiscences used throughout.

Chapter Four

Shipyards

By Phyllis S. Sweetser

There were shipyards along the Foreside, with small building yards in many coves. In these coves the local men would build themselves a small vessel in which to transport goods locally and in many instances to carry loads as far as Boston. Since there were no roads or any other means of transportation, these small vessels were of great importance. Between 1799 and 1809, Prince Sweetser built ships in his own yard on the Foreside, among them a small schooner called the *Retriever* in which he would carry fifty cords of wood and farm produce to Boston. Also, the local men built small rough vessels called gundalows which were made for local use (as farmers later used trucks) to carry produce and supplies and on which livestock would be taken to the islands for pasture for the summer months. Isaac Sturdivant had a fleet of small ships for such use and carried much hay to Boston. These small vessels were usually anchored at Cumberland Town Wharf, later the location of the Spear Yard.

Several years prior to the War of 1812, a vessel of about seventy tons was built at Cumberland Center on land opposite the Cumberland Town Office near the gully. It was built during the summer and hauled to the water in the winter following.

Sufficient snow had fallen by January for the owners to start operations. In order to steer the craft on dry land they rigged out a spar over the taffrail long enough to reach the ground, and when the vessel was in motion it could be easily guided by shoving the stern either way with the help of this crude rudder.

One early morning, eighty yoke of oxen were hooked to the vessel and the trip to the sea was begun, down Tuttle Road. All went well until they reached the top of one of the hills, which had a narrow bridge at the bottom. Here they took off half the team and put them on behind the vessel, to prevent her from going downhill too fast. They had two mill chains and a seven-inch hawser to hold her back with. The bridge was so narrow that it would require considerable skill to steer her across in safety. When about halfway down the hill one of the mill chains broke,

Hutchinson photo, 1966

Cumberland Town Landing.

leaving one string of oxen and the hawser to hold her back. About fifty feet from the bridge, the other chain parted, throwing all the weight upon the hawser.

It seemed as if the vessel must go off the bridge, but just as she reached the structure, the vessel's shoe caught on one of the stringers of the bridge and she was stopped. The teams in front could not get out of the way quick enough and were all tangled up, but the vessel stopped just in time to avoid serious damage, except that Nathaniel Merrill of Cumberland had a leg broken by a falling spar. The overland trip required two days, and on the third, the craft was launched at Cumberland Town Landing.

In those days this work was done gratis, no charge being made for man or team. The owners, however, treated the men to crackers, cheese, fish, coffee, and rum, prepared and served by the womenfolk, who thus got their share of the general good time. This account derived from a newspaper printed in the 1870s concludes, "At the present time such a job could not be done for less than one thousand dollars."[1]

Spear's Yard in Cumberland was one of the most famous of the shipyards on Casco Bay. It was located at the foot of Spear's Hill toward the ocean where the old King's Highway enters present Rt. 88—once US Route 1. This was a family enterprise and under the supervision of David Spear Sr. and David Spear Jr., about 50 ships were built, 30 by the father, 20 by the son. David Spear Sr. was responsible for the building of 6 schooners of 90 to 100 tons, 17 brigs averaging from 250 to 300 tons, 4 ships of between 300 to 400 tons, and 2 barks.

David Spear Jr. built 16 barks, the smallest 250 tons and the largest 583 tons, 3 ships—the largest, the *Dakotah*, being of 1,054 tons burden—and the schooner *Romeo* of 115 tons. The most famous of his barks was the *Grapeshot* of 345 tons, built in 1853. She was a clipper ship and soon earned the reputation of being very fast.

> "William Poole, a notorious and dangerous character, had eluded the authorities and found passage on the *Isabella Jewett*, a steamer bound for Europe. The US Government chartered the *Grapeshot* and she sailed in pursuit of the escaping criminal, leaving port a day later than the steamer. The *Jewett* was scheduled to call

> at Fayal, one of the Azores, and to this place the *Grapeshot* sailed and found the steamer. Poole was immediately taken off and the *Grapeshot* returned with him to the US."[2]

Capt. David Wilson, Hazel Wilson McGoff's grandfather, was the last person from this vicinity to see the *Grapeshot.* He saw her off the mouth of the Mississippi River with a cargo of slaves. She had fallen to the depths of infamy as a slaver.

David Spear Jr. carried on the business from 1842 through 1869, and at times employed fifty workmen in the yard. "When he was only 39 years of age, his last three ships brought losses to him of over $20,000, and he was forced to give up his building yards and other property

Sketch by Eugene Collins, 1958, Courtesy of Yarmouth Shopping Notes

Bark Juniata, *Spear Yard, Cumberland, 1845.*

[including the large Colonial house which still stands across Rt. 88 from the road to the Cumberland Town Landing], to satisfy his creditors. He began life over again as a common laborer, getting less than a dollar a day."[3]

The end of the shipbuilding industry started with the Panic of 1857. Other contributing factors were the coming of steam power, the use of steel as the chief material for ship construction, and the fact that wood for such purposes was becoming scarce and expensive. So it was destined that this wonderful era of shipbuilding should come to an end.

Compiled from articles by Sally Blanchard Maynard and Russell B. Ross.

Endnotes

1. "The ship that ran away on her way to her launching"—adapted from W. H. Rowe's *Shipbuilding Days and Tales of the Sea in old North Yarmouth,* Portland, 1924, pp. 47–49.

2. W. H. Rowe's *Shipbuilding Days in Casco Bay,* 1929.

3. Ibid.

Chapter Five

Sea Captains of Cumberland

By Russell B. Ross

Few people today have any appreciation of the glorious maritime history of the State of Maine. It is difficult to realize the extent and the economic importance of shipbuilding and the manning of the ships built in the 1800s.

William Hutchinson Rowe reports in "The Maritime History of Maine," taken from *American State Papers Commerce and Navigation*, Vols. I and II,[1] the estimated number of vessels built in the yards on the Maine coast from 1820 to 1890, and their tonnage.

The numbers listed for this seventy-year period total 12,587 vessels constructed, an average of about 180 vessels per year.

It is interesting to break down these seventy years into smaller units. In the thirty-year period from 1820 to 1850, 5,318 vessels were built. But you will find that in the first ten years, namely, the 1820s to 1830s, the vessels averaged about 100 tons. During the next twenty years (from 1830 to 1850), the vessels grew in size, averaging from 150 tons to 200 tons.

From 1851 to 1881, the vessels grew not only in size but in number constructed: 6,425. In the 1850s, the clipper ship–building era, ships constructed, such as the *Red Jacket*, ran 2,306 tons. There were ninety clipper ships built in Maine, all built during the 1850s.

The year 1855 saw the crest of the shipbuilding wave, when 396 vessels were built. A better perspective of what this means may be gained when we understand that the tonnage represented by these 396 vessels made up one-third of the tonnage of all ships built in the United States that year.

Of course, the really large ships, the great five- and six-masted schooners, were built later. For example, the *Wyoming*, built in Bath in 1909, was of 3,750 tons burthen (archaic form of burden). She was the largest wooden fore- and aft-rigged schooner ever built.

These vessels sliding off the ways of the Maine shipyards all had to be manned before they could sail to all parts of the world.

"In the year 1860 there were 11,375 mariners in the State of Maine. They comprised almost one-fifth of the population. Of these, 759 were masters of ships. In turn nearly one-half of these 759 masters were in command of Cape Horners."[2] They were truly "Blue Water" men.

In the town of Cumberland, some fifty ships were built at the Spear yard, which was located at the foot of Spear's Hill where the King's Highway enters Rt. 88. Then, too, in Cumberland, but at that time in the town of North Yarmouth, we should mention Division Point on Chebeague Island, where Capt. Ebenezer Hill built five ships: the *Fountain*, *Dash*, and the *Eunice* before he was thirty years of age, and following the War of 1812, the *Decatur* and the *Columbia*. It was on the latter ship that Capt. Hill died while returning from the West Indies with a cargo of molasses; he was buried in Trinity Church yard in New York City. In this area, however, Yarmouth was the shipbuilding center. It is estimated that over 300 ships were built there. With so many ships being built nearby, it is understandable that many sea captains came from homes in Cumberland.

The ancestor of the Blanchard family in this area, from whom many sea captains descended, was Thomas Blanchard, who left England in 1639 and settled in Charleston, Massachusetts. The first Blanchard to move to this area was Nathaniel Blanchard in the year 1743, from Weymouth, Massachusetts. He lived on what is now Rt. 88 where a blockhouse was erected. He was the great-great-great-grandfather of Cumberland's Arthur and Robert Blanchard, and was buried in the Gilman Street Cemetery just off Rt. 88.

This early Nathaniel had a son born in 1728 whom he named Nathaniel. Rowe, in his *Ancient North Yarmouth and Yarmouth*, tells of Nathaniel Jr.'s encounter with the Indians where his "quick ear and action probably saved his life." He heard the sharp click of a gun lock as he walked along a road and saw the eyes of an Indian peering at him from the bushes. He trained his gun on the Indian and retreated until he was out of range. Later Joseph Sweat was ambushed, shot, and scalped at the same spot.

Nathaniel Jr. had a son named Beza who was born in 1765. He married Prudence Rideout in 1792, and they had twelve children. At least three of their sons were sea captains.

> *By the President of the United States of America* Suffer the *Brig Clarice of Portland, Reuben Blanchard,* Master or Commander, of the burthen *Five Hundred & Thirty-seven* tons or thereabouts, encumbered with guns, navigated with *Eight* men.
>
> To pass with her Company, Passengers, Goods and Merchandise without hindrance, seizure or molestation, the said *Brig* appearing by good testimony to belong to one or more of the citizens of the United States to him or them only.
>
> Given under my hand and the seal of the United States of America the *Twenty-Third* day of *December* in the year of our Lord *one thousand eight hundred and twenty-six.*
>
> J. Q. Adams
> By the President
> H. Clay, Secretary of State

Armed with this imposing document, Capt. Reuben Blanchard felt more secure as he engaged in the West Indian and European trade.

Capt. Blanchard was the oldest son of Beza and Prudence Blanchard. He was born in Cumberland on August 24, 1794. As was customary in those days, he went to sea at an early age. At age twenty-seven he was captain of a schooner engaged in the coastal trade. This followed a quite common pattern, gaining experience and seamanship knowledge on small vessels for bigger and better things.

The first ship he commanded was the *Union*. He was shipwrecked on one voyage and the *Union* was lost; of the eleven men on board, all were lost but the mate and himself.

With three other men he had the brig *Morgiana* built, and he commanded her for four years on voyages to West Indian and European ports. In 1845 he made a voyage to South America, and according to a brief biography appearing in the *History of Maine*, published in 1880, it was on the return trip and while he was in command of the ship *Blanchard*, built in Yarmouth, that he was shipwrecked again, this time off the coast of Virginia.

From History of Cumberland County, Maine *Philadelphia, 1880*

Capt. Reuben Blanchard, b. 1794.

Back in Cumberland his father, Beza Blanchard, had purchased a farm to encourage him to abandon a seafaring life and settle down on the farm. This he did; this farm, located on the Greely Road in Cumberland, prospers today under the direction of his great-great-granddaughter, Kay Fowler.

Beza and Prudence Rideout had twin sons born in 1798, Enos and Sewall. Enos followed in his older brother's footsteps and went to sea as a young man. He truly sailed the Seven Seas. His grandson, Robert Blanchard, has in his possession several of the charts he used in his voyages to Spain, the Mediterranean, Ireland, and so forth.

These charts are most interesting. The spelling of places are so different in many instances. Then on these charts Capt. Enos had marked his position from day to day as he crossed the Atlantic. The pencil marks on these charts trace the path and really bring home to one how dependent they were on favorable winds and weather in those days. The paths zigged and zagged and many times they lost ground or they ran far north or south of where it appeared they desired to go. It takes but little imagination to picture them buffeted about by high winds and storms and driven miles off their course. Many times they must have faced discouraging situations day after day. They had to be determined and persevering in those days in that work.

We do not know too much about the ships he commanded. We do know that some of his grandchildren acquired as middle names the names of ships he captained. In Robert G. Blanchard, the G is for *Germain,* and in Arthur N. Blanchard, the N is for *Nile.* The *Germain* and the *Nile* were two of Capt. Enos Blanchard's commands. Incidentally, Capt. William Prince recorded in his log for July 26, 1830: "Spoke the ship *Nile* from New York for Havre and Antwerp." It seems strange that in the broad expanse of the Atlantic Ocean two ships should meet captained by young men from the same small town.

Another son of Beza and Prudence Rideout Blanchard and a brother to Reuben and Enos was Beza Blanchard Jr.

From a scrapbook kept by Mary E. Sweetser, mother of Herman P. Sweetser, there is a clipping from a Portland newspaper of 1895, describing the shipwreck of the brig *Turner.* It was entitled "A Shipwreck of Long Ago."

Photo courtesy of Robert G. Blanchard

Capt. Enos Blanchard 1798–1878

The brig *Turner*, in command of Capt. Beza Blanchard of Cumberland, sailed from Portland on January 30, 1843, for Madeira. Heavy weather was experienced almost immediately, with gales which continued for the first seventeen days. This resulted in the deck load and cargo shifting to leeward, which did not alarm the captain and crew, as the ship was a good sea boat. On February 16, 1843, at four a.m.:

> [while] scudding under close reefed sails, a tremendous sea broke over the stern, swept the man from the helm, and hove the brig on her beam ends. The foremast and bowsprit snapped off as though they had been reed, and the deck load was immediately swept away. [The deck load was lumber.] As soon as possible we cut the lanyards of the main rigging with our knives when the main mast went by the board and the vessel righted, full of water, with nothing on deck but a few thousand feet of lumber and one empty water cask.

They found it impossible to enter the cabin as the floor had been broken up, and everything, including water casks, was rushing from side to side as they floated in the debris, and eventually were broken up so that the men were left without a drop of fresh water. For food they discovered

Photograph by Daniel Dow

Ship Bengal. *Painting by her captain, Horatio Sprague Blanchard.*

they had a barrel of bread wet with salt water, four or five pieces of salt pork, and about two-thirds of a barrel of beef. For eight days they had no water, "excepting a little which some of us caught during a momentary shower, barely sufficient to moisten our lips . . . we found some relief in chewing lead . . . several of the crew drank considerable quantities of salt water, which causes dizziness and slight derangement." On February 24 there was a fine shower of rain and eight gallons of water were caught. On the next day there was another shower and enough water was caught to allow a pint of water per day per man for seventeen days. On that same day a shark was caught and about a gallon of blood was secured which was allowanced out. The shark was cut into strips and hung to dry but the eating of it caused unbearable thirst.

Courtesy of History of Cumberland County, Maine, *Everts and Peck, Philadelphia, 1880.*

Capt. Joseph Blanchard, b. 1803.

On March 13 a barrel was discovered on the larboard side of the cabin and one Joseph Malore, an excellent swimmer, secured it with a rope and the men were able to get it on deck. To their great joy they found it filled with molasses, which helped to alleviate their suffering.

On March 14 a heavy rain squall enabled them to catch thirty gallons of water. But the men drank until they vomited and then drank again. "The effects of drinking too much operated like a physic and for a time increased the inward thirst and fever."

On March 21 fifteen gallons of water were caught, but new afflictions developed about this time. As a result of sleeping on hard boards in clothing which had been soaked in salt water to slacken their thirst the men developed boils and sores.

"During this time five vessels passed in sight of the men" drifting on the battered hulk of the *Turner*. They estimated that two of the ships passed within three or four miles of them. "Only those who have been similarly situated, can imagine our feeling at seeing succor approach thus almost within our reach and we not able to secure it."

On April 3, the lookout cried, "Sail ho." This time they were sighted and watched eagerly as a brig bore down upon them. It turned out to be a French brig, *La Furet*, in command, Capt. Augustine Caulin. By four p.m., all the men, eight in number, were off the wreck and safely aboard the *La Furet*. Since that fateful morning, February 16, they had helplessly drifted, suffering hunger, thirst, and lack of shelter for forty-six days and twelve hours. During this time the wreck had drifted 700 miles to the eastward.

They arrived at Gibraltar on April 13, but were immediately quarantined and barred from going ashore. They sailed for Boston on the brig *Caroline* (built by John Agry at Hallowell in 1828), commanded by a Capt. Hill, and arrived in Boston on May 21, just 111 days after having left their homeport of Portland.

Is it any wonder that Beza Blanchard, the father of these three sea captains, looked for a farm to entice his oldest boy from his chosen career, in view of the above experiences?

Horatio Sprague Blanchard was born to Reuben and Christiana Loring Blanchard on July 4, 1830. In his late teens his parents thought it advisable to send him away from this area where so many were engaged in maritime pursuits. So young Horatio was apprenticed to a man in Vermont to learn a trade.

This did not work out successfully. Horatio left Vermont and came to Portland, where he "signed on" a ship without his parents' consent or knowledge. However, before the ship sailed he was taken sick and had to go to his home on Greely Road.

It is reported that his parents finally consented to his "going to sea." His later life testifies to his success in his chosen field. He commanded a Union ship, the USS *Quaker City* in the Civil War, and later was captain of the ship *Bengal*, a painting of which hangs in the Prince Memorial Library at Cumberland Center, presented by his grandson, John Blanchard.

You wonder as you gaze at this beautiful painting of the *Bengal* if this was the ship on which he voyaged with his wife. It was a common practice for the wife to accompany her sea captain husband on voyages, and on which a son was born who was four years old before the family returned to their homeport. Capt. Horatio Sprague Blanchard lived to be eighty-four years of age, and died February 23, 1915.

Another Blanchard sea captain was the son of Nathaniel and Christiana Loring Blanchard, Joseph, born on June 17, 1803. (Reuben also married a Christiana Loring, but not one and the same.) This Nathaniel Blanchard lived at 102 Blanchard Road in Cumberland Center where the road ended at that time. Young Joseph left home at the rather tender age of fourteen and shipped on board the coastal schooner *Telegraph*. He served, at age eighteen, as second mate on the *Telegraph* for one year. At age twenty he had moved up to first mate on the brig *Echo*, which was later his command.

From History of Cumberland County, Maine, *Everts and Peck, Philadelphia, 1880.*

Residence of Joseph Blanchard, 102 Blanchard Road.

He captained the brigs *Rebecca* and *Catherine*, and then came back to the *Echo,* where misfortune awaited him. The *Echo* was wrecked on Cape Cod and was declared a total loss with cargo, and also the loss of one member of the crew.

Following this disaster he was in command of the brig *Freighter*, and for a period of nine years made regular trips to Point Peter, Guadeloupe. This was followed by two European voyages. In command of the ship *John Cadmus*, he made four voyages to Europe, with some coastal voyages sandwiched between ocean crossings.

By this time he was financially situated so he could have a ship built and own it himself. So he contracted and had the *Cornelia* built, and for the next eight years sailed her to and from European ports. Then he had the *United States* built, which he captained for two voyages before his retirement as a mariner.

The History of Maine (1880 edition) states that Joseph Blanchard "made more trips to the West Indies than any other sea-going man in Maine, having made 84, and 30 voyages to Europe." Truly a remarkable maritime career! Incidentally, Rowe lists the *Telegraph* as built in Yarmouth in 1821, the *Echo* in 1823, the *Rebecca* in 1800, and the *Catherine* in 1833. He also lists the *Cornelia* as built in 1826, but inasmuch as Joseph contracted to have the *Cornelia* built, he would only have been twenty-three years old in 1826, so it appears doubtful that this was the same *Cornelia*. They did give ships the same names at that time, especially if one bearing the name had been reported lost.

Capt. Joe was versatile. He picked up foreign languages as he traveled, and was considered especially fluent in French. When the Civil War broke out, he retired from his forty years of life at sea to his old farm home on Blanchard Road.[3]

One of Beza and Prudence Rideout Blanchard's twelve children was William. He became a farmer and built the house on Rt. 88 at 77 Foreside Road, where Mrs. Sally Blanchard Maynard lived until her death in 2016. He had two sons, Andrews and John Dean, who are listed as shipowners and merchants. Andrews was the owner of the bark *Cumberland* and died in 1855, while John Dean (1810–1873) was a successful shipowner and merchant.

Mrs. Hazel Wilson McGoff's grandfather, David Wilson, was born in Cumberland in 1818. His father, Edward Wilson, came here from Derry, New Hampshire, and married Abigail Spear Atkins, the daughter of the Spear shipyard people. Abigail had married an Atkins who died at an early age. One child was born of this marriage. Then from the Edward Wilson and Abigail Spear Atkins union, there were six children. Abigail Spear Atkins Wilson died, and Edward Wilson married a widow, a Mrs. Buxton, who had several children by her first marriage. From the Wilson-Buxton marriage, there were three children—so there were his children, her children, and their children—all in all, lots of children.

David, one of the three children from the Wilson-Buxton union, ran away from home at age nine. In Portland he persuaded the captain of a ship to take him on as a cook. The captain felt a responsibility for him and took him home with him to live whenever they were in port, and even saw to it that he got some schooling or education. He followed the sea for over twenty-five years and claimed he had visited every important port in the world, with one exception: London. When he retired from the sea he did farming on a small scale. Prince Memorial Library is located on what once was part of his farm.

Edward Wilson had a half-brother, John Wilson, who was also a Cumberland sea captain and lived at the corner of Main Street and Blanchard Road.

An uncle of Mrs. McGoff's, Capt. Edmund Norton, was also a sea captain. Capt. Norton was born about 1853 in Falmouth. After he married Maude Sturdivant, he lived at Cumberland Foreside on what is now Rt. 88, and his house still stands. As a young man he worked up from seaman to first mate on a ship. On a return voyage the captain was taken violently ill, so they put into the nearest port, one of the Atlantic Coast ports, for medical attention for the captain. The captain was immediately hospitalized. The young mate, Edmund Norton, wired the owners of this turn of events and expected that they would send a replacement for the ill captain to bring the ship back to its homeport. Instead, the owners wired the young man to bring the ship back to Portland himself. He was nineteen years of age at the time.

Later he served the town of Cumberland as treasurer for many years, and also founded the Portland Shipbuilding Company, where he supervised the building of many ships, primarily fishing vessels.

Another Capt. Norton was Capt. Charles Norton, an older brother of Capt. Ed. Norton. He was also born at Falmouth in 1852. In his early teens he worked on the Doughty farm on the lower part of Tuttle Road. By the time he was seventeen he was at sea as a cabin boy. Stories are told of his rather adventurous nature as a youth. Reportedly it was common talk around Falmouth Foreside that as a young man, Charles Norton once swam from the Town Landing in Falmouth to Sturdivant Island, a distance of a mile or more. A rowboat followed to keep him in sight. In the cold waters of Casco Bay this was quite an exploit.

It is said of Capt. Charles that he was the only man in the Portland area who would sail a sloop among the islands of Casco Bay on a windy day and deliberately upset her. By pulling on a rope tied to the masthead, while rocking the boat at the same time, he would catch enough wind under the sail to right the boat to an even keel.

In his early thirties Capt. Charles married Lizzie Wilson, daughter of Capt. David Wilson. There were three children by this marriage. The children were all born in the Capt. David Wilson brick house on the site of the present Prince Memorial Library.

Capt. Norton spent his active life in the New England West Indies trade. His square-rigged vessels bore lime and lumber from Rockland and other Maine ports to Cuba, Jamaica, St. Thomas, and Puerto Rico, returning to Boston and Portland with sugar, molasses, guavas, mangoes, and other tropical products. He brought home a number of souvenirs which were placed in the Greely Institute museum in the upstairs hall—rusted guns from ancient Spanish ships in the Caribbean, a full-size stuffed albatross, as well as a sea horse or two, among other marine souvenirs. These pieces were in the museum up to the time the building underwent alterations, about 1940.

Capt. Norton was wrecked three times in his career. He once told of floating around in a pork barrel, his weight ballasting it and holding it upright, with a red bandana fluttering from a nail driven into the chime, until a passing ship rescued him.

His last wreck was in the brigantine *Ernestine* (built in Yarmouth in 1869) that sank in a gale off Cape Hatteras, in 1897. Only one man, the mate Charles Branscom, survived. He clung to the jib boom till it floated ashore. The Merrill family at Cumberland junction once saw this Charles Branscom when he visited town, and he related to them the story of the fate of the *Ernestine*. He stated that Capt. Norton swam five miles that stormy night until within sight of watchers along the debris-strewn beach, and then went down, possibly struck by some floating debris. None of the bodies of the crew were ever recovered from the sea.

One of the most colorful figures around Cumberland Center in the 1880s, 1890s, and up to the early 1900s was Capt. Frederick Crickett. He married into one of the North Yarmouth Baston families, and lived at 276 Main Street. He had daughters named Lizzie, Eunice, and Christine. Lizzie was lively and entertaining and a close friend of Emma Merrill's, who lived in the house next south of the Crickett residence. Christine became a schoolteacher and taught in the District No. 7 School, just above the Cumberland Junction village, about 1902–1903.

Capt. Crickett was a Norwegian. He will be remembered by the old-timers as a kindly man in his sixties. He once taught one of the town's boys to swim. As the captain drove along the Falmouth Road in a buggy, he stopped and made the strokes so graphic to the ten-year-old that the latter made haste to try them out the next time he went up to the Goose Pond. And, following the captain's verbal instructions, inside of ten minutes he found himself swimming, and never lost the knack.

Once, in the Dunn store, a high school principal (Mr. N. Gratz Jackson) on a 20-below-zero morning, asked Capt. Crickett, "How would you like to be out about a thousand miles at sea, Cap'n?" To which the captain quickly replied, "Ha! I'd rather be there than here." Which made good sense, since that far at sea the temperature would probably not have been down to zero.

But the captain worked hard, lived hard, and died hard. It was told of him that on an occasion when his ship was caught in the wintry gale somewhere about a thousand miles at sea—and the rigging was pretty well coated with ice—a topsail got loose from its yard and began to flap and snap in the gale. The captain ordered the nearest crew member to go aloft and furl that ice-coated sail. But the rigging was encased in ice, and

Courtesy of History of Cumberland County, Maine, *Everts and Peck, Philadelphia, 1880.*

Capt. Ephraim Sturdivant, 1782–1868

the man shrank from the prospect. He started to back away from the captain. The captain followed him up as he retreated across the deck, pulled a pistol from his coat, and leveled it at the crew member, advancing toward him. The man, rather than go aloft in the ice-coated rigging, kept backing up until he fell overboard, right over the rail, and was lost in the icy waters. Discipline had to be maintained aboard ship.

Captain Crickett is said to have been assigned to the *Onaway*—the last vessel of the square-rigged variety ever built in Yarmouth yards. She was of about 1,000 tons capacity, and she sailed on most of the oceans of the world. There were other ships under his command, but it appears that the *Onaway* was probably the last one.

About 1907 or 1908, Capt. Crickett fell ill at his home in Cumberland Center with a rare malady. It was said to be a paralysis of the throat. He lost his ability to swallow, and could eat nothing. He lay around for a week or two without getting any nourishment. The doctor confided to the family that there was nothing he could do for him, that he would just have to lie there till he starved to death. It was supposed that the captain was apprised of the prospects. Shortly thereafter, he put a bullet through his head with that same old pistol, killing himself instantly. A tough old bird, Capt. Fred Crickett was, all the neighbors agreed. But he was a likable man and a good neighbor when he was ashore.[3]

Capt. Ephraim Sturdivant was born in what was then the town of North Yarmouth on February 14, 1772. He was the third son of David Sturdivant and Jane Greely Sturdivant. Ephraim went to sea at the age of twelve. Before he reached twenty-one years of age, he was in command of a vessel. He owned vessels and sailed them, trading with the West Indies and Europe. He followed the sea for twenty-eight years.

In 1810 he imported a cargo of Merino sheep from Portugal. He pastured these sheep on Sturdivant's Island, which he owned. This is sometimes called Clapboard Island today, and lies just off the Cumberland Foreside shore.

A letter of marque was issued on June 18, 1812, by President James Madison. This letter of marque gave Ephraim Sturdivant permission to operate the ship *Reaper* as a privateer. She was a schooner of 206 tons and was armed with six carriage guns and seventy-five men. Of course, the large number of men for a vessel of that size came in very handy when they boarded vessels and hand-to-hand fighting occurred. Rowe, in his *Ancient North Yarmouth and Yarmouth*, also places Sturdivant in command of another ship operating as a privateer, the *Ilsley*, a ship of 143 tons, six guns, and seventy-five men.

Capt. Ephraim survived the War of 1812, and when Cumberland was set off from the town of North Yarmouth in 1820, he became its first treasurer, serving until 1832. He gave the town its name, having been granted that privilege by vote of town meeting. He also represented the town in the state legislature, and served two years as a state senator. He served as a Cumberland selectman for many years, where he was followed later by his sons Alvan and Sumner Sturdivant, and grandson Sumner Sturdivant Lowe. Also, in conjunction with Judge Preble, he bought the right-of-way for the Grand Trunk Railroad in this area. He was a member of the first convention, which framed the Constitution of Maine in 1820.

A daughter, Annie, was married to sea captain Marcellus Lowe, who died suddenly while returning from a five-year voyage. Mrs. Lowe took over command of the ship and brought it safely to port. Her son, Sumner, who was born at sea, was the selectman referred to above.

On the hill known locally as "Ephraim's Mount" (behind his house), there were twelve tall pine trees called "The Twelve Apostles." These trees were a sighting or landmark for ships coming into Portland Harbor. The last tree fell in 1935.

Capt. Harold Sawyer owned a journal kept by Capt. William Prince while in command of the brig *Ceres*, dated from 1829 through 1831, and

Courtesy of Cumberland Historical Society

The final Apostle, c. 1917.

also his account book from 1818 to 1830. The account book indicates that he shipped as a seaman on board a brig, noted in the first entry dated April 13, 1818: "This day entered on board the brig, Jonathan Greely, Master—discharged 17th June whole amount of wages $42.00."

By January of 1819, it appears he had taken over a sloop, the *Caleb Strong*, and was engaged in coastal freighting. By October of that same year he was in command of the schooner *Olive*, which in addition to freight also carried passengers. Incidentally, the fare from Boston to Portland was $4—unless one chose to go steerage, where the fare was $3.

By 1828, William Prince was captain of the brig *Ceres* and was crossing the Atlantic regularly. Here are a few notations from his account book:

> June 1, 1830—Paid the corporation of the City of New York for 119 alien passengers from Havre @ $2.50 per head [followed by] "labor $7.37 to clear out the brig and $1.88 to scour the cabin."

> July 11, 1830—The *Ceres* was in Antwerp and the owners were billed by Capt. Prince. "Drink money for Pilots—$5.00." [But on leaving Antwerp the necessity didn't seem as great to treat the pilots as well, as this notation appears:] "Drink money for Pilots, $2.50."
>
> November 13, 1830—"Pd Sheriff bill for cook in Jail—$6.61."

William Prince was evidently a pretty good businessman. He got receipts for many of his expenditures, even though small; for example, one for nineteen loaves of bread—95 cents. It is interesting to note that when the crew was advanced money, many made their mark after their names in the account book. One receipt, on a sheet of paper tucked into the account book, showed where he had paid part of his taxes to the Town of Cumberland in the amount of $3.45, dated December 27, 1834.

Sea captains had to have a pretty good business head. They had to deal in foreign money many times. William Prince paid some bills in guilders, some in English money, some in Spanish dollars. It appears they advertised for cargo, as the cost of advertisements are noted in the accounts. The accounts ran into thousands of dollars on some trips.

The log is fascinating. One section starts August 22, 1829. It is William Prince's first voyage in command of the brig *Ceres*, bound for London from Norfolk:

> First part [meaning the first part of the day] wind from WSW, rough sea and squally weather. At 10 a.m. a heavy squall from NW when we were obliged to take in our light sails. The day ends with a strong breeze from WSW, nasty weather, rough sea.
>
> The Lord is good and gracious to us in giving us so much fair wind and prospering us so far on our passage which I [illegible] to be thankful for, and may it make a suitable impression on our hearts so that we may go on our way rejoicing, praising God daily for his goodness to us and to the children of men.

But nine days later he wrote:

> Light winds from NNE, flying clouds, smooth sea. Saw one brig standing to the westward; very large school of porpoises came around the vessel but could not get one. I anticipate that we are

> drawing on to sounding. If that is the case the ship is ahead of our reckoning. I hope to be in London in one week more. We are always tired of our situation. When I was at Norfolk I wished myself at sea and now I wish myself on shore for I am quite tired of being at sea. The mind of man is always a roving from one end of the world to the other; there is nothing this side of the grave that will satisfy an immortal soul—we must look above this world for that consolation which we need. Lat. by ob. 49° 02' Long 15° 19' Temperature of water 60°.

They docked in London September 9, 1829. On September 29, they hauled away from the dock and proceeded down the river. On September 30, he entered this in his diary: "One man left the brig without leave and stole my boat which cost me two pounds to obtain her again. Stole a watch, two jackets, and a pair of shoes from my crew. Got under weigh again—at night anchored at Gravesend."

There followed about two weeks of gales and rough seas during which time they gained but little. The journal entry for October 17 records:

> Commences with strong winds from SSW, rough sea, under double-reefed sail. At twelve midnight wind hauls to the SSE with rain—at four in the morning a sudden squall from the NW. Scud under double-reefed topsails. The day ends with a heavy gale from NNW, very heavy sea which makes the brig labor bad. I am quite sick of gales and headwinds; such disappointments are enough to make any man sick of the seas. Rigging and sails giving away and we are gaining but little. How long it will last God only knows. I wish I was so situated that I could leave this slavish occupation. I would give three cheers and rejoice and bid old Neptune adieu.

The *Ceres* arrived in Charleston on November 20, so that crossing took them almost two months. Capt. Prince sailed from Charleston February 20, 1830, with a cargo of cotton for Le Havre. He left Le Havre April 14, 1830, for New York, and it is evidently this trip—bringing the 119 aliens to this country—that he mentions in his account book, with expenses for cleaning the brig and scouring the cabin. On this voyage he records that the cook is sick. He later writes, "Ills of life too much to bear; shipload of dirty passengers with some troublesome fools among them." Still later in the voyage he records, "running out of water, wood and provision." This journal brings home the fact that in spite of lots of action at times, at other times it was a monotonous and lonesome life.

On May 19, 1833, he wrote:

> Commenced calm; middle part the same. The day ends, light breezes from the westward, passing clouds, smooth sea and good weather—[gives position] O, how I long to be on shore, for I am tired of being cooped up on a vessel so long at sea without a connection of mine to speak a word [to]. If I had wings I would fly away and be at home.

Then he waxes poetic:

> O, for an angel's wings to soar
> Above the heavy heaving sea
> And reach at once the dearly loved shore
> And dearer friends I long to see.

Capt. William Prince's journal on Sundays may have contained parts of his talk or the prayer from the service he probably held on board ship, weather permitting. This was customary if the captain had religious leanings.

It is amazing to learn of the number of ships lost by shipwreck or foundering. These men did not have the navigational aids used today; therefore, their navigation was not too accurate. For example, Capt. Prince wrote on October 15, 1829: "French captain came on board who informed me that he spoke a Spanish brig that morning who informed him that our longitude is 65 degrees, which has quite disappointed me. Easterly currents and a dull sailing ship [a ship was called *dull* when its bottom was fouled with weeds and barnacles and badly in need of cleaning] has caused this mistake, so that we do not need to look for land until day after tomorrow." They watched for birds as a sign they were approaching land. Prince mentions the gannet as never being seen too far from land. When they thought they were approaching land, they took soundings to determine the depth of the water.

On his forty-fifth birthday Capt. William Prince was at sea. He moaned that many of his shipmates had not lived to reach that age, and wondered why, as he commented that they were no more exposed than he. He thanked the Lord for his kindness to him and for preserving him in dangers and peril.

In 1831 Capt. Prince was a very sick man—so sick that from April 29 to June 5 he didn't make a single entry in his journal. He gave up his command of the brig *Ceres* and came home and spent the summer recovering his health. A Capt. David Gray of Portland took over his command of the *Ceres*.

Later in the fall of 1831, he took command of the barque *Grecian*. This man seemed to have had more than his share of hard luck. On a return trip in 1832 from Liverpool to New Orleans, he reported in his journal, September 25, 1832: "Found the bark making more water than usual; two pumps would hardly keep her face." He spoke the ship *Newport* also bound for New Orleans, and she promised to stay in company with the *Grecian*.

As you read the journal and account of this voyage, you almost live it with the men; you can imagine yourself taking your turn at the pumps—800 strokes per hour—provisions running low, the crew getting restless, the water gaining, stepping the pumping up to 900 strokes per hour. You breathe a sigh of relief when the *Grecian* pulls into New Orleans on November 14, 1832. This had been, however, a seven-week-long strain, and it is not surprising to learn that "William Prince of Cumberland" (as he always signed his name) died at the age of forty-eight.

Almost all we know about this William Prince is what we can learn from his journal. We do know that he was born May 13, 1787, and died in 1835. A William Prince joined the Cumberland Congregational Church in 1807, and it could well have been this William Prince, as he was a very religious man. By paying a tax bill to the Town of Cumberland in 1834, as previously mentioned, and by always signing his name "William Prince of Cumberland," we assume he lived in Cumberland and owned property here.

Endnotes

1. Rowe, William Hutchinson—*Maritime History of Maine.*
2. Rowe, William Hutchinson—*Ancient North Yarmouth and Yarmouth, Maine, 1937.*

3. Norton, Floyd—*Another Sea Captain*, 1970.
4. Hauk, Z. William—*Stone Sloops of Chebeague*, 1967.

5. Acknowledgments for information supplied on

Capt. Enos Blanchard—Robert G. Blanchard

Capt. Beza Blanchard—Scrapbook—Mr. Herman Sweetser

Capt. Reuben Blanchard—Mr. Fred Blanchard

Andrews and John Blanchard—Mrs. Robert Maynard

Capt. David Wilson, Capt. John Wilson, and Capt. Ed. Norton—Mrs. Hazel Wilson McGoff

Capt. Charles Norton—Mr. Floyd Norton

Capt. Fred Crickett—Mr. Floyd Norton

Capt. Ephraim Sturdivant—Mrs. Herman Sweetser (Phyllis Sturdivant Sweetser)

Capt. William Prince—Capt. Harold Sawyer

Capt. Simeon Clough and Capt. John Clough—Clough Genealogy

Other Sea Captains of Cumberland

(Added January 1974)

The homes of many sea captains were located on Tuttle Road in Cumberland. Capt. Enos Blanchard lived in the house at the corner of Main Sreet and Tuttle Road.

Just below the Blanchard Farm and possibly adjoining it was the home of Amos Clough and his family. He had at one time two grandsons living with him, Simeon, born September 28, 1796, and John, Simeon's younger brother. Both of these boys became sea captains.

Capt. Simeon Clough married Mary Wyman, who lived on the farm below the Cloughs, at 291 Tuttle Road. Mary Wyman's mother was Nancy Bradford, a descendant of Gov. William Bradford of the Plymouth Colony. The "Story of the Family of John Clough," edited by Eva Clough Speare, relates that Nancy came from Plymouth to Yarmouth as a girl on one of the vessels departing coastwise. She never returned to Plymouth.

The same source indicates that by 1825, Simeon was in command of the bark *Union*, bound for the Verde Islands and Africa. In 1844, from logbooks and account books, he was captain of the brig *Portland*. He retired from the sea about 1849. He lived on his farm until his death in 1870.

Simeon's brother, John, was captain of the barque *Ontario* in 1845. One winter his ship was frozen in the harbor at Stockholm. He and his mate married Swedish girls. John is buried in the old Eastern Cemetery in Portland.

Capt. Josiah Bradford Clough was the oldest son of Capt. Simeon. He got his training under his father, and by the age of twenty-one was placed in command of a vessel. The West Indian trade was at its height at that time, and he made many voyages to and from the West Indies. In 1850 Capt. Clough was in command of the brig *Watson*, owned by a Portland firm. He was returning from *Matanzas* in thick weather at night, with a cargo of molasses. Nearing Portland, he struck Halfway Rock, and the ship and the entire crew, with the exception of a young Falmouth man, Benjamin Houston, was lost.

Capt. Stephen Clough became quite famous in an alleged attempt to rescue Queen Marie Antoinette in 1793. It is an interesting story. The Clough Genealogy does not establish that Capt. Stephen was a descendant of John Clough, but it is reported that there is evidence that points to that possibility.

On the Wyman side there was Capt. Charles Wyman (1812–1885), Miss Margaret Wyman's grandfather. She tells of hearing her father relate how he remembers his father saying he saw slaves being sold in the slave markets of New Orleans. One of his ships was the bark *T. Vennard*, built in 1857 by J & J. A. Seabury in the Blanchard yard in Yarmouth.

Mr. Harlan Sweetser recalls that there were other sea captains living along Tuttle Road. Some of them were engaged in the coastwise trade. Some of the sea captains Harlan Sweetser recalled were:

> Capt. Barter, who moved here from down east—Washington County way. He commanded ships carrying phosphate rock from the Gulf States, and also made at least one trip to Chile. He lived on Tuttle Road northwest of the Maine Central tracks from about

1893 to the time of his death, about 1908.

Capt. Isaac Sturdivant—as a young man he was in command of ships but later became a merchant.

Capt. Prince Sweetser lived on the Tuttle Road. He had three boys lost at sea. One went west and died of yellow fever.

Capt. Sawyer—lived at 179 Tuttle Road.

Capt. Doughty—lived across from the Tuttle Road Methodist Church. He had a daughter who married a Capt. Johnson.

Capt. Gray—lived where the interstate is located today, near the Conant home.

As Harlan Sweetser points out, because it was necessary to have men to captain the many ships built in this area, it was natural and logical that the men in Cumberland turned to seafaring. And it was logical that shipbuilding became an important industry in this area, with the availability of the materials for shipbuilding: the big pines for masts and spars, the hackmatack (or tamarack) for the knees, and oak for the planking.

In 1860 there were 11,375 mariners in the State of Maine, almost one-fifth the population. There were 759 masters of ships, and one-half were Cape Horners.

A Sea Captain from the 1970s

Granville I. Smith
Interview with editor

If the sea captains of years ago were to return to their native Cumberland shores today, they would be stunned, to say the least! Changes in both training of seamen, and the size of their vessels, are most evident.

One of their contemporaries is Capt. Granville I. Smith of Wildwood Park, Cumberland Foreside. Graduated from Maine Cumberland Maritime Academy in 1947, Capt. Smith sailed as a deck officer for Mobil Oil Co. until 1958, at which time he became a Portland Harbor pilot. In this capacity, he has handled thousands of vessels of all classes, the largest being the tanker *Universe Patriot*. This ship is 990 feet long, 142 feet wide, and can lift 157,602 dead-weight tons. She anchored off Cumberland in Hussey Sound for bunker fuel.

Photo by Donald Johnson, 1970.

Capt. Granville I. Smith

All pilots have master's licenses, and are trained in the latest navigation procedures. Modern equipment is capable of accuracy to +3 feet in channels, and offshore navigation accurate to a ship length in the middle of the ocean, using satellite systems. This is certainly a far cry from the skipper of yesteryear who hoped for a noon shot of the sun, first to determine latitude.

Capt. Smith's license allowed him to command the largest ships afloat under the United States flag.

Chapter Six

History of Chebeague: "The Island of Many Springs"

By Donna L. Miller Damon

When the townspeople of North Yarmouth were deciding what the boundaries of the proposed town of Cumberland would be, they had to consider the waters of Casco Bay as well as the mainland, for Ancient North Yarmouth extended into the Bay. The town fathers had to deliberate over the islands to keep and those to give away. The primary consideration was the distance islanders would have to travel to participate in town affairs. It had been quite a trek for the settlers on Chebeague, Bangs, Bates, and Crotch (now Cliff), to get to town meetings in North Yarmouth; perhaps Cumberland would be closer. Thus the islands closest to Cumberland, as well as the outer North Yarmouth islands lying to the westerly end of the town, were included in the new town. This included Great Chebeague, a portion of Little Chebeague, Broken Cave, Hope, Smooth Clapboard, Basket, Bates, Stave, Ministerial, Bangs, Sturdivant, Goose, Crow, Sand, and Jewell.

The largest and most influential of the Cumberland Islands is Chebeague. Before Captain John Smith explored Casco Bay, or Pilgrims landed at Plymouth Rock, Chebeague was a summer retreat for Maine Indians. Shell heaps are numerous on the banks of Chebeague, and artifacts are frequently found. The Indians enjoyed Chebeague for many years, giving the island its name, which means "Island of Many Springs." When Englishmen first visited Chebeague, they used their imagination as to how it should be spelled. Thus, early records show it as *Chebaccho*, *Jebeage*, *Jebig*, *Chebeag*, then evolving into its present spelling during the last century.

Few Chebeaguers have grown up without hearing the story of how the Indians "really" named Chebeague. Tradition has it that two braves were paddling along in their canoes when they happened by a large wooded island. The brave in the bow pointed toward the island and said, "She big Island." The other Indian agreed, and so Chebeague was named! The Indians were right, for Chebeague is nearly five miles long from Chebeague Point to Deer Point, and two and one half miles wide from Rose's Point to Division Point; it's second only in size to Sebascodegan, or Great Island, which is part of Harpswell. Thompson's Hill on Chebeague has the highest elevation of any point in Casco Bay, 190 feet above sea level.

Early owners got quite a bargain when they acquired this large island, rich in vegetation, shellfish, and an abundant water supply within a few miles of the North Yarmouth mainland. The ancient records are sketchy, but provide a little information concerning the early owners of Chebeague.

The first recorded real estate transaction took place September 18, 1650, when George Cleeves, who held the original grant to Falmouth, deeded Chebeague to Walter Merry. In 1685, Governor Danforth of Massachusetts reiterated this conveyance, saying that Cleeves had conveyed "all that small island in Casco Bay commonly called Chebeag, and now by the name of Merry's Island." Chebeague changed hands again on October 8, 1675. According to Willis's *History of Portland*, Robert Thornton of Canton, in New Plymouth, conveyed Merry's Island to Josiah Wiles of Boston. It is uncertain how Thornton came about owning the Island. Deeds show that the Jordans of Spurwink acquired Chebeague after Thornton, for the sons of Reverend Robert Jordan conveyed 650 acres on Chebeague to Walter Gendall, a pioneer of North Yarmouth, on July 12, 1680. Gendall was killed by Indians near his home at Royall's River, North Yarmouth, leaving his claim on Chebeague to his widow, who in turn gave it to her second husband,

Theodius Moore. Willis, in his history, speculates that this tract of land on the easterly side of Chebeague may have been the site of a fishing station. He based his conclusions on improvements that had been made on this section of land.

The land on the other end of Chebeague had fallen into the hands of Richard Wharton, who was granted 650 acres on the West End of Chebeague by the government of Massachusetts. After the grant in 1683, his administrator, Ephraim Savage, was responsible for transferring this land to the deacons of the First Church of Boston. These men of God planned to use Chebeague for relocating the poor of their parish, changing the name of the Island to Recompense. Luckily, its next owners retained the Indian name, and it was never changed again.

Colonel Thomas Westbrook, a wealthy Falmouth resident, acquired the East End of Chebeague and quickly transferred it to Samuel and Cornelius Waldo in 1743. Neither the Waldos nor the deacons of the Boston Church made any real attempt to settle Chebeague. So for nearly one hundred years, people had been buying the island for speculation, rather than for settlement.

Chebeague's fate suddenly changed in 1746, when the First Church of Boston sold its holdings to Zachariah Chandler. Chandler was the first Chebeaguer. He had moved to North Yarmouth with his parents and ten brothers and sisters from Duxbury, Massachusetts, during the migration of the early eighteenth century. When Zachariah acquired his land, he divided it among his brothers Judah, Jonathan, and Edmond, as well as Jonas Mason, husband of his sister Mary. The Chandlers cut the trees and cleared the land to make Chebeague a settlement. It is fitting that Chebeague's natural harbor is called Chandler's Cove.

We do not know why the Chandlers decided to settle on an island, but one can speculate that the land in North Yarmouth may have been at a premium because of the number of people who were emigrating from Southern Massachusetts. The Chandler settlement seems to have induced others to come to Chebeague. They attended the "Church Under the Ledge" in Old North Yarmouth, as did Ambrose Hamilton, who became Chebeague's next landowner in 1760, also the year that Benjamin Waite, a Falmouth merchant, bought the East End of Chebeague. Both of these men had a profound effect on the island's future settlement.

Benjamin and Abigail Isley Waite's home was on the East End of Chebeague, if in fact they ever lived there. It is presumed that his family lived on Chebeague until 1773, when he deeded his holdings to his brother, Colonel John Waite. Willis says of Benjamin Waite: "He was a respectable merchant before the Revolution; Benjamin died in Falmouth, to which place he had removed." This evidence helps us to conclude that Benjamin lived someplace other than Falmouth, perhaps Chebeague. Another bit of evidence to support the theory that Waite lived on Chebeague for a time are the marriages of two of his sons to Johnathan Chandler's daughters. Benjamin Waite Jr., born in 1756, married Lucy Chandler, while his brother Daniel, born in 1761, married Rachel Chandler. It is logical to assume that some of the Waites must have lived on Chebeague or visited it frequently for these marriages to have taken place. The baptism of Daniel Waite II, son of Daniel and Rachel Chandler Waite, at the home of Johnathan Chandler on Chebeague in 1799, provides a little more evidence to support this conclusion.

Colonel John Waite was a well-respected man in Falmouth when he moved to Chebeague in 1773. A local hero of the Battle of Louisburg, during the French and Indian War, Waite was active in pre-Revolutionary planning in Falmouth. John Waite's tract of land was about 809 acres, sizable in terms of today's lots but ordinary in Colonial America.

None of the old-timers on Chebeague know exactly where Colonel Waite built his house and farm. However, most sources agree that it was on the southerly side near the center of the Island. Evidence exists in the old North Yarmouth records to substantiate this theory, for in 1817, when the discussion of boundaries for the island's school districts[1] was under way, reference was made to John Waite's home. This boundary line ran from the "Northeast of John Waite's house at the First Salt Works Point, so called, on the southeasterly side of the Island." Salt Works Point was in the general vicinity of Central Landing. Years before a landing became a reality at Central, this property was referred to as Salt Works Point in connection with a proposed Town Landing.

Waite remained on Chebeague for a very short period of time. The colonies were in constant turmoil at the dawn of the Revolution. War was certain, and the British were cruising up and down the coast, keeping the settlers in fear. Waite, feeling that Chebeague was open to attack, moved his family from the island in 1774, abandoning a newly completed three-story home and several outbuildings. Tradition has it that some of his livestock roamed Chebeague for many years after his departure. John Waite had appealed to the Federal Court of Massachusetts for protection, but to no avail. Thus, it is not surprising that he became a member of the Committee of Correspondence after his return to Falmouth, helping to formulate the policies during the early days of the American Revolution.

Although Captain Henry Mowatt sailed up and down the coast and eventually attacked Falmouth, not all Chebeaguers felt threatened enough to leave as Colonel Waite had done. The Chandlers had lived on Chebeague for thirty years, raised their families, and were part of the island. Chebeague's other resident, Ambrose Hamilton, had married and raised a family of six children. What an undertaking it would have been for them if they had fled to the mainland! So these hearty Chebeaguers remained. It seems ironic (as far as Colonel John Waite was concerned) that Falmouth and not Chebeague was ravaged by the English!

The Chandlers and the Waites influenced the history of Chebeague, but not nearly as much as did Ambrose Hamilton. He had come to Chebeague, a young man of twenty-six, ready to clear land for a homestead. He bought one hundred acres on the western side of the dividing line from Zachariah Chandler and his brother-in-law Ebenezer Cole in 1761. So Ambrose Hamilton built a home on the northerly side near the center of the island. He was born in North Yarmouth, July 21, 1735, the son of John and Betty Chandler Hamilton, folks of Scottish descent. Ambrose was married to Deborah Soule, on April 28, 1763, by David Mitchell in North Yarmouth. She was the daughter of Jedediah and Tabitha Bishop Soule, born April 22, 1744.[2]

The Hamilton family had maintained a pew in the First Church of North Yarmouth (the "Church Under the Ledge") for many years, so it is not surprising that Ambrose and Deborah were baptized in this church, September 15, 1765. The Chandlers attended the same church. What a cold and lengthy journey it must have been, but this inconvenience was part of living on Chebeague during the early days of settlement.

When the Revolution came, Ambrose Hamilton served on the side of the colonies, helping to defend the seacoast of Cumberland County for six months.[3] He and Deborah had six children at this time, which was only the beginning of the family of fourteen they were to have. Chebeague survived the American Revolution with little or no effects, other than the experiences that some of the inhabitants had while serving in the war.

After the Revolutionary War, Chebeague began to attract many permanent settlers. By the early nineteenth century, the Sawyers, Rickers, Mitchells, Hutchinsons, Thompsons, Doughtys, Bennetts, Webbers, Johnsons, Hills, Rosses, Soules, Curits, and Littlefields were living on Chebeague. Some bought land right away, while others, such as Enoch Littlefield, a stone sloop captain, appear to have waited many years before acquiring land. When Maine became a state in 1821, thirty-five families lived on Chebeague. Quite an increase since the Chandlers came to the Island in the 1740s!

Courtesy of Rachel Miller Sanderson

The center of Chebeague's business was located near the junction of today's Firehouse Avenue and the South Road. Various businesses have come and gone here, from grocery stores and ice cream parlors to a bakery and a post office.

Most of Chebeague's new settlers during the period after the war came from North Yarmouth and the Freeport-Harpswell area. These towns had been experiencing rapid growth for several decades; the islands of Casco Bay seemed good alternatives to the overcrowding on the mainland.[4] Fish was abundant, the land was rich, timber was plentiful, and on Chebeague one could even find a wild sow now and then, thanks to Colonel Waite's hasty departure.

Many Chebeaguers attended "The Church Under the Ledge" and may have persuaded their friends to come to Chebeague and give it a try. Living on an island wasn't much harder than mainland life in wilderness Maine. Both were quite a distance from centers of society. The transition would probably be more difficult for Americans today than it was for their ancestors.

Most of the new residents of the late eighteenth century settled on the West End. The Johnsons, Webbers, and Rickers were well established when the first census of the United States was made in 1790. The Chandlers had been dividing their land for many years, selling it when the occasion arose, whereas the Waites still owned the East End, until 1804, when they sold the first parcels to Benjamin Mitchell, James Hamilton, and Ebenezer Hill.

James Johnson's homestead was located from the westerly side of the "Cricks" (also known as Johnson's Cove), to Sandy Point. James was married twice, first to Hannah Bates and second to Hannah Fickett. His son Barnwell built the original section of Ed Jenks's house in about 1813. When the house was enlarged, the Johnsons used the older part as a store.

Jonathan and Margery Coombs Webber came to Chebeague from Harpswell about 1784. Their property adjoined the Johnson homestead. Unlike all other early holdings on Chebeague, the Webber property was entirely landlocked.

Wentworth Ricker, a Revolutionary War veteran, settled on Chebeague around 1790, bringing his wife Elizabeth and several children with him. His home still stands overlooking Indian Island, a spit of land, on which stands the Lone Oak Tree, one of Chebeague's well-known landmarks. Island tradition has it that Wentworth discovered the tree when it was a mere sapling. Oak trees were scarce on Chebeague at that time, so he nurtured it—and it survived, outliving all other vegetation on the point, as well as many generations of Chebeaguers. Some call it the Umbrella Tree, because of its umbrella-like appearance.[5]

Wentworth Ricker was a very successful farmer on Chebeague, but in addition to his farm he had a very flourishing salt-works operation near his home. Here he manufactured both fine and coarse salt by distilling the water of Casco Bay. This was a common industry around Casco Bay at the time.

Solomon Sawyer's ancestors were among those who settled in the Purpoodock area (now part of Cape Elizabeth) in the 1680s, but were driven back to Massachusetts during the Indian Wars. They returned, and eventually Solomon settled on Chebeague. He was an older man when he and his son Solomon Jr. moved their families to the island at about the same time as the Rickers. The Sawyers first settled adjacent to the Rickers on what is now known as the Sunset Landing property.

As the nineteenth century approached, Chebeague's population was steadily increasing. Ambrose Hamilton's family had grown to fourteen

Courtesy of Donna Miller

Central Landing's deed dates back to 1873 when it was leased by a group of Chebeaguers hoping to improve transportation to the mainland. It was in use for nearly seventy-five years. The buggies at the head of the wharf were waiting to take freight and passengers to their destinations. This picture was taken from a postcard made in about 1898.

children. He had acquired some land at Duck Trap, about ten miles from Camden. Here Ambrose spent a great deal of time. Whether he planned to relocate his family there is not known. He may have bought it as an investment, or as a retreat.

Ambrose's last letter to Deborah is still in the possession of their descendants. Several observations can be made from this letter, sent in August of 1789. One can conclude that he was involved in some sort of business venture, selling and cutting wood. There was little opportunity for Chebeaguers to earn real money on the Island at this time, so this must have been a boost to the meager economy in which the Hamiltons lived. Ambrose's concern for his family's well-being is evident when he inquired about the availability of bread. There was no mill on Chebeague, so all grain had to be ground on the mainland and brought back to Chebeague.

Ambrose never returned from one of his trips "Down East" in 1795. He died in Belfast of typhoid fever. Deborah Hamilton and her oldest sons sailed down to put Ambrose's affairs in order. We do not know if Ambrose had intended to relocate his family to this new property, but Chebeague's history would have been quite different if he had.

As new settlers came to Chebeague, a pattern developed which is typical of many small, geographically isolated communities—namely, intermarriage. Deborah Hamilton planted her children at the roots of most Chebeague families. With the marriage of John Hamilton to Anne Sawyer in 1790, Chebeague was destined to have a population saturated with Hamilton blood. James Hamilton married Mary Webber, Deborah married Richard Hutchinson, young Ambrose took Ruth Sawyer as his bride, while his sister Lucy married Ebenezer Hill. Jane and Jonathan Hamilton married John and Elizabeth Curit, making the Curits and Hamiltons very close. All this in the first generation of Chebeague-born Hamiltons. As they became parents and grandparents, the Hamilton roots became deeply embedded in the soil of Chebeague Island.

The first decade of the nineteenth century brought a change in Chebeague's religion. Until this time, most Chebeaguers had belonged to the Congregational Church in North Yarmouth, but then the Methodist missionaries came. They preached sermons of "hellfire and brimstone" throughout Casco Bay, trying to convert the "natives" to Methodism.

Several men came to the islands preaching the word of God, but it was Edward Whittle who made the first actual conversions on Chebeague. Whittle had been on Long Island before coming to Chebeague, and many thought that he had been sent by God to save them from the evils of the world. Whittle's sermons seem to have been very effective. By the end of the first decade of the nineteenth century, thirty Chebeaguers had joined themselves with the Methodists, disavowing all other religious ties. Deborah Soule Hamilton was so caught up in the Methodist conversion that she wrote a letter to Reverend Mitchell, who had performed her marriage ceremony many years before, expressing her contempt for his church. As a result Deborah was excommunicated from this church on October 15, 1810.

One young man became so inspired that he went into the Methodist ministry. Stephen Bennett was an enthusiastic preacher, dividing his time between Long Island and Chebeague. Tradition has it that when Father Bennett was preaching on Long Island, you could hear his sermons on Chebeague, and vice versa. Stephen was the son of Job and Mary Haraden Bennett. The family had lived in Gloucester and Freeport before coming to Chebeague. Stephen's home still stands on the original Bennett homestead on the southerly side of Deer Point at Bennetts Cove.

Stephen Bennett married Rachel Soule, niece of Deborah Hamilton, linking these two families early in Chebeague's history. Mary Bennett, Stephen's sister, became the wife of David Doughty in 1797, the first of that name to live on the island. It is not known for certain whether the Doughtys moved to Chebeague and induced the Bennetts to follow, but it is a plausible theory based on vital statistics and real estate transactions. The Doughty homestead was on Coleman Cove, a natural harbor that was essential in the Doughty family's fishing industry. The Doughtys have been known as good pilots and astute fishermen from that time to the present. Much of the original Doughty land belongs to the descendants of David and Mary Bennett Doughty.

Ebenezer Hill was one of the first people to buy land from the Waites when they began to sell their land in 1804. He moved to Chebeague from Cousins Island when he married Lucy Hamilton, and became one of Chebeague's best-known residents. Hardly an article is written about

Courtesy of Chebeague Island Historical Society

Chandler's Band from Portland departing from the wharf, having gotten off the Machigonne.

Chebeague without mentioning Master Hill. The son of Hezekiah Hill, a participant in the Boston Tea Party, Ebenezer made his own mark in history.

Ebenezer and Lucy Hill made their home on Division Point. There he built a brickyard and small shipyard. Again to rely on tradition, it is said that Hill built his house of bricks so that he might have a home more impressive than that of Colonel Waite. (That house was razed in the mid-nineteenth century, and the bricks were used to build the Baptist Church building, which still stands.) Ebenezer Hill went to sea at an early age. Being very adept on the ocean, he rose through the ranks and soon became the master of his own ship. Hill built the vessels *Fountain*, *Dash*, and *Eunice* before the War of 1812. The shipyard on Chebeague must have been a very busy place at that time.

Many prosperous merchants and sea captains had watched their fortunes dwindle during the Jeffersonian Embargo. Once war was declared, they eagerly became involved in privateering. Ebenezer Hill was one of

New England's unlucky privateers. Master Hill and his crew were among many who were captured by the British. They spent the remainder of the war in a dark, dingy prison where conditions were deplorable. During Hill's captivity he met Stephen Decatur, the naval hero, famous for his battles with the Tripoli pirates. Decatur was in the Bermuda prison for only a short time but became fast friends with Hill.

The war ended in 1815 and many a weak and sickly sailor was released. Hill and his crew were given an old leaky ship, with orders to get home the best way they could. Somehow they reached New York; there they sold their newly acquired vessel, divided up the money, and headed for home. Hill's share alone was $100. Once back home he began to build a new ship. Chebeague lumber was used for the boat. It must have been a sizable task for the men to haul the timber to the building site near Division Point. This ship was named the *Decatur*, after Master Hill's friend. The brig was 231 tons—quite a boat for such a small community as Chebeague. The *Decatur* was eventually captured by Gibbs, the pirate. Some sources say that it was taken after making a trip to Le Havre, France, with 521 immigrants on board bound for New Orleans; but other accounts report that the *Decatur* ran short of water on this trip, forcing it to come into Portland for supplies, and that it was sunk and captured on a later voyage.

Ebenezer Hill made many voyages to the West Indies carrying various cargoes. A true man of the sea, Hill always assumed the responsibilities of his position as captain. On a trip in 1828, Ebenezer Hill contracted yellow fever. He spent much of the return voyage in his cabin and was making a good recovery when the *Columbia* (his last ship built on Chebeague) ran afoul of bad weather off New York. The crew was shorthanded, for several men had succumbed to yellow fever, so Hill came on deck to bring the ship into port. The elements were too much for the weakened Hill; he had a relapse and died in New York City. Master Ebenezer Hill was buried in New York's Trinity Church Yard. During his illustrious life, Hill earned a place as one of Chebeague's most famous native sons. Ebenezer Hill was not the only Chebeaguer to see action during the War of 1812; no doubt most of his crew hailed from Chebeague. Information was passed down through family members that Hill's brother-in-law, Richard Hutchinson, was also a privateer. Whether he had his own vessel or served on board one of Master Hill's brigs is not known. Job Bennett and his son Job Bennett Jr. were lost on the *Dash*.

Another Chebeaguer who saw action during the War of 1812 was John Ross. Ross served in the North Yarmouth Militia before joining the crew of the USS *Constitution*, better known as *Old Ironsides*. John was the grandson of James Ross, a Scottish immigrant who settled in Gorham, circa 1760. John Ross lived in Gray for a time with his father, Alexander, but near the beginning of the nineteenth century, John and his brothers, Samuel and Walter, moved to North Yarmouth, eventually settling on Chebeague. It comes as no surprise that the Ross brothers married island girls who were granddaughters of Deborah and Ambrose Hamilton, thus linking all Chebeague Rosses with the Hamiltons.

Shortly after his marriage, John left Chebeague to serve on the *Constitution*. When he returned he brought a memento of the voyage. He had carved a walking stick from a sliver of the *Constitution*. Highly polished and adorned with an ivory knob, it has a band of delicate silver near the top with a fine engraving of *Old Ironsides* on one side and "J. Ross" on the other.[6] John Ross was a man of the sea most of his life. He and his sons, Walter and John Jr., were wrecked on Graves Ledge off Boston. They clung to the wreckage of their craft, and were picked up, only to die of exposure before reaching the hospital. While John had settled near the Center of Chebeague, his brother Samuel settled on the East End and was the ancestor of most of Chebeague's East End Rosses. Walter, however, settled on the West End and was the progenitor of the West End Rosses.

At the end of the War of 1812 Chebeague seems to have had a barely subsistent economy. A few people were beginning to haul rock ballast to shipyards around Casco Bay, but for the most part Chebeaguers raised most of their food, and there was always an ocean full of fish, lobsters, crabs, and clams.

Despite their distance from the mainland, Chebeaguers took an early interest in education. In 1817, while Chebeague was still part of North Yarmouth, several islanders petitioned the town to define the boundary line dividing School District No. 8 from School District No. 9 (both of these districts were on Chebeague). Ambrose Hamilton Jr. seems to have spearheaded the petition. A committee was appointed to decide upon an

Courtesy of Rachel Miller Sanderson

Eastern Landing was crowded with people as the steamboat departed, leaving them to enjoy the island resort. (Photo c. 1910)

agreeable division line. The committee consisted of Ebenezer Hill and David Chandler. Three years later in 1820 a proposal was accepted setting the boundary line. This line remained until school districts were dissolved.[7]

Throughout Chebeague's early history there has been little mention of local politics—not because our ancestors failed to participate or were apathetic, but rather because the written records were not complete. Cumberland separated from North Yarmouth in 1821. From that time Chebeaguers' names were always present in town affairs. Chebeaguers voted to separate from North Yarmouth on March 5, 1821. Prior to that meeting Captain Ephraim Sturdivant conducted an informal census of the island in "Old North Yarmouth." His findings showed Chebeague to be inhabited by thirty-five families. Existing records disclose only the names of those Chebeaguers who voted to join Cumberland. Twenty-eight men (this was long before the days of women's suffrage), including four young men who were not heads of households, were in the majority.[8]

The records leave eleven families unaccounted for. Some may have failed to pay their poll tax, but probably not all eleven. The obvious conclusion that comes to mind is that not all Chebeaguers agreed that separating from North Yarmouth was in their best interests. Perhaps they were farsighted enough to realize that problems could occur if Chebeague joined with a different town than its nearest neighbors, Cousins and Littlejohn Islands. This is only speculation, for no written records have been found to support this theory. Noticeably absent from the majority are the Doughtys and Bennetts. (It is unlikely that all the men by those names were off the Island.) Barnwell Johnson, who built the original section of the Ed Jenks' house on the southerly side of Chebeague, is also missing. There is a theory that if this schism existed, it may have been one of the causes of the East End–West End feud.

Zachariah Chandler's dividing line of the 1740s became an invisible barrier between Chebeaguers. Many West Enders agreed with the majority, but ill feelings could have spread after Chebeague joined Cumberland. The separation theory for the feud would explain why Chebeaguers did not object when the Methodist Church property was acquired in 1815 on the West End, but by the mid-nineteenth century East Enders were violently opposed to the erection of the new church on the westerly side of the dividing line. It can also be used to explain why the "Zach Line"[9] was not used as the school boundary line in 1820. There is no definitive answer as to the cause of the feud—but this is a plausible theory. The feud has had an effect on Chebeaguers for many generations. During the nineteenth century, very few Doughtys married East Enders. Most of the womenfolk moved to the Harpswell area where they married and raised their families, while women from that area moved to Chebeague to marry Doughty men. This practice continued into the twentieth century, causing more intermarriage on the East End than might normally have occurred.

Objections on Chebeague did not stop the island from joining with Cumberland when it separated from North Yarmouth in 1821. Participation was an important part of life in the new town of Cumberland. There was no place for apathy in 1821. Despite the difficulties arising from island life, Chebeaguers answered the call to serve at all levels of town government. Monday, April 9, 1821, saw the people of

Cumberland assemble at the Congregational Church to hold their first town meeting. A few hearty Chebeaguers came across the bay and trekked up Tuttle Road to the Center. It seems that only a handful made the trip, for Ambrose Hamilton Jr. and Wentworth Ricker held most of the island positions. Mr. Ricker was overseer of the poor, constable, fence viewer, and field driver, while Ambrose was tax collector for the islands, fence viewer, and tythingman. Both men served as school agents for their districts as well as these other sundry positions. The only other Chebeaguers to hold an office were Solomon Sawyer Jr. and Jonathan Hamilton, who served as field driver and fence viewer respectively. Most of these positions lack prestige in modern terms, but they were essential tasks in early Cumberland government.

Chebeague was not the only inhabited island; Bangs, Jewell, Bates, and Crotch had small populations but were even farther away from the mainland than Chebeague. These isolated islands represented tax revenues, and taxed they were, although they seldom received any benefits from their taxes. Taxing was easy, but collecting was another story. No one enjoyed traveling to these outer islands to collect taxes, so the town was divided into two taxable districts—the mainland and the islands. Persons interested in collecting taxes submitted separate bids, depending on the section of Cumberland they were considering. The person with the lowest bid got the job. Levi Sweetser won the bid for districts in 1825, but what a difference in the bids. Seven cents on each dollar collected on the islands as opposed to three cents on the Cumberland mainland. Collecting taxes on the islands must have been more of a task than Sweetser had thought, for in 1826 his bid for the islands rose to 8 cents/dollar; and finally reaching a high of 9 cents/dollar in 1827. Sweetser may have gone even higher in 1828, for Joel Ricker of Chebeague won the bid with 9 cents/dollar. This seemed to set a precedent, for Chebeaguers usually underbid all other competitors as collectors of island taxes from that time on.

The town meeting of March 1832 serves as the first indication of problems arising between residents of the islands and the mainland. Cumberland needed to invest in a town hall as a meeting place, but problems arose as to where the hall would be built. The selectmen took the needs of the islands under consideration when making plans for the hall's construction. During the early years no islanders served on the Board of Selectmen, so with no one to represent them the people of Chebeague found a drastic manner to voice their disagreement. They were violently opposed to construction of the hall in Cumberland Center.

Judah Chandler and others presented a petition to the town in 1834. It read, "to see if the town will move the town house nearer the center of travel, if so, take measures which may be thought best to carry out the same effect"; if not, "to see if the town will let the Islands with the Southeast of the main be incorporated into a new town, and take any measures to get the same effect." This proposed division was an interesting development for such a new town as Cumberland to experience. Evidently the nucleus of the town's voting population lived closer to the center than the site encouraged by the Islanders and residents of the Foreside. The first motion was defeated 87 to 56, the second defeated 94 to 49. Therefore, most of the people who felt the town should remain intact favored the location of the town hall in the center of town.

A division of a town only thirteen years old could have proven disastrous. Chandler and his delegation were persistent, for they approached the town in May of that same year asking to be allowed to form a new town. The results of this meeting were not recorded, but in the end the town remained unified. The debate must have been strong, frequently reaching emotional terms. Modern-day residents of Cumberland might find these transcripts extremely interesting, with Chebeaguers pleading for independence and Cumberland refusing. The thoughts of independence had subsided by town meeting of 1835. Judah Chandler, who had spearheaded the separation movement, agreed to serve on a committee to do a valuation of the islands. Chandler, Ambrose Hamilton Jr., and Stephen Bennett were also asked to make an inventory of personal property as part of their report.

Chebeague's population had been steadily increasing for nearly fifty years when the first mention was made of the town building roads on Chebeague. The selectmen had been petitioned in 1843 by Jonathan Webber (and others not mentioned) to build a road through Capt. Schofield's (probably Ricker's) farm. The selectmen were delegated to go to Chebeague to determine the best route through this property. No record was made as to the outcome of this study. It was seven years before Chebeaguers pushed for another road. In 1850, this five-mile-long and three-mile-wide island had no roads. "The town voted to accept the report of the selectmen to lay out a Private Way for the use of the town on the Island Jebeage—provided the inhabitants of said Island pay all damages and build the road—said road shall be two rods rather than three as the selectmen had reported."

At first glance this looks like a very unfair decision. The town was allowing Chebeaguers to build and pay for their own road. It must be remembered that this occurred during the period when the town was divided into multi-school districts, tax districts, and even road districts. Paying for the road was no small matter; $150 had to be raised from poll taxes as well as property taxes, levied on the inhabitants of Chebeague. The men and oxen were allowed one dollar per day, while carts and plows were compensated for, at the discretion of the surveyors. Samuel Ross, store proprietor on the East End, and Stephen Orr, farmer and mariner on the West End, served as surveyors. Chebeaguers seemed to have turned out in sufficient numbers to get their road approved at the town meeting, for they also elected their first native selectman, Ebenezer Hill II. Chebeaguers have always been known to support their causes in droves. Hill's election set a precedent which eventually provided Chebeaguers with equal representation on the Board of Selectmen. Traveling on Chebeague was no easy matter before roads were built. Before the construction of the North Road during the mid-nineteenth century, Chebeaguers had to open thirteen gates from the East End to the Church and twenty-one to Waldo's Point! This is evidence enough that a road on Chebeague was essential.

Chebeague had slowly evolved into a flourishing community. The population had increased to four times the 1820 figure. John Morse was operating a store on the East End in part of the old Reuben Keazer house. Several churches had been formed, and the Methodists were building a new house of worship under the auspices of lssac Strout. Just to the northwest of the dividing line, Samuel Ross was in charge of collecting taxes to build a school in District No. 9. Ambrose Hamilton had been justice of the peace for several years, performing marriages and other legal matters. Eben Hill, Stephen Orr, and Samuel Ross had all taken a turn as third selectman for the town.

Courtesy of Norma Sanderson Morahan

Sunset Landing (1908) was part of a land development scheme of the early twentieth century. A large tract of land was divided into house lots, roads were named, and a couple of cottages were built, but Sunset never caught on as a summer colony, and much of the land is still undeveloped.

The Stone Sloops

The most significant activity on Chebeague during the mid-nineteenth century was the rock slooping industry. Also known as stone slooping, the business was run mostly by East Enders, who developed a unique type of craft, which was capable of carrying many tons of great granite blocks and other building stone from the quarries Down East to railheads in New York, Boston, and many other Eastern cities. Chebeague's rock sloop fleet also carried rock and helped in the construction of many coastal lighthouses, breakwaters, and forts. Chebeague stone slooping began on a small scale in the late eighteenth century, carrying small shipments of ballast rock to the many flourishing shipyards around Casco Bay. Through the years they gained prominence by shrewdly investing their profits into bigger and better sloops and equipment.

The average Chebeague stone sloop was about sixty feet in length, twenty feet wide, drew about five feet of water, and weighed about forty-eight and a half tons. The sloops were built nearly flat to enable them to get in close to the shore, making it easier to load and unload cargo. The men from Chebeague preferred to have only one large sail. The boom and gaff were held out clear of the deck by a boom pole. The single mast served as part of the boom derrick, leaving the rest of the deck free to load and unload cargo. This boom derrick was the distinguishing feature of the Chebeague rock sloop. The mechanism used to hoist the stone on board the rock sloop was between the mast and the bow. From the time that Chebeaguers became involved with rock slooping until after the Civil War, this was a windlass operated with hand spikes. The sloop *United States* was launched in 1869, having on board the first steam-operated winch. It was the first time that Chebeaguers had used that innovation.

Stone slooping was a family industry. Usually most of the crew were related to the captain, but this wasn't hard on Chebeague, with frequent intermarriages. The family aspect of rock slooping tended to keep the large profits "all in the family," so when it was time to buy a sloop, Chebeaguers needed little outside investment. The sloops were known collectively as the "Hamilton Stone Fleet." This is not to say that only Hamiltons had sloops, but rather that they comprised a majority of the population. But many other master mariners hailed from Chebeague and bore the names of Ross, Hill, Sawyer, Cleaves, Bennett, Curit, Littlefield, and Thompson, to name a few.

Chebeague boys first went to sea between the ages of nine and twelve, signing on as cook. The large sloops had a crew of five, while the smaller vessels needed only three men. The crew was paid about $30/month, fairly good wages when compared to the national per capita income of the day.[10]

James Hamilton, son of Ambrose and Deborah Soule Hamilton, was a pioneer in the slooping business. He shared his success with his grandsons, giving two of them a sloop of their own. This was a common occurrence; John Hamilton, known as Uncle Jack,[11] gave five of his sons rock sloops. He provided the capital for a sixth son, James Monroe Hamilton, to buy the store which became Hamilton's Co. near the site of the present Stone Wharf. Robert Hamilton, his five sons, and three sons-in-law, comprised one of the most successful slooping families. The following is an excerpt from an interview with Captain Alfred Hamilton, son of Capt. Robert, written in 1928.[12]

> I freighted stone in the *Jenny Lind* from Granite Quarries on the Saco River to the several forts in Portland Harbor. That was during the Civil War and no vessel was allowed to enter or leave Portland Harbor between sunset and sunrise, all vessels being required to fly the American Flag, and I was obliged to hoist my flag from one fort to another in the harbor. The larger sloops were employed on wharf building, government breakwaters, and lighthouse work between Eastport and Delaware Bay. Work was done at Fall River, Jersey City, New Jersey, and in Delaware Bay, and these sloops for many years carried granite from the quarries at Cape Ann, Gloucester. I carried much of the stone for the Boston Post Office. The contractors were Jonas H. French and General B. F. Butler, known as a silent partner in the construction firm. The quarries were at Bay View, Gloucester. Breakwaters for which I carried stone include those at Rockland, Bar Harbor, Portland, Richmond's Island, Saco, Newburyport, Rockport, Hyannis, etc. . . .
>
> I was very busy rock slooping on the Delaware during the years 1874–1875, and my last important work in that line was assistant to James Howard of the US Lighthouse Department in the building of Ram Island Lighthouse. We with 30 men were engaged in this work for two seasons.

Captain Alfred's career is similar to that of many of his contemporaries on Chebeague.

As the market became oversaturated with great haulers, some of the Chebeague men diversified their operation and began to carry building stone used for columns, monuments, and building construction. There was a good market for granite as a result of the Greek Revival style of architecture. The sloops took the stone from the quarries to railheads such as New York, where it was shipped to construction sites. The sloop *Island Belle* carried the granite columns for the addition to the Massachusetts State House in Boston. Other famous buildings made of rock hauled by Chebeague sloops were the State and Navy buildings in

Washington, D.C., the Chicago Auditorium, Chicago Board of Trade, and the post offices in Boston and New York. The last two buildings were constructed during the Grant administration. The granite that backs the Washington Monument was also carried by a Chebeague rock sloop. Captain Sylvester Hill carried stone for several government buildings, but this was his most famous trip as captain of the *M. M. Hamilton.* He took granite from the Rockland quarries to the railhead in New York, and from there it was shipped to Washington. The *M. M. Hamilton* was the largest of the Chebeague sloops. It was 90 feet long and its sail contained 1,003 square yards of canvas. It was built by John "Flatfoot" Hamilton in 1869, at Stover's Cove, Harpswell at a cost of $16,000. Several Chebeaguers owned shares in her; Aaron Cleaves's investment was second only to Hamilton's.

Another use that was made of stone sloops was putting navigational markers on ledges. These stone sloops could usually get in close to the ledges because of their relatively flat bottoms. One extremely difficult job undertaken by Chebeaguers was placing the spindle on Old Man Ledge. The *Jenny Lind* under Captain Hugh Bowen accepted the contract from the Lighthouse Department to drill the hole in the ledge in 1885. The ledge was underwater except for a few hours a day. Frequently there would be six weeks at a time when they couldn't get to the ledge at all. They finally resorted to buying a steam drill to finish the job. They did not finish until the next spring because of ice and cold winter weather. After they finished they took the job of setting the spindle for $1,000, hoping to make up some of the loss that had resulted from buying the drill. They were eventually successful on this very difficult job.

The stone sloops were also used in salvaging sunken craft. Their boom derricks made them very efficient for this line of work. The *United States* and the *Island Belle* lifted the Rockland–Boston steamer, *City of Richmond*, off the rocks in 1881.

The small quarries supplied a great deal of cellar stone in the days before cement was a universal building material. The sloops hauled the stone for the small quarries that used the abundant cellar stone as a way to compete with the larger granite quarries. They also shipped curb stones and paving stones as a means of competition. Many American streets were paved with cobblestones carried on the Chebeague sloops.

The stone slooping business had a very important effect on Chebeague as well as the rest of the country that it supplied with building materials. At one time there was a quarry on Chebeague near Hamilton Landing. It is presumed that the rock they got here was used as ballast or filler, as there are no granite deposits on Chebeague.

From Stone Sloops of Chebeague

The last of the Chebeague stone sloops on her last sail.

The M. M. Hamilton
Boston Bay
October, 1930

The M. M. Hamilton *was schooner-rigged after 1916.*

The Chebeague stone sloopers built three wharfs on the island to use in conjunction with their work. The Stone Wharf, or Hamilton Landing, as it was known, was built of granite hauled and put into place by Chebeaguers. This landing is still in use today. Another landing was built for stone sloops near the site of the present boatyard by the Littlefield family, but this has long since vanished. Lastly, Captain Aaron Cleaves built a granite landing below his house on the north side of Chebeague. This wharf was still used by stone sloops such as the *Lettie Hamilton* in the early twentieth century. The huge slabs of granite are still there, but over the past winters the ice has removed the fill and shifted the granite from its original position. On a high tide Aaron's Wharf is used for swimming, and the loading and unloading of small boats. Frequently slabs of granite would get broken and they could no longer be used for their original

Courtesy of Donna Miller

The rock sloop Lettie Hamilton *lies tied up to Captain Aaron Cleaves's stone wharf at the turn of the twentieth century. Hamilton and Company is visible at the extreme left of this picture.*

purpose. They would be rejected and taken home to Chebeague and used as flower box stands and doorsteps.

Being a stone slooper from Chebeague wasn't always business. Maine winters are usually severe and frequently there is a lot of ice in the bays. The ice and cold weather made this work very difficult and dangerous. As the result of accidents in cold weather Chebeaguers usually came home around Thanksgiving and stayed until spring. They left their sloops on the flats between Littlejohns and Cousins Islands, where they were sheltered and relatively safe even when the Bay was frozen. During the winter months when the men were home, Chebeague was a very busy place. The men put on suppers. They cut a great deal of wood while they were home. Most of the homes burned wood and it was plentiful on Chebeague. The homes were full of company during the winter months and there were great sledding parties. All the children looked forward to winter when their fathers and older brothers would come home. The social life on Chebeague flourished at this time. From the first of April on, the men were seldom on Chebeague. Sometimes they took their wives with them on the sloops, but this was rare. No matter where the Chebeague sloops were, they always came home for the Fourth of July. The sloops would anchor off Hamilton Landing and the men would come ashore. There were parades and festivities. Chebeaguers really celebrated, for they knew it would be the last time that they were all together until late fall. The Fourth of July is still the biggest celebration of the year on Chebeague, a holdover from stone slooping days.

When the men came home in the fall, there was a big slooping trip to Portland. Almost one hundred people could fit on a large sloop. The

From Stone Sloops of Chebeague

The Lettie Hamilton*—the sloop* Aletta L. Hamilton *at Eastport, Maine, 1897*
Length 84.4 ft., breadth 25.5 ft., draft 6.6 ft.

people were gone for several days. This was long before steamboats regularly serviced the island.

Rock slooping was an exciting and lucrative business that brought a lot of outside money to Chebeague, but like anything else it couldn't last forever. Less-expensive building materials were being invented and steam was replacing sails as a means of transportation.

Some of the captains realized that the end was coming to their prosperity. Captain Alfred Hamilton built his new home, Hamilton Villa, in 1871. The next summer he took in Chebeague's first summer boarders. This was to be the beginning of a new era on Chebeague. By 1900 many of the sloopers had followed Hamilton and reinvested their capital into building boardinghouses and hotels.

At the dawn of the twentieth century Chebeague was beginning a transition from a closed, ocean-oriented society to one that catered to tourists from all over America. Chebeague was caught up in the pre–World War I summer resort boom. Some Chebeaguers converted their homes into hotels and boardinghouses, while others accommodated

Courtesy of Donna Miller

The Hamilton Villa, built by Captain Alfred Hamilton in 1871, was the first Island home to take summer visitors.

Courtesy of Rachel Miller Sanderson

Chebeague Island Field Day was the biggest event of the season for a decade. People filled the field, now part of the golf course, to participate in games of all kinds. A parade and a baseball game were high points of the celebration. The Bayview House is at the extreme left, Old Hillcrest, center, and Summitt House, on the right. (1910)

tourists in spare rooms. Of Chebeague's fifteen hotels and boardinghouses only the Hamilton, Sunnyside, and new Hillcrest were built as hotels.

The Hamilton Villa, operated by Captain Alfred E. Hamilton, was the first boardinghouse on Chebeague. This large colonial house with green shutters could accommodate thirty guests in 1903, but as the islands' transportation improved, a cottage annex was built. The Villa prospered for many years.

The old Hillcrest was the best known of the early Chebeague hotels. Charlie Hamilton renovated his home to accommodate boarders about 1895. At first it could accommodate only 15 guests, but by 1916 the capacity had increased to 140. The dining room seated 300 people. (Many of the tourists who boarded at private homes ate at the hotels.) The old Hillcrest was the scene of many social activities before it was destroyed by fire on August 3, 1923. The Hillcrest fire was the most disastrous in Chebeague's history. Three people died, eighty-seven lost all their belongings, the entire hotel complex was lost, along with the Bayview House, Howard Hamilton's boat house, and John Seabury's home. The loss was estimated at over $100,000, but this did not stop Charlie Hamilton. The next year he built the new Hillcrest, which is still in operation under the proprietorship of William Shuttleworth.

The Summit House, now know as the Dick Seabury House, was operated by Clinton and Addie Hamilton. This establishment once housed eighty-six people, and operated for over thirty-five years.

Still another important East End hotel was The Hamilton, built by Harry Hamilton in 1904. He had operated the Woodbine Cottage, but recognized the need for a larger, more elaborate facility. Elegant and modern in every way, the Hamilton could house over one hundred guests. The floors were highly polished hardwood, the beds white iron, the lights furnished by acetylene gas. The first floor had a large fireplace in a large reception hall. A 200-foot piazza surrounded the hotel. The

Courtesy of Donna Miller

The Hamilton Hotel, built by Harry Hamilton in 1904, was the fanciest of all Chebeague hotels.

Courtesy of Norma Sanderson Morahan

Caldwell's Bowling Alley (1911) sat behind the Bellevue Cottage (known today as the William Whitney house) on the East End. This was a popular attraction from 1909 to 1915, when it was destroyed by fire.

Hamilton changed hands many times, continually undergoing renovations, but in the late 1930s the bottom fell out of the tourist business on Chebeague, and the Hamilton Hotel was razed.

Several other boardinghouses flourished on Chebeague: The Bellevue operated by Henry Caldwell, who also ran the bowling alley, the Orchard Cottage run by Granville and Becky Hill, and Bertha Seabury's Sea Breeze were all on the East End. On the North Road was Cleaves Villa, Caroline Cleaves, proprietor; the Island View House (formerly Pleasant View Cottage), run by Lincoln and Josie Hamilton; the Bradshaws' Juniper Lodge, and the Grannell Cottage operated by Sadie and Jennie Grannell. The Central House run by Selden Hill was near the Island's center. Armordale, operated by Mrs. M. A. Charleston, and Jenks' Sunnyside Hotel were on the West End.

The tourist industry affected most aspects of Chebeague's economy. New stores, tearooms, and gift shops were opened; many Chebeaguers met the boats and carried tourists to the hotels on hayracks, while others did sundry other jobs needed in the tourist business. Even the post office was affected by tourism. Postmaster Henry Bowen made Chebeague a class-A post office by having thousands of postcards printed, and placing mailboxes at convenient locations on the island; 1,734 postcards went through Chebeague's post office on one Monday morning in 1906.

The social life increased with tourism. The hotels sponsored joint field days. In 1905 over 1,000 people had gathered on the East End by 10:00 a.m. to participate in the activities. A golf course was laid out on David Hill's farm, and tennis courts sprang up all over Chebeague. This summer migration changed Chebeague's society in nearly every way.

Some industries existed independently from the tourist industry. The Fenderson Clam Factory, Quimby's Blacksmith Shop, and Uncle Ambrose's Cobbler Shop were nearly independent from the summer tourists. The most independent of all Chebeague industries was the West End fishing industry. Men engaged in all kinds of fishing based their operations at Coleman Cove. Fishing vessels were continually in and out of the Cove, headed for the Grand Banks. Many West Enders were lost at sea while earning their livelihood in this dangerous business.

Courtesy of Norma Sanderson Morahan

Coleman's Cove and Western Landing about 1910. This cove has been the center of Chebeague's fishing industry for nearly 200 years. The fifth house from the right was Stephen Doughty's store. Western Landing was first known as Westman's Landing. Kate Westman ran a boardinghouse at the head of the wharf.

Courtesy of Rachel Miller Sanderson

The Methodist Church on Chebeague Island was built in 1855 by Isaac Strout. The present parsonage is across the street. The center building is thought to be the oldest intact structure on the island, dating back to the eighteenth century. At one time it sat across the road and served as the parsonage for the church.

World War II brought many changes to Chebeague. Island boys served from Russia to Australia. While they were gone, the US Army came to Chebeague. Casco Bay was strategically situated during World War II, as the North Atlantic refueling station was on Long Island, so troops were stationed on many of the islands. It is interesting to note that twenty Chebeague girls married soldiers. This brought new blood to the island, and four families remained and raised their families on Chebeague. Herman Riddle, Scott St. Cyr, John Slowick, and Jasper Smith were all stationed on Chebeague during the war.

There is so much that should be recorded about an island like Chebeague if space allowed; for example, its colorful characters (Billy Hill, the only man to outshoot Annie Oakley, was born and raised on Chebeague); religious development (Methodist, Episcopal, and Catholic services all take place at the United Methodist Church); economic base (most Chebeaguers are either self-employed or retired); education (Chebeague's High School was started by Carroll McKusick in 1902 and was closed in 1956); folklore (the Ghost of the Haunted Cellar still roams Parker's Woods); social structure (the schism between islanders and newcomers has existed for many years); recreation (many people take advantage of the facilities of the Chebeague Island Boat Yard); transportation (passengers depend on Smith's Water Taxi for transportation, while the mail and freight service depends on Casco Bay Lines); and politics (many Chebeaguers have served well in town politics). All this and much more needs to be said about Chebeague, for Chebeague is a separate and distinct community from Cumberland. They share a form of government, but there the similarity ends. Chebeague is an island and that in itself says a lot. Chebeaguers are a unique breed of people, "for yet there is a difference; there are some who cannot forget what their ancestors knew in this place, the remoteness, the silence, the imperviousness of the surrounding sea—the sense of being an Islander, and therefore, in some ways different from all men."[13]

Endnotes

1. To be more fully discussed under "Education in Cumberland" (see Chapter 13).
2. Jedediah was one of three brothers who moved from Duxbury, Massachusetts, to North Yarmouth, Maine, in the 1720–1730s. These Soules became prosperous shipbuilders in the area. They were descendants of John and Priscilla Alden, Alice Southworth Bradford, George and Mary Soule, all early settlers of the Plymouth-Duxbury area.
3. For more information on Chebeague and the Revolution, see "Cumberland in the American Revolution" (Chapter 7).
4. Overcrowding refers to farmland, and should not be confused with today's overcrowding. Large farms were essential because of family size and limited agricultural technological knowledge.
5. The longevity of this tree may be attributed in part to Ellis Ames Ballard, a summer resident, who was very interested in all aspects of Chebeague life. Mr. Ballard had tree surgeons come to the Island in order to examine the "Umbrella Tree" and treat it.
6. This cane is now in the possession of Waneta Hamilton Cleaves, John Ross's great-great-granddaughter.

7. This dividing line does not coincide with the original division between Waite and Chandler.
8. The following is a list of heads of households living on Chebeague in 1820; an asterisk indicates that they voted for joining Cumberland.

David Bennett
Stephen Bennett
William Bennett
* Asa Chandler
* John Chandler
* Judah Chandler
* John Curit
David Doughty
Nathaniel Doughty
* Ambrose Hamilton
* Charles Hamilton
* David Hamilton
* James Hamilton
* John Hamilton III
* Jonathan Hamilton
* Ebenezer Hill
* Richard Hutchinson
* Samuel Hutchinson
Stephen Hutchinson
* Alexander Johnson
Barnwell Johnson
James Johnson
* Enoch Littlefield
* Benjamin Mitchell
* Benjamin Mitchell Jr.
* James Mitchell
* Joel Ricker
* Wentworth Ricker
* John Ross
Samuel Ross
Walter Ross
* Solomon Sawyer II
* Solomon Sawyer III
* Rufus Soule
* William Thompson
* Jonathan Webber
Richard Webber
* Simon Webber

9. Zachariah Chandler's division line.
10. The US per capita income in 1886 was $326; the captain's share on the sloop *Yankee Girl* that year was $1,659.
11. This distinction must be made, for six John Hamiltons lived on Chebeague at this time.
12. *Portland Sunday Telegram*, July 15, 1928.
13. From *The Maine Islands* by Dorothy Simpson.

Many thanks to the following Chebeaguers who contributed pictures and information to this book:

Gail E. Barker, photography
Alice Cleaves Blackwell
Shirley Burgess
Vera Hamilton Cobb
Katherine Morse Devereaux
Earle E. Doughty Sr.
Hattie Curit Dyer
Marion T. Friis
Ruth O. Libby
Albion and Helen Miller
Ellsworth and Melba Miller
Norma Sanderson Morahan
Carrie Ross Morse
Martha Ross Newcomb
Joan Bennett Robinson
Ernest Ross

Elsie Ross Hamilton
Martha K. Hamilton
Raymond Hamilton
Leroy Hill
Lucy E. Hill
Edward M. Jenks
Russell Ross
Rachel Miller Sanderson
Lida Hamilton Small
Carol J. Todd
Frances Ross Todd

For more information on Chebeague Island, Maine, one may consult the following sources:

Dunn, William. *Casco Bay Steamboat Album*. Camden, ME: Down East Enterprise, Inc., 1969.

Hauk, Z. William. *The Stone Sloops of Chebeague*, 3rd ed. Portland, ME: Frost Mimeograph Co., 1967.

Merrill, Thomas R. *The Church on Chebeague*. Chebeague Island, ME: The Chebeague Island Methodist Historical Society, 1960.

Miller, Donna L. *The Ancestry of the Hamiltons on Chebeague*. Unpublished manuscript, 1971.

———*Chebeague: An Early Summer Resort*. Unpublished manuscript, 1971

———*Stone Stooping Chebeague Style*. Unpublished manuscript, 1971.

Tinker, Katherine P. *A Few of the Hamiltons on Chebeague*. Manuscript at Maine Historical Society.

Todd, Carol T. *Sociological Study of Chebeague Island*. Unpublished manuscript, 1973.

Weld, Stanley. *A History of the Great Chebeague Golf Club*. Chebeague Island, ME: Shoe String Press, Inc., 1962.

———Account Book of Sloop *United States*. In possession of Donna L. Miller.

———*Casco Bay Breeze*. Portland, Maine, 1900–1920.

———Cumberland, Main—Vital Statistics.

———Scrapbooks kept by many Chebeaguers, some available at Chebeague Island Library.

———*Stalk Book of Sloop* Yankee Girl. Available at Chebeague Island Library.

Chapter Seven

Cumberland in the American Revolution

By Donna L. Miller Damon

Cumberland was still part of Old North Yarmouth during the Revolutionary War, so it is frequently difficult to distinguish events within that town. Shortly after the Battle of Lexington and Concord, military watches were set up on the coast of the town at strategic locations. All of the North Yarmouth inhabitants (except islanders) were on the alarm list. The military companies took turns keeping the six watches manned. Two shots were fired from one watch to the next to signify the changing of the guard. The town's arms were checked and swivel guns put in place in preparation for an encounter with the enemy.[1] Even the meetinghouse was armed, and a watch was scheduled for "the Lord's day."

By May of 1775 the town of North Yarmouth realized that they must organize some governmental agency to serve as a liaison between the town and the Continental Congress. Therefore, old North Yarmouth joined many other towns throughout the colonies and set up a committee of correspondence. It was also decided that the watches that had been set up in April would remain, and any citizen refusing to stand watch would be fined six shillings. Consequently nearly every citizen from

North Yarmouth served in defense of the town and could be regarded as Revolutionary War veterans.

The threat of British invasion was very real as Henry Mowatt sailed the Maine coast, with British warships keeping seacoast communities in constant terror. A Minuteman organization was established under Lieutenant Benjamin Parker. In June of 1775 these troops were paid twenty-two pounds, three shillings, and four pence to compensate them for their service. The British threat was so real that on July 3, 1775, a law was passed in the town preventing any vessels belonging to the town or any of its inhabitants from supplying the British troops or navy with wood or fuel. This was a year before the Declaration of Independence was signed in Philadelphia, but North Yarmouth was on the road to revolution. An interesting note is that although the town refused to cooperate with the British in any way, the Town Warrant began "In His Majesty's Name . . ." until the official break in 1776.

Throughout the summer of 1775 tensions continued. The town worried about protecting its islands. Should they outfit privateers to patrol the bay? A committee of safety was appointed to deal with such questions. John Lewis, Col. Powell, Silvanus Prince, John Gray, and Col. Jonathan Mitchell served on this committee. John Hayes was the representative to the liaison committee between neighboring towns which was responsible for mustering soldiers. The town was called upon by the Continental Congress to provide fifty-four coats of homemade "Cloath" in order to provide Continental troops with warm clothes for winter. North Yarmouth was doing its share. The town barely escaped burning at the hands of the British, under Captain Mowatt, but neighboring Falmouth was not as fortunate. The people of Old North Yarmouth must have had many sleepless nights, as Falmouth (the City of Portland) was burned to the ground. Other towns had sent troops to help defend the seacoast of Cumberland County at this time, and North Yarmouth shared in the expenses incurred by the troops. After Mowatt left Casco Bay, the Cumberland area was never really threatened again during the Revolution. Several residents served in the Penobscot Expedition under Col. Jonathan Mitchell in 1779, but that took place down east.

Men from the area that was to be Cumberland saw action in other parts of the country. Laura Herrick Wyman, great-granddaughter of

Nehemiah Porter, told the story of his exploits at Bunker Hill to her daughter, Margaret Wyman. Nehemiah fired sixteen shots, and then his ammunition was gone—"I fired and scattered," he was fond of telling. The children of the neighborhood never tired of hearing the stories of the "Old Pensioner," so named because he received a veteran's pension from his Revolutionary War service. He was present at the laying of the cornerstone of the Bunker Hill Monument when it was dedicated by Lafayette, June 17, 1825. The forty survivors of the battle rode in a barouche (an open carriage) drawn by four white horses. On his return old Nehemiah said "Phew! They had some nice rum there!" Some of the Cumberland lads were not as fortunate as Nehemiah Porter. William Rideout contracted smallpox at Valley Forge during the tragic winter Washington was quartered there. The illness resulted in total blindness. His father started from Cumberland on horseback, leading another horse. He reached Valley Forge and brought Billy back. "Blind Billy Rideout" lived a long and full life in Cumberland.

Chebeaguers Who Served in the Revolutionary War 1775–1781

Enos Chandler
Ebenezer Cole
Nathaniel Doughty
Ambrose Hamilton
Benjamin Mitchell Jr.
Wentworth Ricker
Solomon Sawyer
David Upton
Benjamin Waite
Col. John Waite

Men of Cumberland Who Served in the Revolution

Joab Black
Col. Ozias Blanchard
Seth Blanchard
William Buxton
Amos Harris

Robert Maxfield
Nehemiah Porter
Thomas Pratt
William Rideout
Rev. Amasa Smith
Burrel Tuttle
Zebulon Tuttle

A Look Back through the Revolution

An interview with David Hamilton (1797–1893) published in a Portland paper on December 28, 1891. (Source: Leah Hamilton Webber, great-granddaughter of David Hamilton)

GREAT CHEBEAGUE, MAINE, DECEMBER 28: Our venerable friend, David Hamilton, now in his 95th year, hale and hearty, with a clear mind and a relish for a social chat, talked to the *Globe* correspondent a few days ago at his seaside home on the west side of Chebeague. With Mr. Hamilton was his wife, now in her 84th year, the two having traveled along life's journey 59 years together.

"I was born on this island November 4, 1797, and have just passed my 94th birthday. My father Ambrose Hamilton was also born on the island. He lived to be almost 93. His father, also named Ambrose, was born in Scotland, and with two brothers, one of whom settled on Cousin's Island and the other on Walnut Hill North Yarmouth, came and settled here.

"I have heard my grandmother tell about the war of the revolution, and how she saw Portland burned up, fired by the English, when my father was four years old. Just before the War of 1812 all the spruce trees on the island died. There was some worm or insect that killed them. The woods were all full of vapor in the tops of the trees. Colonel Waite of Portland, who owned one-half of the island, let the people cut out this dead wood free, and we sold it for about nine shillings a cord to the distilleries in Portland. There were about fifteen of them at that time making rum. Rum used to be pretty plentiful and cheap in those days, and about everybody used it.

"I was in the woods picking raspberries when the *Boxer* and the *Enterprise* had their fight during the War of 1812. It was in the month of August. There was some lively firing of the heavy guns, and I could hear the sharp firing of the small arms too. It was not long before the *Enterprise* carried the *Boxer* into Portland. I was about fifteen years old and was in the woods working when the news came that the war had closed. Guns were firing in Portland. Father came up from watering the cattle and said he had met old Mr. Johnson and asked him what that firing was about. 'Peace. Peace,' said the old man, throwing up his hands for joy.

"One remarkable thing in my life is that I have never had a doctor, but I have gone for the doctor a good many times for others. One winter I went 21 times in an open boat to Yarmouth for the doctor. I suppose my great strength and long life comes from chopping so much wood when I was young. It is estimated that I have chopped 1,500 cords of wood in my day. I began when I was nine years old.

"When I was a boy we used to go to Yarmouth to church. I remember the parson, Tristram Gilman at Yarmouth, who was a very old man. He wore a beautiful white wig, and when a boy I used to think his hair was white because he was so good. There was a great revival on this island 63 years ago, under the Methodists, and about everybody on the island got converted.

"I never have rode on a steamboat or on the cars. Since the steamers began to run to Harpswell some 16 years ago, I have not been on one. I have rowed a boat many a time from Portland to Chebeague in a tough northeast gale."

The old gentleman lives in the house which he built and owns. It is related of him that he said that he did not intend to get married until he was worth $1,000, and he reached that figure at the age of 35 and then married.

Endnotes

1. Swivel guns were placed by the old Church Under the Ledge to be fixed as an alarm. Another gun was placed near John Gray's home on the Foreside at the foot of Tuttle Road.
2. For a complete list of North Yarmouth privateers, see *The History of Cumberland Co.,* published by Everts & Peck, Philadelphia, 1880, page 343.

Chapter Eight

The War of 1812 and the Mexican War (1846–1848)

By Donna L. Miller Damon

The War of 1812

Much of the activity of the War of 1812 took place on the sea. The United States Navy was not very strong, so it was necessary to use private vessels in public service. These privateers were authorized to seize British ships, keeping the bounty as their pay. This was a very lucrative business, so anyone who had a ship of any size outfitted it as a privateer. The crew's share of the prize was usually sizable, so there was no trouble manning the ships. Privateering was not all easy money. Many ships were lost, and many American seamen spent the war in dark, dingy prisons. Several privateers hailed from the North Yarmouth area. It is difficult to tell which crews were from Cumberland, but it is reasonable to assume that many Cumberland men participated in this business. Both Ephraim and Joseph Sturdivant had vessels under their command.[2]

Jacob Blanchard, Levi Sweetser, and Lemuel Wyman enlisted in the army in September 1814. They were stationed at Fort Burroughs. The war was nearly over when they enlisted.

Many residents served in the militia defending the homeland. Nearly every Cumberland surname is represented on the roster of militia members.

The War of 1812 was an unpopular war, but the country was new and in a very vulnerable position, so many Cumberland residents participated in the war in various capacities.

War of 1812—Cumberland

Jacob Blanchard
Ellen Cleaves
William Cleaves
Alexander Merrill
Samuel Merrill
Levi Sweetser
Lemuel Wyman

War of 1812—Chebeague

Jobe Bennett
Jobe Bennett Jr.
Ebenezer Hill
Richard Hutchinson
John Ross

The Mexican War (1846–1848)

The Mexican War had little effect on people of the Northeast except for isolated individuals who served in the war. David Webber, born on Chebeague in 1822, was the only Maine survivor of the war when he died in 1918 at age ninety-five.

His early years were spent on the Island, and at age eleven he signed on as mess boy on a fishing vessel. When he was twenty-two, he entered the United States Revenue Service, serving on board the cutter *Morris*.

On April 24, 1846, the United States declared war on Mexico. In May an order was issued detaching the *Morris* from service on the Portland Station and ordering that a full crew be recruited. They took on a store of munitions and naval stores and set sail with sealed orders not to be opened until they were off Cape Hatteras. These orders told the cutter to report for duty in the waters adjacent to Key West, in and about the Gulf of Mexico. While headed for its destination the *Morris* was wrecked by a hurricane in October of 1846. The vessel was beaten onto its side and was held down by broken spars and wreckage, and the only chance of saving anyone on the ship lay in clearing away the wreckage which was dragging it down. The captain called for volunteers, but only David Webber and a young black man named John Young responded. They climbed up the slanting masts and were thrown about during their climb, but finally succeeded in cutting away all the ropes and broken spars. Thus the ship righted itself and all officers and crew members were saved.

Mr. Webber refused the offer of a Congressional Gold Medal for heroism because he felt that he was simply doing his duty.

The vessel had been virtually destroyed during the storm, so once into port the crew was discharged. Webber continued in the Revenue Service for many years. He later served on board the *Caleb Cushing,* which was captured by Rebels (during the Civil War) who were nearly successful in taking the ship to the South.

Based on information found in old scrapbooks of newspaper clippings.

Chapter Nine

Cumberland's Role in the Civil War

By Donna L. Miller Damon

Abraham Lincoln's election provided a catalyst for the volatile situation that had existed between Northern and Southern societies since the "Great Compromise" of the Constitution. The differences between the agrarian South and the industrial North became too difficult for the politicians of the era to settle in the halls of Congress. The time for compromise had passed! The Southern states began to secede, resulting in the firing on Fort Sumter, April 12, 1861; and so the Civil War began.

The War of Rebellion touched the lives of all Americans. People in the North saw their families and friends march off to a war geographically removed from their daily experiences, while Southerners saw their Northern "brothers" overrunning their farms and cities, making everyday existence a terrifying experience for soldier and civilian alike.

The Northern citizen's knowledge of the war was gleaned through newspaper articles and personal accounts of returning soldiers. Maine, the farthest removed of the New England states, sent many of its men to Southern battlefields. Again and again the towns in Maine were called on to fill their quotas in order to replenish the Union Army.

Cumberland never shirked its responsibility. Throughout the war the town continued to supply soldiers, often at the expense of borrowing money on ten-year notes. During the first year of the Civil War several men from Cumberland had been caught up in the patriotic surge for glory, making a town effort to raise recruits unnecessary. Thus, the Town's first official action pertaining to the Civil War did not take place until July 21, 1862. The citizens met to see what action they would take in order to raise volunteers for the Union Army. The Warrant also included an article requesting the development of a plan to raise money to pay the soldiers.

The result of that July meeting was the following plan: Each "volunteer" for the army was to be paid $100, provided that nineteen persons could be induced to enlist, but only those physically fit for service could qualify. The town treasurer was authorized to borrow $1,900 on the best possible terms, in order to pay the volunteers needed to fill the quota. But men were slow in coming forth, so another meeting was held the next month. The original proposal was amended to allow the men to receive their money when they enlisted, rather than wait until the quota had been filled.

The quotas became increasingly more difficult to replenish. Men seemed reluctant to voluntarily leave their homes to go to war. In September of 1862, the Town of Cumberland augmented the bounty for volunteers. By enlisting for nine months, men could receive $110 in addition to the regular army pay. Soldiers who were drafted received $100. This mention of conscription took place before Congress instituted the draft on March 3, 1863. The men were to be paid when they were drafted or enlisted. In addition, $10 per month was to be paid to the volunteer or his heirs at the expiration of his term of service. The bounty and monthly pay were also extended to the naval volunteers, providing that they were accepted as part of Cumberland's quota. This plan seemed to have solved Cumberland's recruitment problems for a while, as the largest percentage of Cumberland residents enlisted in the Civil War at this time.

The Federal Conscription Law was passed in March of 1863. Cumberland voted to comply with the law by implementing a threefold plan. Three options were open to draftees: 1) They could receive $300 from the town and go to war, 2) take the $300 bounty given them and use it to buy a substitute, or 3) give their bounty to the United States Treasury and stay at home. A plan for everyone! Quite different from the days of the Vietnam War, when young Americans left the country rather than fight in an objectionable war.

Many Cumberland men were tempted by the $300 bounty. It was a great deal of money to the average man in a rural community. The bounty was even higher than the average per capita income of the United States in 1863, which was $259 per year. Not all draftees took advantage of the bounty; some found it more profitable to furnish a substitute and stay home to pursue lucrative careers in established business ventures. In all, twenty-two men from Cumberland turned their bounty over to a substitute; fourteen came from the mainland, while eight hailed from Chebeague. An interesting note concerning these Chebeaguers is that they were all involved in the rock sloop business. The margin of profit far exceeded the $300 bounty offered by the town. These men were busy hauling building stone, constructing breakwaters and navigational aids, as well as working on the construction of Fort Gorges, taking several years to complete this Civil War fort, which was obsolete before it could be used. They may have felt that their contribution to the country's war effort was better made at home, while a substitute could do their fighting on the battlefield. Economics were not the only reasons for obtaining substitutes. On the mainland, relatives exchanged places for various personal reasons.

Several men from both the island and mainland were drafted but never reported for service. We may assume that they chose the option of turning their bounty money over to the government.

Again and again the townspeople voted to allow the treasurer to borrow sufficient money to pay the volunteers and draftees needed to fill Cumberland's quotas. The money was to be raised at the cheapest possible rate, not to exceed 6 percent for a ten-year period. The men were paid in town script issued by the treasurer. With every new quota, Cumberland went deeper in debt. In November of 1863, Cumberland borrowed $7,200, but that was not enough. They authorized a loan for $2,000 in January 1894; and so the spending went on and on.

Even with monetary compensation, the quotas were hard to fill. The draft's options made it ineffective. Eleven interested citizens petitioned the town to call a special town meeting to discuss a method of raising soldiers to meet the call of August 1864. A committee was formed with the specific duty of filling the Cumberland quota. The committee, comprised of William Prince, Robert Dyer, and Stephen Orr, were to receive

$25 for each man accepted for service in the Union Army. This plan put the community $2,700 further in debt.

By September 1864, State funds were running low, making it necessary to advance their men $300, as the State's bounty, when they qualified for service. This was made in the form of a loan to the State at the lowest possible rate of interest. Everyone was paying for the Civil War, as taxpayers could attest.

The plans changed at a special town meeting in January 1865. Robert Dyer was appointed as the sole recruiting agent. The townspeople didn't realize that the Civil War was nearing an end. Soon Cumberland was faced with the dilemma of filling another quota. Money was a primary consideration, for Dyer was to complete his task at the least possible cost to the town.

Many private citizens had been contributing funds in order that the town could meet their commitments to the soldiers. This had been done with no assurance for repayment, until the January 1865 meeting, nearly six months after the quota had been filled. Due bills were actually issued to the subscribers of the Volunteer Fund of July 1864, in March 1865. Many of these interested citizens or members of their families had served in the earlier years of the war.

The people of Cumberland must have been relieved when Lee surrendered to Grant at Appomattox. Now the country could return to normal. Friends and loved ones would return home, quotas would no longer plague town officials, nor would any more money have to be borrowed—or so they thought. Cumberland had borrowed heavily; and now it had to be repaid. In 1868, they had to borrow the money to pay the notes that came due that year. The repayment of Civil War debts took many years, causing many hard feelings. Chebeaguers thought of seceding from the mainland over a seemingly disproportionate amount of the war debts which were charged to the islanders.

Cumberland overcame its debts and internal disagreements resulting from the Civil War. Although no battles were fought in Cumberland, the War affected the lives of all the townspeople. Over 130 people from the Town of Cumberland served in the Civil War. Military Lists appear in Appendix V.

The Underground Railway in Cumberland

By Margaret G. Wyman

It is well known that from the beginning of the anti-slavery conflict until after the outbreak of the Civil War, much of the North was pro-slavery.

Even in Cumberland Center "at a special meeting called in regard to the draft, several parties came, armed with pistols and revolvers, prepared to resist the draft."[1]

Many slaves, fleeing from the Southern states and their pursuing masters, were helped by a carefully organized system which came to be called "The Underground Railway." Their abolitionist benefactors often faced great danger to themselves in sending the fugitives by various means from one so-called "station" to another, until they finally reached Canada or some other place of safety.[2]

In the early 1840s these fugitives often obtained help in Maine, for Portland became the center of several important routes to Canada.[3]

Perhaps because of the great secrecy that was necessary, there are only a few stories that link Cumberland with this compassionate and exciting undertaking. This information has been handed down in families where stories, repeated with great pride, were told to the children and grandchildren of those who took a small part in "The Underground Railway."

The story most often told is that Deacon Nicholas Humphrey, who lived in the house which is now the parsonage of the Cumberland Center Congregational Church, was the head of the Underground Railway in Cumberland. In her brief "History of the Town of Cumberland," written in 1921, Mrs. Fred Sweetser relates that at one time a slave was said to have been hidden in a chamber above the country store, which occupied the lower part of the building.

It was confirmed to some extent by the following story often told by my mother, Laura Herrick Wyman. Since she was most accurate in relating any story about the past, it seems an acceptable source.

In the early years of their marriage her parents, Charles and Mary Herrick, lived at 363 Tuttle Road in the house across from the fire station.

On at least one occasion they hid and cared for a slave overnight. They too said that Deacon Nicholas Humphrey was the head of this organization.

One nearby "station" may well have been a part of the same "branch" of the Railway: the old red house on the southeast side of the road at the junction of Routes 9 and 115 in North Yarmouth, and owned by Miss Mary E. Dolloff. She says that slaves were hidden there, and that she can show a room made especially for that purpose. It seems quite probable that other families may have been involved, but, as far as we know, no one can verify the somewhat vague tales that are still heard now and then.

Experiences of a Cumberland Man during the Civil War

From the Diary of Hollis True

By Elizabeth S. Baxter

Hollis True enlisted in the US Army in Portland, Maine, on July 24, 1862. After spending some time at Camp King, he was sent to Fredericksburg, in which he served in Co. E, 17th Maine Volunteers. Much of the next few months were spent in that general area. April 1, 1863, while at Belle Plains, Mr. True's company was reviewed by President Lincoln. The following is an account from his diary describing the camp where he was stationed, and several battles:

On May 4, 1863, the Company crossed the Rapidan and arrived at Chancellorsville. They camped for the night and the next day they fought until dark, with 10 killed and 60 wounded. The next day they drove the enemy about 1 1/2 miles, but then the Rebels drove them back again. It was hard fighting all day and the losses were very heavy. During the next five days, there were several skirmishes and his company was forced to fall back, but on the 12th, they marched to Laurel Hill and charged the enemy, taking 7,000 prisoners and some artillery. Mr. True carried the State of Maine colors during the battle that day. There was very little fighting during the next couple of weeks, but on one occasion the enemy was apprehended while trying to capture the Union Wagon Train. True's company drove them back, taking 300 prisoners. On May 24th they crossed a small river, under heavy fire. Nearly out of rations, they camped three miles from the Chickahominy River. While on picket duty, Hollis True found some potatoes in a cellar, which he ate and thereby eased his hunger. Hollis True found the Rebels to be very sociable when they visited together after making an informal cease-fire. At that time one of his fellow Union soldiers deserted and joined the Rebels.

Soon Hollis True saw another side of war. On June 15th, they crossed the James River and camped about three miles from Petersburg. On the morning of the 16th, the enemy began shelling. Hollis True was hit by a minie ball that broke his thigh. He lay wounded on the battlefield, guns firing all around him. Four men from his company volunteered to go onto the battlefield for the wounded. Hollis True was carried to safety by his friend Tom Rideout from Bruce Hill in Cumberland, one of the volunteers. He was then taken to a hospital where an overabundance of flies made him very uncomfortable. His leg was swelling very badly and he felt that the doctor didn't "know any better than a sheep," but the nurses were very kind. On the 26th True was sent to the hospital in Washington. He arrived on the 28th and his leg was dressed. He was much surprised by a visit from his mother and from a Dr. True, a relative stationed there. His leg had swollen as large as his body, but Dr. True's treatment saved his life. He was transferred to Dr. True's ward, where water was continually dripped on his leg, to keep it cool. From the 30th of June to the 14th of August he writes of progress and bad days with his leg. His days were brightened by visits from his mother, Dr. True's family, and ladies from Maine. True also wrote of the constant threat that the Rebels might attack Washington. Wounded men poured into the hospitals, as well as men stricken with sunstroke. While Hollis True was at the hospital Harrison Jenkins took care of him. Jenkins had joined the war from Massachusetts, but when his company fell ill with dysentery, he became an aide at the hospital. After the war he moved to Cumberland, where he lived for the rest of his life and was a neighbor to Hollis True.

Hollis True went nearly a month without writing in his diary. On September 12th, he told about a nurse taking a piece of bone out of his leg, and on the 27th he writes of getting up for the first time in three months. When he recovered he returned to his home on 16 Blanchard Road in Cumberland.

Endnotes

1. Source: Laura Wyman's scrapbook, from an article about the old town house appearing in the *Portland Press Herald* in 1927.
2. Siebert, "The Underground Railway," published 1898.
3. Ibid.

William Merrill Memorial Monument

By Harlan H. Sweetser

William Merrill, the son of Captain Reuel Merrill and Lucy Knight Merrill, was born in 1844. Dr. Sumner Berkovich and his wife, Dr. Barbara Berkovich lived at 66 Winn Road, his ancestral home, until his death. She still lives there. He had one sister, Emma C. Merrill, and two brothers, Louville H. and Edwin B. The latter died at the age of eighteen. Both William and Louville served in the navy during the Civil War.

In the early part of his manhood, William Merrill held a position with the Forest Paper Company of Yarmouth, Maine, and lived there. He

Sketch by Lena G. Foster, 1949

William Merrill's boyhood home at 66 Winn Road.

married Ada Mountfort of Falmouth and lived in that town for a time. They had one son, Edwin R., who graduated from the University of Maine in 1891 with a degree in mechanical engineering, and in 1894, he received an honorary degree from the same institution. He settled in Columbus, Ohio, and was engaged in designing mining machinery. In 1928, he had the William Merrill Memorial erected. He was killed in an accident in 1934.

In the latter part of his life William Merrill owned and lived in the residence at 259 Main Street. His wife Ada died in 1910, and he died in 1927.

Inscriptions on the William Merrill Memorial Monument

FRONT PANEL: In commemoration of the men of Cumberland, Maine, who served their country on land and sea in all wars of the nation.

RIGHT PANEL: The demands for loyalty to a country is as great upon the sons as they were upon the sires. The safety of the country lies in the intelligence, the moral character, the patriotism of its citizens.

LEFT PANEL: Cumberland honors her sons and daughters who have shown by their loyalty, self-sacrifice, and devotion to preserve and cement the Union in the days of the Civil War, 1861–1865.

Courtesy of Cumberland Historical Society

William Merrill Monument.

Chapter Ten

History of the Post Office in Cumberland

Compiled by Editor and Bruce Hazelton

"One of the transportation concerns of our Colonial forbears was that of the postal service. In the early days mail was entrusted to ships or to post riders on horseback . . . By this means a postal service between Boston and Portland had been established as early as the year 1707, but it was very irregular. Post riders made irregular trips over the old Post Road. Travel by stagecoach first occurred when Joseph Barnard, a post rider of Kennebunk, operated a two-horse wagon between Portland and Portsmouth in January, 1787."[1]

Early post office records indicate that there have been three post offices established in Cumberland. The first was established as Cumberland East on June 2, 1821, at Poland's Corner (now the intersection of Tuttle and Middle Roads) with James Prince, the first postmaster. Its name was changed to Cumberland on August 23, 1821, with William Buxton the new postmaster. His salary was $60 a year. Charles Poland, for whom the corner was named, became the third postmaster December 22, 1842.

The first railway to serve this area was the Atlantic & St. Lawrence R.R. (now the Canadian Pacific), built in 1847–1853. A larger post

Old postcard (c. 1930)

Showing corner of J. L. Dunn's store (present 277 Main Street), where post office was for many years, before moving to Farwell Avenue.

office building was built near the stop at Poland's Corner in 1849, with Jacob Merrill the fourth postmaster.

When David Gray, a printer by trade, became postmaster in 1853, the post office was moved to his print shop. He lived in what was later the Conant house, which stood at the end of Tuttle Road on the present Interstate 95, and which has been moved to the top of Spear's Hill on Route 88. In 1870 John N. Dunn, the station agent for the Grand Trunk R.R., became postmaster, and the post office was moved to the station. The post office was moved to a store at the crossroads (Tuttle and Middle) when Edward H. Trickey was appointed postmaster in 1895, and it remained there until the office was discontinued March 30, 1918.

The second office to be established was Cumberland Center, May 16, 1826, with William Bird as postmaster. In 1849 the office was in a corner room in a house situated on the site of the currently unoccupied Shell station, with Col. Samuel True the seventh postmaster. In December 1878 Everett Blanchard was appointed eighth postmaster and served seven years. The store at the Center operated by Everett and his brother Fenwick quartered the post office, located just below the Silas Rideout house, at 277 Main Street. The store and office burned, and the mail was handled in a small building nearby, then owned by Dr. Moulton. This little building was occupied as a dry-goods and notion store, operated by Mrs. Elizabeth Powell and shared with Nellie H. McCollister, the postmaster. Blanchard's store was rebuilt and the post office was moved into the new store. The Blanchards sold their interest to James L. Dunn, who became postmaster in 1892.

The Rural Free Delivery was established in the United States in 1896 and came to Cumberland in 1902. Sylvanus Porter, a citizen of Cumberland, was an influence in politics at that time, and through him it was established in this town. His sons, Samuel and Ralph, became the first two carriers, both serving for many years.

Norman Hulit was appointed postmaster in 1936, and saw the post office moved to Farwell Avenue in 1947. Business in the post office increased faster than the population, and the number of call boxes

Collection of Phyllis Sweetser

RFDcCarrier, Samuel S. J. Porter, delivering the mail to Jeannette Sturdivant, Tuttle Road, 1904.

Hutchinson photo

Senator Margaret Chase Smith speaks at the dedication of the post office, November 7, 1965.

increased from 32 in 1936 to 180 in 1947. The stamp sale increased from $300 in 1937 to $12,000 in 1965, and a larger staff became necessary. This caused the building of a new addition which was dedicated on November 7, 1965, with a surprise visit from Senator Margaret Chase Smith, who spoke briefly. Mr. Hulit served till July 31, 1970, when his sister, Frances Hulit Nelson, became the

Photograph by Daniel Dow, 1975

US Post Office, Farwell Avenue.

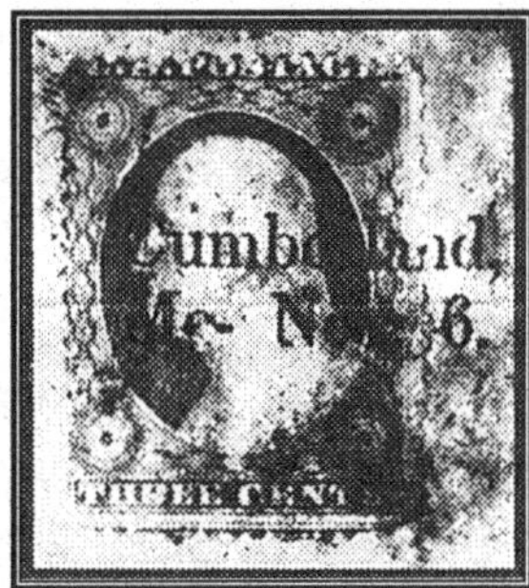

Cumberland, Maine, pre-cancels "finest examples of early pre-canceled stamps."

officer in charge. She was appointed postmaster on April 3, 1971, and served till Rena M. Lamson became postmaster in September, 1972.

The third office to be established was West Cumberland, January 28, 1846, with Greenleaf Mountford, postmaster. It was located in a store at the top of Morrison's Hill. The postmastership of West Cumberland was held by two families during its fifty-four years of existence. Mrs. Hannah Mountfort, Greenleaf's wife, succeeded him in 1873, and James W. Mountfort was appointed in 1875. The Wilsons followed: Lorenzo Hale Wilson in 1878 and Alnah L. Wilson in 1883. The West Cumberland post office was discontinued December 20, 1900.

Cumberland, Maine, pre-cancels "finest examples of early pre-canceled stamps."

Cumberland has the distinction of providing stamp collectors with the first undisputed pre-canceled stamps in the United States. In the late 1850s these pre-canceled stamps originated on mail sent out by the school book publishing firm of Sanborn and Carter of Portland, Maine. The stamps were applied to the envelopes and the pre-cancel was printed, along with the partial address, in David Gray's Print Shop at Cumberland and mailed by him as postmaster through the Cumberland Post Office.

Stanley Ashbrook in his book *The United States One Cent Stamp of 1851–57* (Volume II) states: "The Cumberland, Maine, pre-cancels are the finest examples we have of early pre-canceled stamps."[2]

A complete list of postmasters appears in Appendix VI.

Sources

Material for this article is from "History of the Post Office in Cumberland" written by Herman P. Sweetser, for the occasion of the dedication of the new post office in 1965.

1. Herbert A. Jones—*The King's Highway*, pp. 17, 22. Other information from *Maine Postal History and Postmasters* by Sterling Dow, 1943, published by Severn, Wylie, Jewett Company of Portland, Maine.
2. Bruce Hazelton.

Chapter Eleven

Churches in Cumberland

The Congregational Church of Cumberland

By Herman P. Sweetser

The first church in this territory was organized on November 18, 1730, the tenth church in the Province of Maine, and for twenty-three years it was the only church in this large area called North Yarmouth. It was called the Church Under the Ledge and stood in what is now Yarmouth, on the point of land created by the Prince's Point Road (Gilman Street) leading off Route 88. The doorstep of the old church is still the front step on one of the dwellings there. "From this ancient church, five churches have been organized in the original territory of North Yarmouth . . . In the year 1794, the Northwest Congregational Society of North Yarmouth was formed. This is the present church at Cumberland Center. It was the third daughter of this venerable mother."[1]

This church grew out of a great religious revival when over one hundred young people were converted and wanted a church of their own, and nearer to their homes. The rough structure of the building was put up in 1794. It was located where the present church driveway is now. "It was about 40 feet square with a hip roof and a modest steeple in the central point, was provided with galleries along three sides of the interior. The pews were square as was the custom in those days . . ." As soon as

Courtesy of Cumberland Historical Society

The Church Under the Ledge.

this new house of worship was up, and long before it was finished, a new church organization was formed.

Twenty male members of the First Church, having obtained a dismission for that purpose, together with Reverend Tristram Gilman, pastor of the First Church, and Mr. Rufus Anderson, met on September 3, 1793, and subscribed to a mutual covenant including a confession of faith drawn up by Reverend Gilman. This formed the "Second Church in North Yarmouth." Mr. Anderson became the first pastor. Reverend Amasa Smith became the next pastor in 1806, and remained until 1820. When Reverend Samuel Stone, a graduate of Bangor Theological Seminary (1821–1829), was pastor, the town of Cumberland was established and the name of the church changed to the "Congregational

Church in Cumberland." He was responsible for the establishment of the Sunday School and the mid-week prayer meetings.[2]

"During the pastorate of Reverend Isaac Weston, the fourth pastor, two great revivals are recorded. The second revival came during the summer of 1831, at which time the meetinghouse had been torn down because it was practically in the right-of-way for a new County Road, giving settlers in the Androscoggin Valley a more direct route to Portland. The revival meetings were held in the new barn of Captain Enos Blanchard. Meanwhile, the present meetinghouse was erected. . . . The new church was built by contract at a cost of $2,150 and the old church torn down for $500, with many of the old timbers used for the new church. . . . This church was consecrated with prayer before a timber

Courtesy of Cumberland Historical Society

Cumberland Center Congregational Church, 1905.

Collection of Herman P. Sweetser

Silhouette of Joseph Smith, master builder of four churches, Congregational, Foreside Methodist, West Cumberland Methodist, and Tuttle Road Methodist.

was lifted. Colonel Joseph Smith, son of Reverend Amasa Smith, was the master builder. The church was dedicated on November 8, 1831.

"The next pastor was Reverend Joseph Blake, whose pastorate was the longest of any minister of this church, from March 3, 1841, to April 18, 1859. During this time, the brick parsonage (306 Main Street) was built, and at that time considered the best house in town. The bricks were made in the old kiln behind Prince Memorial Library. Mr. Blake set the elm trees in front of the house and around the church.

"During the pastorate of Reverend Ebenezer S. Jordan, a pipe organ was procured and installed in the rear of the church through the efforts of Captain Enos Blanchard in 1860. During this period a bell was placed in the belfry."[1]

Funds for carrying on the church were obtained by assessing the pews. If the tax on a pew was not paid, that pew was sold at auction after due notice. Deeds to the pews were recorded in the Registry of Deeds, as parcels of real estate are recorded today. Raising money by subscription did not begin until after the Civil War, and then only in part, as many people retained the deeds to their pews and paid accordingly for many years.

The church lost many members during the Civil War. Three men were killed in the Battle of Antietam, and one or two in most of the major battles where Maine regiments were engaged. Also with the opening of the West, many church members emigrated to new homes in that region.

Photograph by Daniel Dow, 1975

Original parsonage for Congregational Church, 306 Main Street.

Many of the early church members were seafaring men, and at one time, there were thirteen retired or active sea captains in the church.

In a sermon by Reverend T. S. Perry, delivered on the eighty-fifth anniversary of the church, September 1, 1878, is the following paragraph:

> One remarkable feature in the membership of this church is the large numbers that have joined it from certain families. Of all the members of this church, not less than seventy-five have borne the name of Blanchard; forty-six the name of Prince; forty-eight the name of Sweetser; thirty that of Merrill, and many other names often recur in the lists of this church.

Extensive remodeling of the church took place in 1906 under the direction and capable work of Mr. Oren S. Thomes. The organ and choir loft were moved to the front of the church, and the present pews

Photograph by W. Chester Rideout, collection of Herman P. Sweetser

Old-timers who helped celebrate the 100th anniversary of the Congregational Church, September 21, 1893. L-R front: Mrs. John (Margaret) Wilson, Mrs. Benjamin Sweetser, Mrs. Enos (Joanne) Blanchard, Mrs. Asaph (Sarah) Buxton, Mrs. Blake, a former pastor's wife, Mrs. William (Harriet) Blanchard, Miss Jane Merrill. L-R back: Samuel Sweetser, Capt. Beza Blanchard, John Blanchard, Josiah Haskell, Silas Rideout.

installed. In 1916, the church was raised and the vestry established beneath it.

On August 29, 1943, the church celebrated its 150th anniversary with a day of delightful exercises. During the morning church service, most of the congregation were appropriately dressed to represent their ancestors (as shown by the accompanying picture), and a poem entitled "The Country Church," with the names of many of the older people, written by Nellie L. Sweetser, was read by Mrs. Harlan H. Sweetser. The organ was played by Mr. Linwood Crandall.

In 1959, a building project got under way for many needed repairs to the church and parsonage. By 1962, it became imperative to have a new Parish House to accommodate the growing church and all its activities. The old brick parsonage was sold to enable the church to purchase more

Sketch by Lena G. Foster, 1946

Congregational Church, after 1916.

Courtesy of Cumberland Historical Society, collection of Herman P. Sweetser

Congregational Church Celebration 1943. Families represented include Blanchard, Barter, Fickett, Burnell, Chase, Doane, Sweetser, Porter, Wyman, and Warren.

land beside the church, and the home on the property became the parsonage. The new Parish House became a reality in 1964. The whole church plant is in constant use with all the usual church and community activities, plus Project Head Start in the Parish Hall and Project Main Stream in the vestry. Thus, this fine old church continues its good life.

Sources

Compiled by editor from:

1. *History of the Town of Cumberland*, by Mary E. Sweetser, 1921.
2. Booklet entitled "One Hundredth Anniversary of the Congregational Church, Cumberland Center, Maine, September 21, 1893."

   From histories written by Herman P. Sweetser and Harlan H. Sweetser.

   List of church ministers found in Appendix IV.

collection of Herman P. Sweetser

Older members of Congregational Church, 1943. L-R front: Mrs. Philip (Annie) Sturdivant, Mrs. Archie (Laura) Wyman, Mrs. Frank (Alice) Doughty, Mrs. William (Emily) Wilson, Mrs. Albert (Evelyn) Sweetser, Mrs. Charles (Elizabeth) Greely, L-R back: Fred Adams, Arno S. Chase, Horatio H. Herrick, Edward B. Osgood, Samuel S. J. Porter, Edward Warren, and Samuel Ross.

Photograph by Daniel Dow

Congregational Church Parish House dedicated September, 1964.

Update of Cumberland Congregational Church

by Barbara Blanchard Garsoe

Nine ministers have served the Cumberland Congregational Church since 1976. Each has contributed to the church, helping it to grow to where it is today. There are now approximately 400 members, with an increasing number of youth group members. The growth is not just in numbers; the church voted unanimously in April 2001 to make our church an open and affirming church in the UCC.

In 1989, a connector was added to incorporate the parish house and the church into a whole. An elevator was added, enabling persons with disabilities and older people to attend church and its functions. One member did not attend church for seventeen years, but the addition of the elevator allowed her to return to services every Sunday.

Back in 1981, the organ was completely restored, new windows were added, and the sanctuary was spruced up with new carpeting and a restructuring of the choir loft.

The church celebrated its 200th anniversary in 1993 with a series of special events. On one Sunday, members dressed in period costumes, and one youth group member, turned minister, gave the sermon. The service featured old hymns from the 200 years. Another event was a special exhibit arranged by the Cumberland Historical Society so that church members could see the collection of church archives and artifacts. A stone to honor the ministry of Amasa Smith, the church's second minister, was placed at his grave in the Old Congregational Cemetery. Stitching it all together, Cumberland quilters made a commemorative quilt featuring the life of the church, and this quilt now hangs in the parish hall.

The Methodist Church

(Now Foreside Community Church at Cumberland and Falmouth Foreside)

By Emilie Cram

This church, one of the historic landmarks of the two towns, stands on the line dividing Cumberland and Falmouth. In 1789 the first religious services were held on this site in a log church, which burned in 1792. Another was built in 1793, and this one burned in 1804. Services were then held in a schoolhouse across the road until the present edifice was built in 1811 as a Union Church. Three Sturdivant brothers, Joseph, Ephraim, and Greely, all North Yarmouth Congregationalists, were the central figures in erecting this building. The choice site overlooking beautiful Casco Bay was given by William King York on the Falmouth side, and by Ephraim Sturdivant for the part in Cumberland.

For many years the residents of the respective towns sat on their own side of the Church, and the preacher was required to preach from first

Courtesy of Emilie Chase Cram

Foreside Methodist Episcopal Church, 1910.

Know all Men by these Presents, That I Greely Sturdivant of Cumberland State of Maine

for and in consideration of the sum of Ten dollars

to me in hand, well and truly paid, at or before the signing, sealing and delivery of these presents, by Joseph Sturdivant of Cumberland State of Maine

the receipt whereof I the said Greely Sturdivant do hereby acknowledge, have granted, bargained and sold, and by these presents, do grant, bargain and sell unto the said Joseph Sturdivant Pew No Twenty nine on the lower floor of the Methodist meeting house situated in Cumberland & Falmouth State of Maine aforesaid

TO HAVE AND TO HOLD the said granted and bargained Pew unto the said Joseph Sturdivant his heirs, executors, administrators or assigns, to his only proper use, benefit and behoof forever. And I the said Greely Sturdivant do avouch myself to be the true and lawful owner of the said Pew and have in full power, good right, and lawful authority to dispose of the said in manner aforesaid: And I do, for myself heirs, executors, and administrators, hereby covenant and agree to warrant and defend the said Pew to the said Joseph Sturdivant against the lawful claims and demands of all persons whatsoever, unto him the said Joseph Sturdivant his heirs, executors, administrators, or assigns.

In Witness Whereof, the said Greely Sturdivant have hereunto set my hand and seal this twenty sixth day of August in the year of our Lord one thousand eight hundred and fifty seven

Signed, Sealed, and Delivered in Presence of us,

Ephraim Sturdivant

Sarah J. Stiller

Greely Sturdivant

Cumberland SS August 26th 1857 Personally appeared the above named Greely Sturdivant and acknowledged the above instrument to be his free act and deed before me Ephraim Sturdivant Justice of Peace

Collection of Phyllis Sweetser

It was 1857 when Greely Sturdivant bought pew No. 29 at the Methodist meetinghouse on the Cumberland-Falmouth town line, for ten dollars.

one and then the other side of the pulpit, so as to preach in both towns. Some of the early preachers were Rev. Joel Winch and Rev. Martin Reuter. In 1824 a Methodist minister, Rev. Joshua Taylor, was appointed to the pastorate. During the history of the church some fifty or more pastors have ministered to the church and community, some of whom were leading members of the Maine Methodist Conference. Many changes have taken place in the building, going from foot warmers to stoves, one in Cumberland and one in Falmouth, to a modern heating plant and a fine addition to the thriving Foreside Community Church.

In 1920 a cellar was installed underneath the church to add more room. A Fellowship Hall was built in 1953, the Sunday School addition was built in 1981, and the new offices were built in 1998.

History of West Cumberland United Methodist Church

(Formerly the Methodist Episcopal Church)
Blackstrap Road, West Cumberland, Maine

By Kenneth R. Dorr

The First Methodist Episcopal Church Class was formed in West Cumberland about 1800. A Society was formed in 1813 with Edmond Alien, clerk.

The Reverend James Jacques was regular pastor in 1825, with a church of fifteen members, including John Marston and wife, Sarah Wilson, and members of the Jordan, Brackett, and Winslow families.

The meetinghouse was erected in union with the Universalists in 1813. Ozni Harris, Hezekiah Winslow, and Jonathan Pearson were the committee.

The church became a separate appointment in 1844, and from 1844 to 1974 has been under the appointment of fifty-five pastors.

In 1848 the meetinghouse was rebuilt and dedicated. After a long time of being closed, it was reactivated in August 1963.

A parcel of land was donated to the church by Annie C. Copp in 1963, and in 1964 an additional parcel was acquired. A Parish Hall was

Photograph by Daniel Dow, 1975

West Cumberland Methodist Church.

constructed on this land, located on the corner of Blackstrap and Methodist Roads, which was dedicated by Bishop Matthews in 1969.

Rev. Kingsley Strout became pastor in 1967, and has continued to the present time (1974). There are thirty-seven members presently on the rolls of the church.

Source of Early History

Excerpts from the Church Record, copied from the Church Record of 1905–1963, being a history copied by Wm. Bragg (minister 1894–95) from the History of Cumberland County.

Update of West Cumberland United Methodist Church

By Nancy Latham

The first Methodist Episcopal Church Class was formed in West Cumberland about 1800. A society was formed in 1813 with Edmond Allen, clerk. A meetinghouse was erected at first in union with the

Universalists. Ozni Harris, Hezekiah Winslow, and Jonathan Pearson were the committee.

The church became a separate appointment in 1844, and from 1844 until 2005, there have been about sixty-five pastors. The church was rebuilt and dedicated by Rev. Joseph Jenne in 1848. The parsonage was built in 1844 and is located at the site of the Norton Farm, about a quarter-mile up the road. It was actually two houses that were hauled there and put together. Rev. J. S. Rice did much of the carpentry work himself.

Blackstrap Road was originally the old stagecoach road from Portland to Lewiston. Between the church building and the road were sheds or stalls where the parishioners could tie up their horses and park their carriages and wagons while attending church.

In the early days the church was heated by stoves in the back corners of the sanctuary. It was discovered when a furnace was moved into a newly constructed room under the church, in 1967, that the underpinning was of hand-hewn timbers. In fact, some of the shavings were still on the ground and were dry after 160 years of being in place. Thus it can be seen that this church was built on a firm foundation.

There are a few remnants that are hanging in the church today that give some of the early history. Among these are certificates from the Epworth League for the Willing Workers and the Methodist Episcopal International Sunday School Council, certifying that the Truth Seekers were a recognized adult Bible class.

There are also pictures hanging of three of the early influential parishioners of the church: Levi and Sarah Wilson and Loemma Wilson. "Poor old lady" was the remark of Loemma Pearson Wilson when she stood before the portrait of herself, which was done in 1920. Loemma lived from 1831 until 1924, so she was about eighty-nine years old in the picture. According to the article written up in the October 24, 1920, Portland *Sunday Telegram*, Loemma never failed to keep her appointments while sitting for her portrait, done by the well-known Joseph B. Kahill in his studio in Portland. She would take the trolley from her home on Morrison's Hill. Both Loemma and her husband Nathaniel B. Wilson were active in the Methodist Church, and their house was a stopping place for all the presiding elders and ministers of that faith in their travels over the circuit.

Hanging in the church is a beautiful ornate chandelier with a story to tell. It originally hung in the Wilson Tavern, now the Norton Farm. Nathaniel Wilson and Sarah Pride Wilson, Loemma's father-in-law and mother-in-law, were the owners at the time. Family tradition has it that Sarah Pride Wilson was a woman of strong character, and headed a genuine temperance movement in the community of her residence by stopping the sale of liquors in the tavern, which was conducted by the earlier Wilsons at the ancestral home for the accommodation of travelers to and from Portland. The marriage of her daughter Martha was always referred to as "Sally Pride's temperance wedding," and from her day no liquors for use as beverage were ever allowed in the house. The chandelier now hanging in the church came from the tavern. It still has the globes advertising Old Gold whiskey. Though some of the lanterns have since been converted to electricity, others are the original kerosene lanterns.

A parcel of land was donated to the church by Annie C. Copp in 1963, and in 1964, an additional parcel was acquired. A Parish Hall was constructed on this land located on the corner of Blackstrap and Methodist Roads, which was dedicated by Bishop Matthews in 1969.

The church is now called the West Cumberland United Methodist Church. A new altar was built about 1950. The parsonage was sold to Maurice and Donna Beal for $5,500.00 on December 12, 1962. The church porch was replaced in 1991. Accessibility ramps were added to both the church and Parish Hall in 1995. A new addition to the Parish Hall was added in 1997 that allowed for a pastor's office and storage space; the added cellar allowed the furnace to go downstairs. Both the church and the Parish Hall have been painted inside and out in the last five years. Our latest project was the expansion and paving of the parking lot. Our next major endeavor was to build a new booth at the Cumberland Fair.

Our services are on Sunday mornings at 10:00 a.m. Pastor Tom Frey currently serves at the pulpit. We invite you all to join us.

Universalist Church on Morrison's Hill at West Cumberland

Land for this church was deeded to the Universalist Society in 1847 by Ephraim Morrison. In size it was eight rods (a rod equals five and a half yards) on the street and ten rods back.

On June 19, 1869, he deeded another ten rods back for a burying ground—for which the town paid $25. This little church is a monument to the piety and way of thinking of our forefathers. Ephraim built the house now occupied by Brian and Lynda (Wilson) Jensen at 5 Mill Road. Lynda is Ephraim's great-great-granddaughter. As time went on, the church became neglected and the cemetery was in sad condition. In the early 1920s, devoted women who had attended it when young, started a movement to get the yard cared for and the church reopened in the summers. Services were conducted by the much loved Dr. Harry Townsend of the Westbrook Universalist Church. A Ladies' Circle was formed and the feeling for Universalist teaching was nurtured.

As time went on, changing conditions led to the sale of the church in 1958 to the Pentecostal Society of the Apostolic Challenge, with Reverend Leo Sadler as the present minister.[1]

The church disbanded for a while, but has been reestablished.

Source

1. By Evelyn Thurston Jones, a great-granddaughter of Ephraim Morrison.

Tuttle Road United Methodist Church

By Marion Larson Chandler

The church on Tuttle Road was built by the people of the neighborhood in 1882 as a place for community worship. The nature of the endeavor was strongly interdenominational, and the decision to join the Methodist Conference was based mainly on the necessity of ensuring a source of ministerial supply.

Photograph by Harlan F. Burr

Methodist Church on Tuttle Road.

Pastoral leadership came from Reverend Eliazar Hutchinson, minister of the church on the Cumberland-Falmouth town line, which Cumberland Methodists had been attending for fifty years. Its location stressed the union of the two congregations who were represented by joint trustees. This arrangement continued after the erection of the Tuttle Road Chapel, and Mr. Hutchinson continued as pastor of both churches.

Before either church was built, the Falmouth-Cumberland Methodist Episcopal Society had been organized in the area by Methodist preachers and circuit riders from Portland, among whom were Reverend Joel Winch, Reverend Edward M. Whittle, Reverend Martin Ruter, and Reverend Joshua Taylor. "Reverend Elisha Duran, a local preacher for many years, rendered valuable services at Tuttle Road."[1]

The *Cumberland and North Yarmouth Register* gives the following summary:

> The two societies near the Foreside, which were united under one pastor, were included in the Falmouth and Cumberland circuit under the care of Reverend Joshua Taylor, a local preacher. In 1842, Reverend Phineas Higgins was stationed here and these two became a separate charge. The church at Cumberland was erected about 1882. The one located on the town line at Falmouth Foreside, so called, was erected about 1831. Previous to occupying these buildings, the services were held in the local schoolhouses. The new, neat little church previously mentioned was built during the pastorate of Reverend Eliazar Hutchinson.[2]

In 1886, under the leadership of Reverend W. P. Merrill, a revival was held at Tuttle Road which resulted in a growth of membership. That year the new building was dedicated as the Cumberland Methodist Church at a service that filled it to capacity. The principal speaker was Reverend Lauriston Reynolds of the Yarmouth First Parish Congregational Church. Music was furnished by the choir of that church, directed by Dr. Augustus Hannibal Burbank. As a dedication gift, the Yarmouth church gave the pulpit that is still in use at Tuttle Road.

The chapel on Tuttle Road and the church on the town line continued under the same minister with joint trustees until 1915. At that time, the Cumberland church was made a separate and independent charge with its own official board. The first quarterly conference met June 3, 1915.

Since that time, the Cumberland church has shared ministerial support with the following Methodist churches: Yarmouth, 1915–1927; Falmouth Foreside, 1928–1943; People's (South Portland), 1945–1956; Washington Avenue, 1957–1974; Chebeague Island, 1974. Small membership and no pastoral connection made the years around 1944 trying ones in the history of the church. The stubborn faith of trustee Alfred W. Doughty kept the church alive until its forces could be rallied and its survival assured.

Church social functions were held in homes until 1924, when a building given by Mr. Doughty was moved to the church grounds. This was enlarged in 1947 and again in 1967. In 1952, a room was added to the rear of the original church building.

Besides the weekly worship service, present church activities include family nights, a senior and a junior choir, a Youth Fellowship, a thriving church school, and the program of the United Methodist Women. There are now 105 members at the Tuttle Road Church who worship, serve, and fellowship together in the same spirit of inclusion that marked the church at its beginning.

Update of Tuttle Road United Methodist Church

By Wahneta Dahlgren, church historian, 2005

For years we shared a minister with various Methodist churches in the area. In 1979 we had our first full-time pastor.

Plans began in the early 1980s to build a larger church to accommodate a growing congregation. In the mid-1980s extra land around the church was purchased. This began with the pastorate of Michael Davis and continued with John Neff. In 1988 a three-year fund-raising campaign was launched. Due to limited funds the decision was made to contruct a multipurpose sanctuary which would allow us the space to continue the Swedish Meatball Suppers, Christmas Fair, and the other activities of the congregation.

Doughty Hall, the church's parish hall, was taken apart. One portion was sold and moved to the Blanchard Road to be used as an artist's studio. It's located near a small brick building that once served as Cumberland's town hall. The other portion was dismantled.

In August 1992 ground was broken and construction began. On January 17, 1993, the transition was made, during church service, from the little old church to the new building. Within this building is an efficient kitchen with a full cellar below. Pews from the old church were moved to the new building and used for a number of years. Consecration Sunday took place January 31, 1993, with Bishop F. Herbert Skeete, Resident Bishop of the Boston area.

Those on the building committee were:

Eileen Wyatt, co-chairperson
Jonathan Hathaway, co-chairperson

Barney Baker
Peter Burr Sr.
Charles Cox
Wahneta Dahlgren
Mildred Fochler
Pamela Gleason
Philip Hunt
David Matthews
John Rand
Jack Sampter Jr.
Peter Smith
Russell Stevens
Everett Wiley
Roger Wilmot Jr.

Michael E. Davis, pastor
John W. Neff, pastor
Mark Monson Alley, pastor

The little old church building became Sunday School space. Investigative work was done to see if the building, built in 1882, could be added to the list of Historical Buildings. Due to the fact that metal railings had been installed at the front doors and the openings of the doors had been changed to comply with fire codes, we did not qualify.

In 1999, the narthex, a connector building between the old church and the new church, was built. Within this area are four Sunday School rooms, a nursery, and a reception space. At this time the old church building underwent some renovations, creating the pastor's office, secretary's office, Sunday School room, and a small chapel area that is also used by the Sunday School. In renovating the old church, care was taken to preserve as many of the original features as possible so if at a later date the building were to be restored as a chapel, it could be done. The exterior walls were not changed, the metal ceiling left intact when the ceiling was lowered, and the original overhead lights were reinstalled in the chapel area.

In 2000, new movable pews were placed in the church. The old pews, put together with square nails, went to homes of various parishioners. A few were placed in the chapel and the narthex.

The church acquired a large bell in January 1996, given to us by the Mechanic Falls, Maine, Methodist Church when that church closed. It was cast in Cincinnati, Ohio, in 1892, and weighs about two tons. At present, September 2005, it is waiting a permanent place on the church grounds. During the early summer of 2005 a memorial garden was installed, with a dedication and consecration of ashes taking place on July 31, with Rev. Mark Monson Alley and Rev. Meg Queior officiating.

In late autumn 2005 a parsonage was placed on the grounds.

Present membership is 212. Two services are held each Sunday—a contemporary service at 9:00 a.m., and a traditional service at 10:30 a.m.

List of ministers in Appendix IV.

Sources

1. *History of Methodism in Maine 1793–1886,* Alien and Pilsbury, 1887, p. 298.
2. Mitchell, Russell, and Strout, *Cumberland and North Yarmouth Register*, H. E. Mitchell Publishing Co., 1904, p. 40.

Chapter Twelve

History of Taverns in Cumberland

By Robert G. Blanchard and Harlan H. Sweetser

The Prince Tavern

The Prince Tavern, now 371 Tuttle Road, is located at the intersection of Route 9 and Tuttle Road, diagonally across from the Congregational Church at Cumberland Center.

The land on which this tavern is located was first acquired on August 7, 1733, by John Powell, one of the original proprietors of ancient North Yarmouth, at the drawing of lots by which he drew #70, one of the 100-acre lots in the early subdivision of the town. This land remained in the Powell family until October 18, 1781, when it was sold by Jeremiah Powell to James Prince, yeoman, for 60 pounds, for the northerly half of lot #70, and in 1793, he sold one acre of this land for use as a burial ground, now the Congregational Cemetery. Ownership was later transferred to his son, Joel Prince, who became proprietor of Prince Tavern. The main highway ran under the archway where stagecoaches stopped and horses were changed from a stable of fifteen stalls. Overnight travelers were accommodated in the spacious house. It is not known how long this establishment served as a tavern, but in 1829, Joel Prince sold the homestead to Nathaniel Blanchard, who in 1833 sold it and seventy-four

Collection of Robert G. Blanchard from a postcard (c. 1925)

Prince Tavern.

acres of farmland for $3,000 to Captain Enos Blanchard. His son George became owner in 1874, and his son Arthur became owner in 1935, until his death in 1972. In 1974, it went out of the family when it was sold to Dr. William Wyatt. It is now a coffee shop named "Doc's Place."

Chase's Tavern

Chase's Tavern was located on Route 9 opposite its intersection with Winn Road. The tavern served the travelers over the old road from Falmouth (now Portland) to Walnut Hill and New Gloucester. In the old days the road from Portland to Walnut Hill joined what is now called the Winn Road at the former frame schoolhouse, converted into a residence at the corner of Winn and Field Roads, then followed the present Winn Road to Route 9, through Cumberland Center and on to Walnut Hill Congregational Church, and thence on to New Gloucester. Later, another road was laid out from the junction of Route 9 and the Winn Road to Falmouth Corner over the Longwoods Road.

This tavern being situated at the intersection of three important roads must have served a very useful purpose in providing hay and grain for oxen and horses, and lodging and refreshment for travelers. It was in use from shortly after the Revolutionary War to sometime after the Civil War.

Some of the owners were Joseph Drinkwater, Albert E. Drinkwater, Charles Lane, and Gilman Thurston. The tavern burned to the ground about 1898, the event being remembered by both Herman and Harlan Sweetser.

Courtesy of Margaret Wyman, from Laura Wyman's scrapbook (c. 1921)

Leighton's Tavern.

The Leighton Tavern

The Leighton Tavern, now a private residence, was located on the Gray Road at the intersection of Route 100 and the old Gray Road, about a half-mile north of Skillins Road. It is the oldest and best known of the old Cumberland taverns, and was built about 1800 by Andrew Leighton.

This tavern being situated on the old stagecoach road from Falmouth (now Portland) to Bakertown (now Lewiston) was a popular stopping place for travelers and teamsters hauling freight by ox teams, which might average only seven miles in a day. In the early days it was doubtless a stagecoach stop for refreshment for both man and beast.

Andrew Leighton, the builder and first proprietor, was born in 1762 and died in June, 1830. He had seven sons and one daughter. Two of his sons, Joshua and Robert, served before the mast during the War of 1812 on the vessel *Dash*, a renowned privateer which sailed out of Porter's Landing in Freeport. Both men went down with the vessel when it was lost in 1815.[1] The other sons were William, Moses, Nicholas, James, and Ezekiel. The daughter's name was Mercy.

The fine old building is now a residence, and until quite recently has always been occupied by descendants of the original Leighton family.

This old tavern, now owned by Lee and Holly Thibodeau, was moved in 1970 by then-owner David Stanley to a new location at Schooner Rocks at Cumberland Foreside, once the land belonging to the estate of John and Jeremiah Powell.

Source

1. This is the vessel called "the Ghost Ship of Casco Bay." See Chapter 21, "Tales and Legends."

Chapter Thirteen

Education in Cumberland

Early Schools of Cumberland

By Phyllis S. Sweetser

In 1727 the division of lots on the Foreside of the town of Cumberland took place. There were 104 home lots drawn, as shown on the old map in Chapter 1. Aside from these were two ministerial lots intended to be used for a meetinghouse and parsonage, and a 200-acre lot for the benefit of schools. This was situated on the Cumberland-Falmouth town line just behind the present church and cemetery. The first record of a school was that of the schoolhouse on lot #60 on the Tuttle Road near the Foreside Road, where Daniel Mitchell taught, beginning in 1764.

In 1788 William Martin, a London businessman who had come to America with his family, purchased the Jeremiah Powell estate at Broad Cove and moved his family to this town. Here, in the Powell mansion, his daughter Penelope Martin, educated in England, with the assistance of her two sisters Eliza and Catherine, in 1790 established a private school for girls, which is remarkable as being one of the first institutions in this part of the country to undertake the higher education of women. It was a boarding school in which were taught the branches now included in our high

> school course, as well as those accomplishments then deemed necessary in a girls' school. It became prosperous and well known throughout the state, attracting pupils from a distance because of its reputation for imparting a thorough education. The Misses Martins' School was conducted in North Yarmouth till the family removed to Portland in 1804, and there the school was continued, being one of the first in New England to bring to it the cultivated Christian elegance of the old world.[1]

Other private schools were held in old homes which are still standing—one the present McCarty house on the old Drowne Farm at 306 Tuttle Road, the other on the Top Knot Farm at 100 Middle Road. The latter was conducted by Squire William Buxton and his wife Mary and their daughter Maria. Squire Buxton had served as an officer in the colonies before he settled down to life at home as a schoolmaster. Pupils came from as far away as Bethel and Cape Elizabeth. Two of the girls who attended this school left their marks: Their names scratched on a pane of glass and dated 1839. They were Phoebe Buxton and Capt. Ephraim Sturdivant's daughter, Hannah, who later married a Capt. John Smith and lived in Japan for many years.

When the first Cumberland town meeting was held in 1821, it appropriated $550 for the support of schools for the coming year. This was the largest amount appropriated that year for any purpose.

The schoolhouses supported by this fund were built in different sections, or districts of the town.

> Pupils attending the one-room schools varied greatly in age and intelligence, as all pupils from ages 5 to 25 were accepted. They provided their own books and the teacher, who was not very well educated himself, had a large task before him at the opening of school to arrange his pupils into classes. The same system of teaching continued as before the incorporation of the town. The man who supervised the districts was called a school agent. His duties were to see that the teacher did his (or her) work well and to hire a new one when the old one was driven out by his pupils.[2]

At one time there were fifteen districts in the town of Cumberland, but usually only fourteen as shown on the accompanying map.[3] An old

SCHOOL REGISTER.

Register of School District No. 13. Town of Cumberland

EXPLANATIONS AND DIRECTIONS.

SCHOOL REGISTER.

SCHOOL REGISTER.

SCHOOL REGISTER.

School Register, 1853.

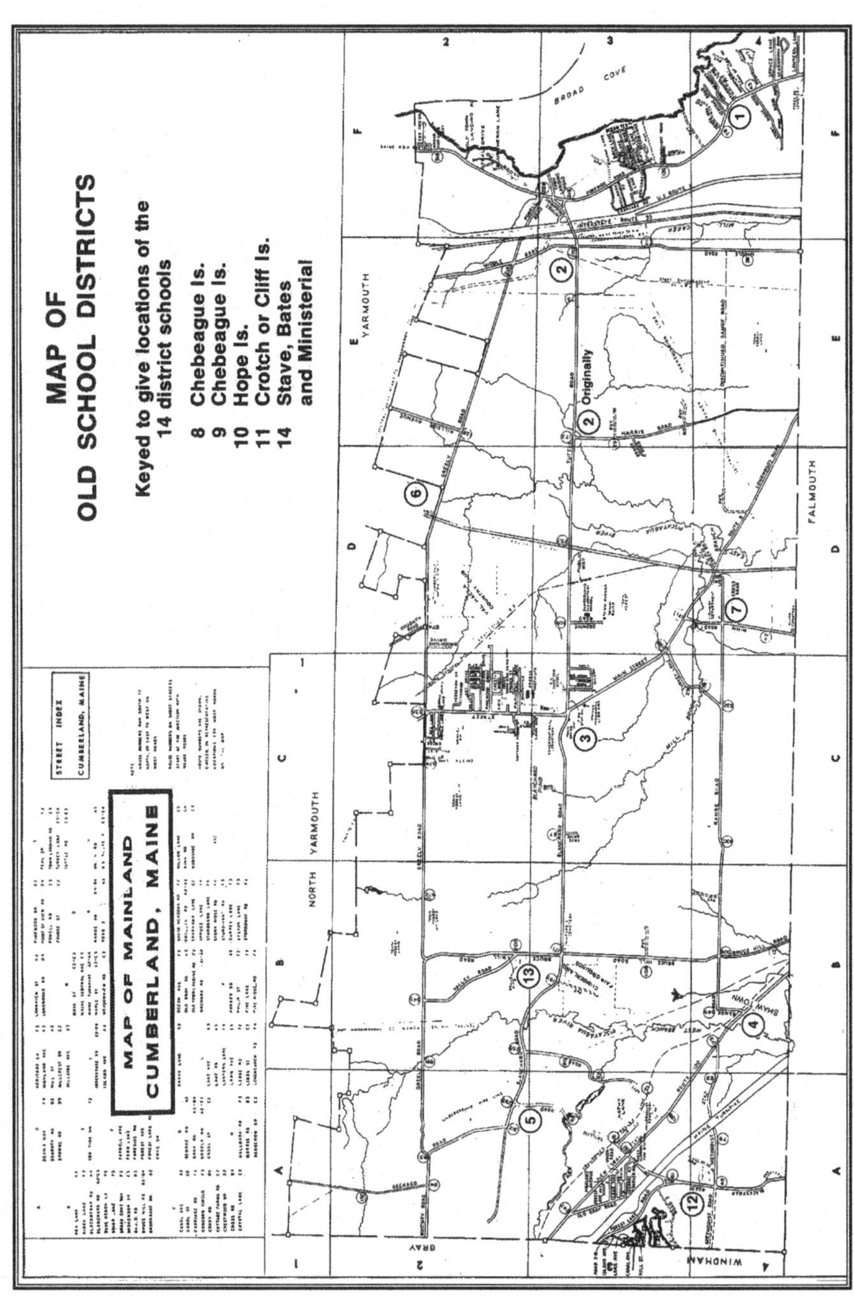

Map courtesy of Cumberland town office

Photo by Donald Drew

The schoolhouse at Winn and Range Roads, District #7.

Register from District 15 dated 1853 is explained as follows: "The number of school districts would rise and fall. Perhaps this was because the population in one district became so low as to justify closing the school and sending the scholars to a neighboring district. In 1838, the selectmen voted to form a new school district from districts now numbered 2 and 3 . . . Said plan is placed on file and marked School District No. 15."[4]

A few of these old schoolhouses still exist—No. 3 became the Cumberland Town Office; No. 7, at the junction of Winn and Range Roads; No. 2, a dwelling nearly opposite the Tuttle Road Methodist Church; No. 13, a dwelling on the Bruce Hill Road; No. 5, the old Gurney schoolhouse now a dwelling moved westerly on Skillins Road; No. 4, an old store at Shawtown; and No. 8, the present Historical Society on Chebeague Island. No. 2 was once at the south corner of the Harris and Tuttle Roads, but was moved by oxen to its present location in 1854. The E. K. Sweetser Grammar School was built in 1913—named for the old schoolmaster Ezra Knight Sweetser, whose widow donated that part of his former property for the purpose.

Singing schools constituted the chief social activity in many New England communities in these days, and Cumberland was no exception. "One of the earliest was taught by Benjamin Sweetser, called Master Ben, who was the village schoolmaster during the early 1800s. He also taught singing school in the good old-fashioned way for many years, and the really fine voices of his wife and twelve children furnished no inconsiderable part of the music. It was quite an event in the village when Master Ben called a meeting of the 'Silver-Grays' at the little brown schoolhouse. On such occasions the old folks for many miles around came to rehearse the music of their younger days, as found in the 'Cumberland Collection,' a compilation of sacred and patriotic music made by the old master himself."[5]

Another singing school was held in a large open room above Capt. Nicholas Humphrey's store near the street between the present Congregational Church and parsonage. This was taught by Samuel Chase of North Yarmouth and Capt. Reuben Blanchard of Cumberland, who taught there around 1851 between his voyages to sea.[6]

In West Cumberland there was a singing school held in a room over a store at the top of Morrison's Hill, as well as a dancing school. Around 1878 there was a dancing school in the old Cumberland Town Hall.

During the 1920s Cumberland became part of School Union 13 comprising Cape Elizabeth, Falmouth, Cumberland, and North Yarmouth.

Collection of Dean Blanchard

District #1 schoolhouse was on the Foreside. It burned in 1950 after half a century of disuse.

Sketch by Lena G. Foster,
taken from an old painting belonging to Ruth Blanchard Norton,
whose parents attended this school in the late 1800s.

District School #6 was on Greely Road.

During the 1940s Cape Elizabeth withdrew, leaving the three other towns. Then in January 1963, Falmouth withdrew. Union 13 was dissolved when School District 51 came into being in February, 1966.

By 1950 the new elementary school on the Drowne Farm was built and occupied on Thanksgiving weekend. All the work of moving the contents of the small schools was done by volunteer labor.

Thereby ended the use of the widely scattered grade schools in the various districts, and a new era was begun, under the guidance of William H. Soule as superintendent of schools.[7]

Endnotes

1. W. H. Rowe, *Ancient North Yarmouth & Yarmouth, Maine*, 1636–1936, pp. 301, 302.
2. From *A History of Greely Institute 1868–1935* by Mary E. Sweetser.

3. Information supplied by Harlan H. Sweetser and Cumberland Town Reports from 1874, 1875, and 1881.
4. *The District Schools of the Town of Cumberland in the Nineteenth Century* by Nancy P. Hutchins, 1971.
5. From "An Evening at Master Ben's," from an old scrapbook belonging to Mary E. Sweetser. A copy of the *Cumberland Collection* songbook is in the Cumberland Historical Society.
6. From p. 16, *History of the Town of Cumberland,* by Mary E. Sweetser, 1921.
7. List of superintendents in Appendix III.

Schools of Cumberland 1950–1974

By Mabel I. Wilson

The decade of the 1950s was one of great progress for the Cumberland School system. During the war and early postwar years, the population had grown, but no new construction had been possible. Under the leadership of Supt. William H. Soule, the nine-room elementary school had been constructed in 1950 for consolidation of grades K–6, the four-room Chebeague Island School replaced the three old buildings there, and a new wing was added to Greely Institute in 1957, providing library, science and home economics laboratories, classrooms, and administrative facilities, with commercial and junior high school rooms in the old section.

This seemed like a great accomplishment at the time, but it was soon to be dwarfed by the growth and construction of the 1960s. The large elementary classes moved up, and even larger kindergarten classes entered. It again became necessary to house classes in old Union Hall and temporary rooms in Red Men's Hall. On June 1, 1959, a new survey committee with representatives from the school committee, selectmen, planning and budget committees met, with School Committee Chairman Richard Sweetser presiding. Robert Cram was elected Chairman of the Survey Committee. Meetings were held in August and throughout the fall to study needs and formulate plans to care for them.

Paralleling these studies were those on a School Administrative District for Cumberland. In 1957 the Maine Legislature had passed the Sinclair Act to encourage small towns to organize into such districts with minimum high school enrollments of 300, by subsidizing new construction and increasing the subsidy on operational costs by 10 percent. In addition the debt ceiling was raised from 7.5 to 12.5 percent. The succeeding Legislature approved the formation of smaller districts provided they contract with another town for their secondary students, with both towns receiving an 18 percent building aid. Meetings were held with neighboring towns. Those interested were North Yarmouth and Pownal. Supt. Henry Perkins and Asa Gordon of the State Department of Education then met with representatives of Cumberland and those two towns to explain the organization, operation, and benefits of a district. A three-town committee for further study was selected, with William Chandler and Fred Logan representing Cumberland.

The school and survey committees felt that Cumberland's problems were much too urgent to await a district, and that they should proceed to develop long-range plans that could be used either in a district or alone. It appeared that it was only a matter of time until the Greely Institute building would be inadequate and that an entire new high school should be built, leaving Greely Institute for the junior high and upper grades. Several locations were studied and an engineering firm employed to study soil conditions. The area behind Greely Institute belonging to Arthur Blanchard and Sidney Bennett was determined to be the most desirable. In addition it offered the advantage of close proximity to Gyger Gymnasium for use in conjunction with the new high school for a time. It was acknowledged that, while it would cost less to build the entire school at one time, the town debt limit would not permit that plan without a School Administrative District. Therefore the committee recommended that the construction should take place in three stages. Part "A" would be a classroom wing that could be used for the junior high school and upper elementary grades for a time. Part "B" would be a science wing which together with "A" and Gyger Gymnasium could then house the high school. Part "C" would be a new gymnasium and probably a "cafetorium."

The 1960 town meeting authorized the appointment of a building committee to employ an architect to furnish complete plans for the classroom wing to satisfy immediate needs but designed to become a part of a future high school, and to obtain firm bids for the construction. Bruce Potter was elected chairman. The three-stage high school was planned for 450 students but with provisions for expansion to as many as 1,500, with additional wings.

Part "A" was approved, constructed, and occupied as planned in the fall of 1961, followed by Part "B" plus the administrative wing and industrial arts building, and with high school occupancy for September 1965.

During this time the elementary enrollments had continued to grow. A second subprimary room was added to the Sweetser School in 1964, and a portion of the cafeteria taken over for a classroom. An addition to the elementary school was being considered. It seemed desirable to take another look at a School Administrative District.

Votes had been held twice on a District with Pownal and North Yarmouth in the fall of 1962, and again in the spring of 1963—and had been rejected by Cumberland both times. North Yarmouth had declined a District with Pownal for the purpose of contracting with Cumberland. North Yarmouth entered into a five-year contract with Cumberland, and Pownal made similar arrangements elsewhere.

In November 1964, the Cumberland and North Yarmouth School Committees asked a group of citizens composed of Richard Sweetser, William Garsoe, William Chandler, Robert Walker of Cumberland, and Gloria Burrell, Walter Young, and Theodore Warren of North Yarmouth to work with them in another study. They studied the data previously prepared and the proposed building programs, and attempted to determine how much could be accomplished and at what cost if the towns (a) continued separately, or (b) formed a School Administrative District.

They expanded their numbers and formed subcommittees to study and report on enrollments, finance, and construction, and on curriculum, transportation, and legislative acts. The committees worked throughout 1965 and came up with a detailed report in October, recommending the acquisition of the George Burgess property, the immediate construction of a sixteen-room elementary school, the physical education plant and cafetorium at the high school in 1967, and further junior and senior high school additions in 1970. This would all be feasible only if a district were formed. Otherwise only the elementary building could be undertaken in Cumberland, and North Yarmouth would have to add on to its Memorial School.

They recommended a vote on the District as soon as possible, and held area meetings to explain their findings. Cumberland voted January 14, and North Yarmouth January 15, 1966, and both approved the District with a good majority. MSAD 51 became legally operative February 7, 1966.

The transition from School Union 13 to Maine School Administrative District 51 was a smooth one, with school board members becoming district directors. Clifton Turner, previously chairman of the Cumberland Committee, was elected chairman and Donald Smith of North Yarmouth, vice chairman. Vaughn Lacombe, Union 13 superintendent, was given a five-year contract as district superintendent.

The first actions included naming a committee to meet with Mr. Burgess to discuss the purchase of his property and appointing a citizens building committee and arranging a meeting with them. Fred Logan was elected chairman of the building committee. Their first action was to ask that the name of the new high school be changed from the previously suggested Cumberland High School to Greely High School and Greely Institute to Greely Junior High School—a request approved by the directors. Recommendations of the survey were discussed together with a suggestion of director Andrew Bunker that a swimming pool be considered along with the high school gymnasium.

Over the next weeks, plans and recommendations were developed by the building committee and accepted by the board. Part one was to construct a sixteen-room elementary school, including a multipurpose room, kitchen facilities, and an administrative section on the Burgess property, then under option. These plans provided for future expansion by the addition of another sixteen-room wing. Part two provided for the addition to Greely High School consisting of a gymnasium, locker rooms, swimming pool, auditorium, music room, arts and crafts, and necessary accessory spaces, with provision for future library and additional wings.

The proposal was submitted for vote and approved on April 23, 1966. Final plans were completed and submitted for bids in late summer. When bids were opened, it was found that all exceeded the appropriations. Plans were carefully reviewed and adjustments made where possible without causing incurable deficiencies and sent to the voters for the additional necessary funds. These were provided and construction begun.

The elementary school was ready for occupancy in September 1967. At the September meeting of the board of directors, Mrs. Mabel Wilson was informed by Chairman Clifton Turner that at the December, 1966, meeting in her absence, the board had voted to name this school the Mabel I. Wilson School, honoring her for her many years of devotion to schools as member of school committee, board of directors, survey and building committees. A public open house was held the evening of October 18.

Shortages in materials delayed completion at the high school, but the gymnasium was ready for the basketball season and the pool was opened for use on January 8.

Chairman Audrey Hutchinson and her committee planned a May 22, 1968, dedication of the two schools, with ceremonies at the Wilson School, and a parade to Greely High School where a second dedication program was held.

The new building made it possible to completely integrate grades one through six of North Yarmouth and Cumberland mainland. Kindergarten classes were housed in two rooms of Sweetser School and one of North Yarmouth Memorial. First graders were in Memorial, second and third at Cumberland Elementary, and fourth, fifth, and sixth in the Wilson School. Grades K through six of Chebeague attended school on the Island, but seven through twelve were transported to Greely Junior and Senior High Schools.

Supt. Morton Hamlin, directors, survey and building committees continued their studies in order to anticipate needs in time to meet them with adequate facilities. Those they foresaw were a library resource center at the high school, renovation and remodeling of "Old Greely," an addition to Wilson School, and paving and drainage of driveway and parking lots at the high school. This package was voted upon and rejected July 28, 1969.

On February 4, 1972, three separate articles were offered for vote for (a) the library resource center addition to the high school, (b) renovation of "Old Greely," and (c) grading and paving of driveways and parking areas at the junior and senior high schools. The library was again rejected, but the other two articles were approved.

All bids on the renovations again exceeded estimates and another vote was necessary to authorize additional funds. The project finally got under way in December. Three classes had to be moved out of the building and installed in Gyger Gymnasium, while the senior high school shared its gym and the pool with the junior high physical education classes. The century-old Greely Institute building was structurally sound and the outside appearance was carefully preserved. Inside, partitions were removed, ceilings lowered, floors carpeted, new stairs, new heating system, new electrical wiring, and lighting fixtures installed. An addition at the rear provided a safe fire escape under cover. The additional classroom space made it possible to enlarge the library in the new wing by removing a partition and adding another classroom space. The work was completed in time for September occupancy. On October 25, dedication ceremonies were held with Mr. Linwood Crandall, former teacher and principal of Greely Institute for twenty-eight years, speaker of the evening.

On April 24, 1973, the library resource center was approved. This was designed to include a principal's office and teachers' work room, but with partitions that could be easily removed if more library space should become necessary. This was planned for occupancy in the fall of 1974.

In 1974 a new survey committee with Dr. Frank Reed as chairman was appointed. They inspected buildings and held a series of meetings with Superintendent Morton Hamlin, Elementary Supervisor Reginald Dews, and principals and teachers of all buildings. As this is written the study is still under way, but it is already evident that there are very pressing needs in the mainland elementary schools. Not only has the enrollment continued to grow, but new services have been added, and in addition to crowded classrooms, classes are being conducted in closets, storage rooms, and halls. With additional programs now mandated by state law, the situation can only become more acute.

The high school will continue to grow as the larger classes already in school move ahead. It appears that some students will be denied Industrial Arts classes this fall because of limited facilities.

The towns must soon decide upon more building, double sessions, or twelve-month schools. Under the new law, the state now pays the entire cost of construction, so any building program must first be authorized by the State Department of Education.

List of superintendents of schools in Appendix III.

Update of Cumberland Schools

By Jill Storey and Carolyn Small

The Mabel I. Wilson School was renovated and expanded in 1991. The Wilson School was used for kindergarten through third grades. The North Yarmouth Memorial School was used by the fourth, fifth, and sixth grades. In 1999, the Drowne Road School was reopened. The new Greely Middle School was opened in 2004. The Wilson School includes kindergarten through second grades, the North Yarmouth Memorial School includes fourth and fifth grades, and the Drowne Road School is used for the third grade. The old junior high school is now used as the cultural arts center. The grand opening was held in January of 2006. Many members of the Gyger family attended the event.

A large addition was added to Greely High School, opening for classes in September of 2008. The wing built on the original Greely Institute in 1957 was torn down to accomodate the driveway to the Greely High School addition.

Mort Hamlin retired in 1987. Judy Stallworth was superintendent for two years after Mort Hamlin. Dr. Nye then took over as superintendent. Frank Harrison was hired as an interim superintendent for Dr. Nye. In 1992, Dr. Robert Hasson Jr. was hired and remained so until 2015. Jeffrey Porter is the current superintendent of schools.

History of Greely Institute

By Herman P. Sweetser

Greely Institute was established by the will of Eliphalet Greely. Mr. Greely was bom in 1784 on the Greely Road, which was named after his ancestors. In 1812 he married Elizabeth Loring, his childhood playmate. He became a sea captain but left the sea at an early age to settle in Portland. He became president of the Casco National Bank during its second year of organization. He remained as president for thirty-three years and was mayor of Portland for ten years.

Although he had no children of his own, he felt that the children of his hometown, between the ages of twelve and twenty-one, should have free education.

Collection of Phyllis Sweetser

Greely Institute before 1928.

In his will dated January 27, 1858, he left $27,500 to the town of Cumberland: $20,000 to be invested in a trust fund; $6,000 to erect the building; $1,000 for "philosophical apparatus"; and $500 for a school library. The will stated that the building was to be of a simple style of architecture, neat and substantial in manner, should have two stories, and be built of brick and granite with a slate roof. This was supplemented by his wife, who gave four acres of barren pastureland purchased from Enos Blanchard, thus determining the site of the school. This spurred the town to act promptly with the construction so that Greely Institute was opened on September 28, 1868, with the accompanying notice being in Captain Nicholas Humphrey's store, at the present Congregational Parsonage. The lower floor was finished with a study hall, a small classroom, and a combined principal's office and library. A portrait of Mr. Greely painted by a relative, Mr. Alson Greely, and a clock were hung on the wall of the main room. The second floor was a large room for assemblies and public functions with a stage across the

Greely Institute.

THE FIRST TERM OF THIS INSTITUTION WILL COMMENCE ON

MONDAY, SEPTEMBER 28,

Under the instruction of

T. JEFFERSON EMERY, A. M.

It is desirable that all who expect to attend the school should be present, if possible, on the first day.

Wm. Russell,
R. H. Rogers,
Samuel Ross Jr. } Trustees.

Cumberland, Sept. 23d, 1868.

Courtesy of Cumberland Historical Society

Greely Institute opening notice.

front. The building was dedicated September 29, 1868, with the following program:

Dedicatory Prayer—Rev. Isaac Weston

Addresses by Rev. E. S. Jordan

N. L. Humphrey, Esq.	Asa Greely, Esq.
J. Sturdivant, Esq.	Benjamin Merrill, Esq.
Dr. Hall	Mr. Emery, Principal

In 1870, a Bowdoin College classmate of Mr. Emery's, Charles Chamberlain, came to Greely as a teacher of botany. His classes were much interested in growing things, and he decided to plant trees and beautify the grounds of the Institute. He knew he could count on the cooperation of the people in the area and on his students. So in the spring of 1871 a day was chosen and a grand holiday proclaimed. Farmers came with oxen and horse teams, plows and shovels; the land was leveled and spread with loam. Mr. Chamberlain made a chart, stakes were located according to his plan, and trees were set by the students, who put their names in cans buried beside their tree. Many of the trees still stand as a living memorial to those early students and Mr. Chamberlain.

Another evidence of local interest was indicated by a student campaign, suggested by the next principal, George M. Seiders, to raise money to buy a cabinet organ, and a bell for the belfry, which was first used in 1872. By this time there were nearly 200 pupils, some of whom were tuition students from other towns, who lived with families in Cumberland. Mrs. Nicholas Humphrey and Mrs. Samuel Sweetser were long and lovingly remembered because of their kindness toward those pupils who lived in their homes.

Prior to 1880 no graduations were held and there were about 145 students who attended. The first graduation was held in June 1880, with six graduates—three young ladies and three young men. They were Roland Blanchard, Addie Dunn (True), Annie Leighton (Whitney), Edward B. Osgood (for whom the Osgood room in present Greely Junior High is named), Lena Pinkham (Hamilton), and Edward Warren. In 1883 the Alumni Association was founded.

Courtesy of Mrs. Howard B. Clough

Faculty and students of Greely Institute (c. 1888).

For some years the selectmen as trustees had little interest in the operation of their school; $250 a year was the extent of the town appropriation. There were only two teachers, with an occasional student helper, and the average attendance faded to thirty-five or forty.

With encouragement from the town and guidance by the State Department of Education, Greely Institute became incorporated by the Legislature of 1913. A board of trustees was elected by the town and included the selectmen, as provided by Mr. Greely's will. In 1914, the town appropriated $1,000 and conditions bettered immediately. The school became a class-A high school (having a course in agriculture, with Arthur Harris as the first teacher) and permitting students to enter college without taking college examinations. Dana Jordan had come to Greely as principal in 1912, and many advances were made during his stay. A course in home economics was started with the first teacher, Margaret Seavey. A house at 310 Main Street was remodeled as a dormitory and home economics classroom and laboratory. In 1914 Union Hall, now the building used as the office of the maintenance department, was purchased by the Alumni Association to be used as a gymnasium. Records show the following persons to have been trustees at this time:

President	George M. Seiders
	Mabel R. Brown
Treasurer	Frank H. Chase
Secretary	Herman P. Sweetser

In 1916, a building program renovated the upstairs hall of Greely Institute, put in water and new toilet facilities, and a better heating system. A kitchen was remodeled in Union Hall, providing a laboratory for the class in cooking, and the first hot lunch program for schoolchildren was started under the guidance of Lucille Dark as home economics teacher.

In 1928 an unusual event took place. The town had already established one of the first town forests in the state. Ernest Rand (a selectman trustee) wanted to increase the interest in this forest. With the cooperation of the class in agriculture he directed the planting of an acre of young pine and spruce trees on the Drowne Farm field adjoining the original forest acreage.

The Drowne Farm, which came into possession of the town through the will of Mrs. Elizabeth Drowne in 1907, is the only 100-acre plot which remains as originally laid out by the first surveyors of the town. Located on Tuttle Road, it was owned for many years by Captain Isaac Sturdivant before Mrs. Drowne, his daughter, gave it to the town. Under her will the benefits derived from the farm were to be used for educational purposes. It was appropriate that a town forest be planted by students. That first acre of trees established Cumberland as the seventh town in Maine to adopt a town forest.[1]

In 1929, a new wing of three stories to match the old building was added and dedicated in an all-day celebration in May. This wing provided a science laboratory; a home economics room with four unit tables with sinks, and three sewing machines, two of which were electric; and a room for the classes in agriculture.

In 1930 the junior high school came into being. In 1934 the first course in manual training (known as "Shop," later called industrial arts) was introduced with funds furnished for vocational training through the Smith-Hughes Act, which was also beneficial to the home economics and

From school brochure, 1940

Gyger Gymnasium and Greely Institute.

agricultural departments. The first shop was in the top story of Union Hall and taught by Raymond Corey. It was later moved to the basement of Gyger Gymnasium and now is in a building of its own on the expanded campus.

The first basketball game was played in 1904, in an outdoor field with baskets fastened to the top of poles. Around 1911 arrangements were made to allow basketball to be played in Union Hall, then the church vestry. Conditions were far from satisfactory, with wire shields built around the two wood-burning stoves located in opposite corners of the room. The kerosene lamps were also protected and at best furnished insufficient light. However, other schools in the area had little better facilities. The community built up great interest in the games and crowded into the limited space along the walls. After the building became school property, hanging balconies were built, the stage removed, and the floor strengthened. Three famous basketball championship teams practiced and played in this room and won fame in the county. The teams of 1928 and 1929 brought to a climax three years of championships, and thereby won the Cumberland County Conference (Triple C) Trophy. The players were

Stanley Blanchard, Raymond Corey, Howard Lowe, Robert Nelson, and Leigh White, coached by Myron Leighton.

The girls also played basketball, with class schedules so arranged as to give them practice periods.

The first Greely school orchestra was started in 1927 when Ernest Herrick, who lived next door (to the northeast), volunteered to train the students on various instruments. Ever since that time the school has had great interest in band and orchestra. In 1935, at the suggestion of Principal Otto Davis, the Gilbert and Sullivan operetta *H.M.S. Pinafore* was produced by the pupils under the direction of Robert Stetson, superintendent of music. It was presented in the Red Men's Hall to a crowded house and was so successful that other Gilbert and Sullivan works were presented for a number of years.

In 1937, the Federal Public Works Administration program was studied by trustee Herman Sweetser and selectman trustee Ernest Rand, and thoughts became centered on possible financial aid for a gymnasium. Plenty of cold water was splashed on this suggestion, but persistence won out. In 1938 the Greely Institute PWA Project No. 1097F was accepted at a special town meeting. The town paid little more than half the cost. Work was begun in October on the campus on the northeast side of Greely Institute. The gymnasium was dedicated on June 9, 1939, with the following program:

Music
Prayer
Music

Introduction of Chairman of Meeting—Ernest Rand, for the Town
Herman P. Sweetser, Chairman
Representing the Federal Emergency Administration of Public Works, Francis X. Slane, Asst. Regional Engineer

Music

Representing the Alumni Association, Walter H. Barter
Representing Greely Institute, Eleanor Stevens
Dedicatory Address—Judge Scott Wilson, Pres. of the Board of Greely Institute Trustees

Music
Benediction

The building was named the Gyger Gymnasium in honor of John T. Gyger, who was superintendent of schools from 1928 to 1939. His portrait hangs in the entrance hall of the gymnasium. He died one week before the dedication of the building. The building was occupied in 1939. Classrooms in agriculture and shop, and later a laboratory, used most of the basement where also modern toilets, locker rooms, and showers were installed for the gymnasium classes and visiting teams.

Around 1939–40, the State Department of Education attempted to withdraw the retirement funds already contributed by teachers of Greely Institute with the argument that Greely Institute was a private academy and not a free high school. Judge Scott Wilson, president of the board of trustees, at the request of the treasurer Alfred Doughty, hastened from Calais where he was sitting at Circuit Court, stepped into the fray, and after providing the state superintendent of schools with the facts, Greely Institute was declared a free high school.

With the new Gyger Gymnasium available, Union Hall was of no particular use. A farmers' workshop program was available with federal

Portland Press Herald—Portland, Maine — Tuesday Morning, October 26, 1948

Greely Institute Has Open House To Celebrate Remodeled Building

(Special Dispatch)

Cumberland Center, Oct. 25.—Greely Institute held open house tonight when townspeople viewed the remodeled home economics department and new classrooms constructed in the school's old gymnasium.

The new home economics four-unit electric kitchen, believed one of the most modern in the state, was installed at a cost of about $2,500 while nearly $10,000 was spent to remodel the old gym into a two-room junior high school.

Part of the money for the alterations was taken from the $24,000 voted the school at annual town meeting and part from a fund set up by the trustees.

Also open to inspection were other classrooms and Gyger Gymnasium. Teachers were present in the various classes to greet the public and answer questions. Girls in the home economics department acted as guides and served cookies and punch.

Principal Linwood T. Crandall reported there were 34 pupils taking the home economics course and 41 in the junior high classes. Both classes were reported a little larger than a year ago.

Present also to greet the public were Miss Evelyn [illegible], home economics instructor, Jeff [illegible], representing the company that installed the kitchen equipment; Miss Florence Jenkins, head of the State Home Economics Division, State Department of Education, and Miss Mildred Turney and Miss Louise Pettenger, both teacher-trainers with the State Home Economics Division; Herman P. Sweetser and Alfred W. Doughty, trustees, and Supt. of Schools Ralph B. Motz.

By Press Herald Photographer Libby

OUR JOB FINISHED—Herman P. Sweetser, Greely Institute Building Committee chairman, hands plans and specifications for the remodeled building at Greely to Glenden B. Dean, representing the Cumberland selectmen, as a symbol that the building job has been completed. Looking on, left to right, are Howard C. Blanchard and Alfred W. Doughty, trustees of Greely Institute.

Courtesy of Margaret Wyman

From Laura Wyman's scrapbook.

aid taking most of the expense for equipment. This program appealed to the local farmers, and it was requested and obtained and set up with William Farwell, the agriculture teacher, as supervisor. It was a great help in repairing and rebuilding farm tools and equipment, with its power saws, welding equipment, hoists, a forge, and other tools. So Union Hall was still being useful.

In 1946 the addition of a commercial course made four vocational courses. The Greely shop course was chosen by Gorham State Teachers College for practice teaching. In a statewide survey of schools receiving vocational aid, only eleven had four operating courses, and Greely Institute was one of them.

In 1948 an appropriation of $9,700 was made by the town to remodel Union Hall for schoolrooms. All foundation supports were replaced, the floor strengthened, the walls braced, the ceiling lowered, and partitions and closets built. The ell was enlarged for toilets and the heating system. This building was then used for the junior high, and the upstairs Greely Hall, which had been housing junior high, was remodeled for more classrooms for the high school.

During these years the music department was growing bigger and better under the guidance of Mr. Stetson. The orchestra was playing for graduations and the band marching in the Memorial Day parades. Both band and orchestra sometimes joined Falmouth for concerts and other activities. All this helped increase alumni and community interest in the school, and with help from the Men's Club and Parent Teachers' Association, new uniforms were purchased for the band, the old film projector was replaced, and curtain and drapes for the Gyger Gym stage were provided.

In 1953, by a vote taken at town meeting, the trustees of Greely Institute were to surrender all property of the Institute to the selectmen of the Town of Cumberland for the purpose of establishing a free high school in accordance with Section 103, Chapter 37 of the Revised Statutes of the State of Maine of 1949, as amended. In July 1953, the formal transfer was achieved and the Corporation of the Trustees of Greely Institute was dissolved.

In 1955, due to crowded conditions in the school, the town voted to finance and build a one-story addition to be added to old Greely Institute. This addition provided two new science labs, a home

Courtesy of Cumberland Historical Society

Eliphalet Greely's portrait hung in the Greely Institute's first formal library.

economics room, a library and study hall, and four new classrooms. This permitted the junior high to use most of the original building and first addition. This new wing was put into use in 1956–57.

By 1957 the change in farm operation in this area began to be felt in the school. Fewer boys were interested in agriculture, and the course was discontinued. Industrial arts under Byron Rawnsley's able guidance was more and more in demand, leading eventually to a wholly new building by 1965.

In 1957–58, with Linwood Crandall as the very capable principal, the status of Greely Institute was studied by the State Department of Education and accreditation policies outlined. These requirements were to become effective in July 1960.

In 1959 a big step forward was achieved by having the first guidance department director added to the faculty. Vaughn Lacombe had an office in the old Greely building, and his department was a great success and has been continued ever since.

A school library was another requirement for accreditation. By this time Mr. Thomas Burden was principal of the school. He and Superintendent Perkins arranged to have Mrs. Phyllis Sweetser, librarian of Prince Memorial Library, become a member of the faculty and school librarian. So in the summer of 1960, Mrs. Sweetser organized and established a program and an acceptable supply of books, assuring cooperation with the town library. This first functioning library was set up in the Osgood room of the new one-story wing. With this accomplishment and further improvements in the science department, the State Department of Education was satisfied and issued a five-year Certificate of Accreditation beginning in 1960.

Courtesy of Cumberland Historical Society

Mrs. Sweetser and students in the Greely library.

In 1961 the first section of a new three-part high school plan (Part A) was completed, with twelve new classrooms. The junior high and grades four, five, and six were moved temporarily to that building, giving the high school five more rooms.

In 1963 the speedy growth of the school required acceptance of Plan B, as well as the construction in 1965 of a new building for industrial arts.

In 1965, with William N. Farwell—a longtime successful member of the faculty—as principal, heading a faculty of 22 members, with 294 students, the town budget for Greely Institute was $151,000.52. Quite a contrast to the early days, when the principal, one assistant, and 35 pupils had a budget of $250.

Interest, meanwhile, was growing for the formation of a School Administration District to contain Cumberland and North Yarmouth. This was achieved in February 1966. So, the formation of SAD No. 51 brings to a close the history of Greely Institute and changes the name to Greely High School, which opened in 1967.

Sources

1. Town Forest article by Ruth Burnell, p. 20, Bulletin of Greely Institute, 1928.

Compiled from histories written by Mary Osgood Sweetser, Herman P. Sweetser, and Donna Martin Berry.

Union Hall

By Robert G. Blanchard and Herman P. Sweetser

Union Hall was built around 1868 for the Cumberland Center Fair, which was held for the most part on the pastureland in back of the burying ground, and owned by Capt. Enos Blanchard. On this land a one-third-mile racetrack was laid out and constructed. In 1874 Capt. Blanchard deeded a lot 110 feet by 82.5 feet on which the hall stood, to the Agricultural Hall Co., for $35.

In October 1877 the Cumberland Center Farmers Club held a fair on the Union Hall grounds—a two-day affair with dinner served at the Town Hall.

Photograph by Daniel Dow, 1974

Union Hall.

In March 1878 after reconstructing the building with two fine halls, done under the able supervision of William E. Wilson, Union Hall was dedicated with an address by Rev. T. S. Perry and music under the direction of Capt. Enos Blanchard. The upper hall was used for meetings of the "Lodge of Good Templars," the Cumberland Farmers Club, and evening meetings of the Congregational Church. The lower hall, which with a balcony had a seating capacity of 400, was used for entertainments, Lyceum programs, etc., as shown by the accompanying poster. Howard Buxton was a truly professional singer who traveled with the show *Comical Brown*.

Dramatic Entertainment

—BY THE—

Cumberland Dramatic Club,

AT UNION HALL,

CUMBERLAND CENTER,

Thursday Evening, March 30,

When will be presented the new Centennial Drama, in two acts, entitled

One Hundred Years Ago

Or, OUR BOYS OF '76,

CAST OF CHARACTERS.

Obed Sterling, a Quaker,	Herbert N. Pinkham
Ephraim Sterling, his son,	Herbert A. Merrill
Elmer Granger, a young patriot,	Geo. Blanchard
Uriel Bosworth, a Quaker convert,	D. M. Prince
Pretzel, a Dutchman,	A. Howard Buxton
Ginger, a Negro,	Chas. G. Thurston
Burke, Tories,	W. E. Wilson
Blucher, Tories,	Carroll D. Prince
Rachel Sterling, the Quaker Mother,	Mrs. Annie Blanchard
Ruth Sterling, her daughter,	Lena C. Pittee
Prudence Granger, Elmer's sister,	Della S. Whitney

The scene of the Drama is near Philadelphia, July 4, 1776.

BETWEEN THE ACTS,

A READING, by	Mr. GEO. BLANCHARD
SONGS, by	Mr. A. H. BUXTON
A READING, by	Miss LENA C. PITTEE

Doors open at 7, Curtain rises at 7-45 precisely

Admission 20 cts. - - Children 15 cts.

Bagley, Printer, Portland.

Poster, courtesy of Robert G. Blanchard

Cumberland's observance of the National Centennial in 1876.

When the Cumberland Center Fair was discontinued, Mr. Oren Thomes bought the whole property for $800 in 1880, and in 1885 presented it to the Congregational Church for a vestry. The church had been holding public suppers put on by the Ladies' Circle in the hall for years. In 1895 an addition was built to provide better kitchen facilities and also to provide a small dressing room for the stage. Circle suppers continued to be in vogue, as well as dinners for town meeting. In October 1889, the Sawga Tribe of Red Men started using Union Hall for their ritual work. They continued to meet here until December 1914.

By this time a new vestry had been built beneath the Congregational Church, and the Ladies' Circle relinquished all claims to Union Hall. So the alumni of Greely Institute had a campaign to raise funds which permitted them to buy the property and present it to the school. It was then put to use as a gymnasium where both boys and girls played basketball. It was also used as the home economics laboratory, and the manual arts workshop was on the second floor, from which a fire escape was built.

As Greely Institute was enlarged and Gyger Gymnasium was built, Union Hall was used for other purposes. By 1948 it was remodeled and used as a junior high school. In 1961 it became the school cafeteria, and then was used for various classrooms during the process of building new schools. In 1968 it became the administrative offices for the superintendent of schools. It is now the maintenance department office.

Chapter Fourteen

Railroads in the Town of Cumberland

By Charles D. Haseltine

Public transportation through the Town of Cumberland came into being with the development of various stage lines running out of Portland. According to the Portland City Directory of 1850, there were two such lines passing through Cumberland. The Portland, Augusta and Bangor Mail Stage left the Elm Hotel in Portland daily at nine p.m., passing along the Foreside to Brunswick and beyond. The Portland, Gray and Andover Mail Stage was scheduled to leave American House at seven a.m. on Tuesday, Thursday, and Saturday, running along what is now Route 100 through West Cumberland, Gray, Poland, and South Paris. By the year 1850, the steam railroads were coming into existence and the stage lines were on the way out.

Since then the Town of Cumberland has been served by two different railroad systems, and at one time by two different electric railroad companies, all being shown on the accompanying map.

Steam railroading through Cumberland began with the opening of the Atlantic and St. Lawrence Railroad as far as North Yarmouth in 1848, connecting at Yarmouth Junction with the Kennebec & Portland Railroad for Brunswick, Bath, and later, Augusta and Waterville. The

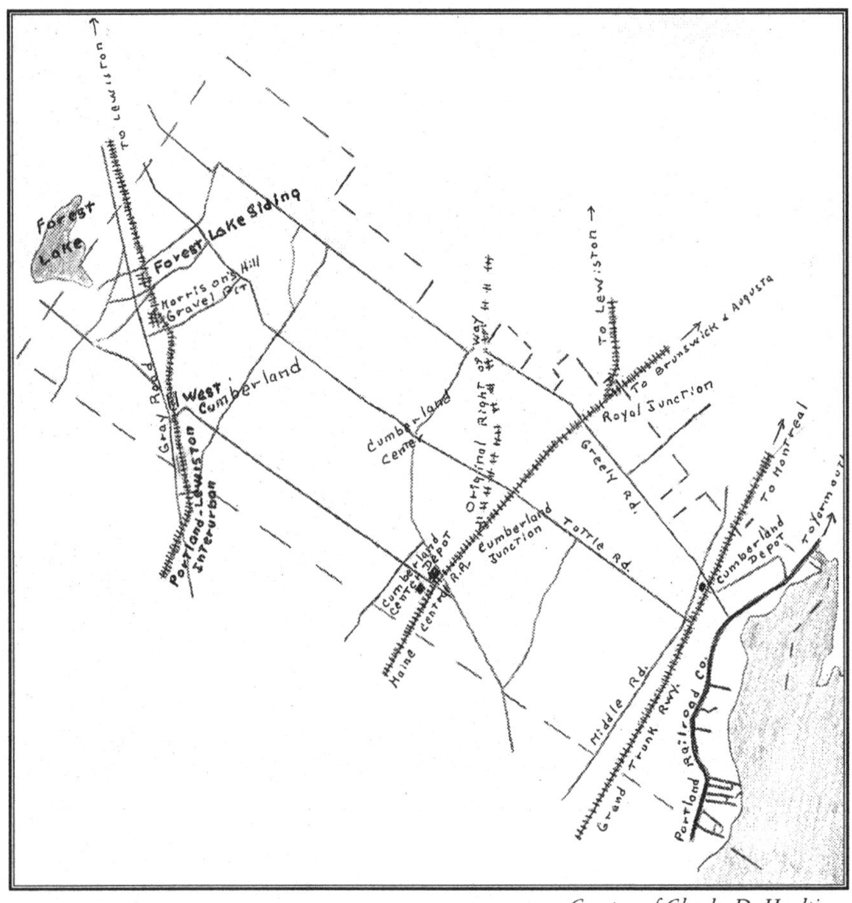

Courtesy of Charles D. Heseltine

Railroad lines through the town of Cumberland.

> *The Portland and Kennebec was opened from Yarmouth Junction to Portland in 1867. It had been in running order from Augusta to Yarmouth Junction, where the passengers took the Grand Trunk road for Portland. There was a serious accident at the crossing on Tuttle Road, and several workmen were killed.*
>
> *—Mary Eliza Osgood Sweetser*

Courtesy of Charles D. Heseltine

Atlantic and St. Lawrence No. 11 "Danville," built by the Portland Company (1852), would have been one of the first steam locomotives to run through the Town of Cumberland. Later sold to the Portland and Oxford Central, 1867.

Courtesy of Charles D. Heseltine

The Grand Trunk had a reputation for handsome locomotives. This one, posed at East Deering in 1926, was a familiar sight to those waiting for trains at the Grand Trunk's Cumberland station.

Cumberland Junction Village (New Boston) about 1915, on the occasion of the Stanley Cattle Auction.

Atlantic and St. Lawrence road became the Grand Trunk Railway, and currently is a portion of the great Canadian National Railway.[1]

The second steam rail line through Cumberland was the extension of the Kennebec and Portland Railroad from Yarmouth Junction into Portland. In 1871 this road was merged with the rapidly growing Maine Central Railroad system, and a connection was built from a point near the Cumberland depot to Danville Junction to link up the so-called "back road." This connection was designated Cumberland Junction, and the depot carried that name for many years.[2]

> The freight house was the busy place in the Junction village, locally known as New Boston. The "way freight" every weekday brought the assorted things consigned to Cumberland people: barrels of flour and sugar, a hogshead of molasses for E. B. Osgood, who ran a butcher shop and store up on SHE Street [so called because at that time there were almost no men living on it, but mostly widows and

Photo by Floyd W. Norton

unmarried women], from the Corner by the church over the Greely Road; similar things for James L. Dunn who ran the general store 50 yards below the four corners, with all manner of sundries and appliances, even to a piano or an organ now and then, kitchen ranges and bed-springs, cream separators, gallon cans of maple syrup and all sorts of spices, condiments and furnishings required to run the homes of the town. Not to mention the stacks of tin lard pails and other containers embossed or labeled for F. R. Sweetser & Son, who ran a processing and packing plant up on Blanchard Road, as well as other stacks of tin lard pails bearing the name of E. B. Osgood, the other packer in town. Some of those stacks of pails for these men would run 10 feet in length, with four or five stacks at a shipment.

On a Monday morning that freight house might be well-nigh empty, but after the "way freight" had come out it would be stacked to the roof. At this time, during the early 1900s, there would be at least 40 trains a day, half of them passenger trains,

> passing through Cumberland Junction. There were seven tracks in the yard, including three main lines to Lewiston and Brunswick—and four side tracks.[2]

In 1911 the Maine Central built a new route of about six miles in length, to eliminate heavy grades through New Gloucester, and the new connection became known as Royal Junction and remains in service today. With this change, the station at Cumberland Center became an agency station. According to the Maine Register for 1910–11, Henry G. Adams was the first agent appointed to this position. The 1922–23 edition of the Maine Register lists Ernest N. Herrick as agent, and none follow this date. This was during a period when station agents were acquiring shorter working hours and many small stations were being discontinued as

Photo and caption by Floyd W. Norton

Cumberland Center Station about 1934, after the Royal Junction tower had gone into operation, and only an agent was employed at Cumberland.

Courtesy of Yarmouth Shopping Notes

"Ox-Bow" or "Oxtail" Curve.

agency stations. The agent's main duty was to report passing trains, and the new interlocking tower built at Royal Junction could provide this service.

Following World War II, the Maine Central Railroad, like many another steam rail line, made a valiant effort to stave off declining passenger service by acquiring a dozen modern streamlined coaches, but as gasoline rationing was a thing of the past, the public once again was to forsake the railroads in favor of their family cars, and passenger service went into a deep decline. On September 5, 1960, the final scheduled passenger train on the Maine Central Railroad left Vanceboro at 11:30 p.m., ending at Portland Union Station at 6:30 a.m. the next morning. This was the last passenger train to run through the Town of Cumberland.

Residents of the Town of Cumberland, particularly those along the Foreside, must have been delighted with the news of the chartering of the Portland and Yarmouth Electric Railway on November 31, 1894. This would provide a more convenient mode of transportation than that which the steam railroads could offer. While the funding of this project took some time, actual construction of the road commenced during 1897, and progress was made despite several legal entanglements.

Access to Portland would be via Tukeys Bridge, which the City of Portland was about to replace with a new span. Both the Portland Railroad Company and the Portland & Yarmouth road were invited to contribute the sum of $20,000 each as their share for laying rail across the span. The Portland & Yarmouth road, none too adequately financed, made a counterproposal of paying a fee of $800 annually for a period of one hundred years—or until 1997! A compromise was worked out, however, permitting them to pay the sum over a ten-year period.

Courtesy of Charles D. Heseltine

A standard pose for cars on the Portland and Yarmouth road, one being off the rails! Open car No. 10 is at the left, while closed car No. 23 stands by.

Courtesy of Charles D. Heseltine

Car No. 10, "Arbutus," poses outbound on Forest Avenue, bound for West Cumberland and Lewiston in 1923.

As the line would be a side-of-the-road operation through Falmouth and Cumberland Foreside, it was discovered that through the Town of Cumberland the poles of the Postal Telegraph Company were on the site selected for the laying of the rails, and the telegraph company was unhappy about relocating them. A judgment by the courts finally brought about a solution, with the poles being moved and the street railway paying the costs. By the first of August, 1897, rails had reached the Cumberland-Yarmouth town line and workmen were strengthening Martins Point Bridge so as to support the weight of the heavy electric cars. A brick car barn was being built on Washington Avenue in Portland, and a wooden car house in Yarmouth Village.

Regular service commenced on this line August 18, 1898, with motorman John D. Bennett handling the first regular trip. Service was hourly at the beginning, but shortly thereafter cars ran every thirty minutes from 6:00 a.m. until 11:30 p.m.

The route extended from the corner of Elm and Congress Streets in Monument Square, Portland, through Elm and Oxford Streets to Washington Avenue, which it shared with tracks of the Portland Railroad Company, swinging into Veranda Street at East Deering, crossing Martins Point Bridge and following alongside what is currently Route 88 through Falmouth and Cumberland Foreside to Yarmouth. To dodge various outcroppings of ledge, the rail line crossed the highway no less than four times from one side of the roadway to the other. A particularly distinctive feature of this line was so-called "Ox-Bow" curve, where the line was built on the side of a hill twenty or more feet above the highway and from which a delightful view of Casco Bay could be viewed. The Yarmouth line, so-called, was considered the most scenic of all lines of the Portland system.

The Portland & Yarmouth Electric road built a popular pleasure resort near the Falmouth-Cumberland town line known as Underwood Springs. A casino featuring shore dinners and other recreational facilities drew vast crowds during the summer months and added greatly to the financial returns of the company. The site of this park was the favorite of the Algonquin Indians in a bygone day. With the opening of this park the railway scheduled cars every fifteen minutes throughout summer afternoons and evenings. Unfortunately, it was burned to the ground August 14, 1907, and the casino was not rebuilt, the Portland Railroad having both Riverton Park and Cape Cottage Casino to offer the public, and the property was soon thereafter disposed of.

Initial rolling stock of the Yarmouth road consisted of single truck cars both closed and open, the latter for summer service, of course. It also had a rotary snowplow for combating the drifts following winter storms. As the line was of a suburban character and the single truck cars had a tendency to develop a galloping motion when operating at full speed, derailments seem to have been a common thing along the line.

For a period of nineteen years the Town of Cumberland was served by a high-speed interurban line rated as the finest electric railroad in the East. This was the Portland-Lewiston Interurban Railroad chartered in 1907 and put under construction over its own private right-of-way early in 1910. It was unique in that there was no public stock offering, the promoters putting up their future earnings in the Lewiston electric light plant they owned as security for the sum needed to build the railroad.

Construction of the thirty-odd-mile private right-of-way began at Littlefields Corner, Auburn, and the following year construction began on the Portland end of the line. All work was done by pick and shovel, using horse-drawn dump carts and earth scoops. An electric locomotive was acquired as soon as some rail had been put down, and gravel from a private pit at Morrison's Hill was hauled along the line for use in ballasting. The contractors were pioneers in building reinforced concrete spans over the various small streams, and one remains today near Route 100 at West Cumberland.

Construction was completed in late 1913, but the roadbed was permitted to remain idle through the winter to allow for settlement. It was unfortunate that the road's builder, W. Scott Libby, died suddenly, but two weeks before the grand opening of the line. The first regular service commenced July 2, 1914, and a full hourly schedule commenced a couple of weeks later.

Intended as a high-speed, limited-stop, interurban line, the road fully met all expectations, using heavy interurban cars geared to a top speed of sixty miles an hour in a day when sixty miles an hour was a mile a minute! Green plush seats, luggage racks, and a smoking compartment were found in each car, and each carman was issued a pair of white kid gloves to wear while handling the Pullman-type stair straps or adjusting the trolley ropes and so on.

Within a short time residents along this line protested to the Public Utilities Commission and requested additional stops other than the five which initially were provided. As time passed, the Public Utilities Commission brought about a relaxing in this strictly limited stop service, and in its last years there were few limited runs. Fare from West Cumberland to Portland was thirty cents, with monthly commutation tickets available at a discount.

Electric freight and express was also handled along this line, and throughout its length were many small freight and milk platforms where nearby farmers were able to ship their milk and farm produce into Portland or Lewiston. The Portland-Lewiston Interurban was without a

Courtesy of Charles D. Heseltine

Citizens along the Foreside join hands with street railway men in helping to break out the line during the winter of 1920, in which occurred the "Blizzard of the Century." High centers of snow between the rails froze, causing cars to leave the tracks.

peer in the six New England states and, without doubt, was fondly remembered by old-time residents of the Town of Cumberland, as well as other communities.

The final trip over the line was made June 28, 1933, with the last trip from Lewiston arriving early the following morning. At about the same time the final run was arriving in Portland from Yarmouth.

Thus, by a chance coincidence, both electric lines serving the Town of Cumberland ceased operation on the same date.

The trolley freight and express business expanded greatly during World War I when our steam railroads were taxed to capacity. It was over this Portland-Falmouth-Cumberland-Yarmouth route that the large trolley express cars, often hauling one or more trailers, carried on their operations from the Lewiston area, via Brunswick and Freeport into Portland, and over which the nightly Waterville Night Freight passed, being the longest streetcar run in the New England states. Portions of this old roadbed still remain, and can be seen along the Foreside road in parts of Cumberland.

The winter of 1920 was an exceptionally difficult one, as heavy snows followed by freezing rains served to fill the track centers with ice, which tended to derail even the heaviest of cars. Trolley service along the Foreside came to a halt despite the valiant struggles of the street railway plow crews. Residents along the route turned out with picks and shovels to bear a hand at opening up the track, but for several days car service was at a standstill.

The inhabitants along the Foreside were possibly among the more affluent in the area, and were known to acquire automobiles at an early date. Records show that, while in 1910 there were but four automobiles in the Town of Cumberland and but five in both Falmouth and Yarmouth, a dozen years brought about a great change in the figures. The area served by the Portland Railroad in 1910 accounted for but 538 motor vehicles in all, while by 1922 there was a total of 10,634. For this reason, passenger riding along the Yarmouth line dropped rapidly following the First World War. With the posting of the fall schedules in 1921, service through to Yarmouth was cut to an hourly basis, with alternate cars running only to Town Landing, later only to Madockawando Landing. On September 1, 1929, the Yarmouth-Freeport-Brunswick trolley service was abandoned.

The Portland Railroad Company continued to maintain their hourly service to Yarmouth until June 29, 1933. Public notices had been posted for the discontinuance of the line a week prior to this date, but the Public Utilities Commission had not determined which of four bus applicants it would favor with a franchise, and requested that the road continue operations until replacement vehicles could be made ready. The Maine Central Transportation Company, which was operating a Portland-to-Rockland service, was granted the authority.

On June 29, 1933, George V. Olmstead left Monument Square with his car at 11:15 p.m. for Yarmouth. Although the car was full on its leaving Portland, but eight passengers were aboard when it reached its destination. Passengers on the final run included Freeman Brown, Wallace Brown, Albert Olmstead, Clyde Richardson, H. S. Drown,

Lester Chase, G. S. White, and F. B. Fish Jr. John D. Bennett, retired trolley motorman who had run the first trolley car over the line thirty-five years previously, was unable to make the trip as he had planned.

The car returned to Monument Square at 1:08 a.m. the following morning. At the same time, the Portland-Lewiston Interurban was completing its final trips. Thus, the Town of Cumberland lost the service of both its electric roads almost at the same instant.

Endnotes

1. See chapter 3, on Poland's Corner.
2. Floyd W. Norton's "Hand-Hewn History of Maine and its Representative Town of Cumberland," 1970.

Chapter Fifteen

Industries on the Mainland

By Phyllis S. Sweetser and Antoinette N. Packard

This list was copied from George Blanchard's diary, dated February 25, 1865:

In Cumberland Center

23 Houses
16 Barns
2 Stores
2 Shoemaker's Shops
2 Blacksmith's Shops
1 Joiner's Shop–Carpenter
1 Town House
1 Schoolhouse
1 Church
2 Unoccupied Buildings
Total: 51 Buildings
Population in 1865 was 92—probably only males being counted.

Some of the industries mentioned in these old lists could well have been Col. Samuel True's blacksmith shop, operated by him and his son

Courtesy of Portland, Maine Evening Express, *March 24, 1964*

Col. True's village blacksmith shop (c. 1880).

Edward in the 1850s. This was situated on the site of the present Gulf station at 296 Main Street.

In the 1870s–80s, Silas Rideout painted carriages and wagons in a garage at 279 Main Street. Around 1875–1880, Benjamin B. Sweetser was a wheelwright with his carriage shop on Tuttle Road near the railroad tracks. He made carriages and heavy farm wagons. Those were hard times, and his grandson Harlan H. Sweetser tells that most business was done by barter, and that one year the only money he received was eight cents!

A Mercantile Directory for 1884 gives the following statistics:

Population 842
Adams, John S. & Son—Blacksmiths
Blanchard, E. L.—General Store
George Blanchard & Co.—Stock Farm
John E. Dunn—Cumberland Depot General Store

Leighton & Wilson—West Cumberland Lumber
Merrill Bros.—Cumberland Center Butchers, Packers
Osgood & Dunn—Cumberland Center General Store
S. M. Rideout—Cumberland Center Blacksmith & Carriagemaker
Benj. Whitney—Cumberland Center Carriages
Wilson, N. B. & Son—West Cumberland General Store

The Osgood & Dunn store listed above stood in front of Union Hall and was torn down. Mr. Dunn then built a dwelling for his mother at the present 299 Main Street. He then had his general store at present 277 Main Street.

In the late 1890s there was a corn canning shop, located at the present 231 Main Street, run by Charles E. Herrick and his son Horatio, where many of the young people of the town found seasonal employment. A later corn shop, about 1906, was located on the southeast side of the tracks near Cumberland Junction, known as the Cumberland

Photograph by Floyd W. Norton, 1907

Corn shop at Cumberland Junction.

Photograph by W. Chester Rideout, courtesy of Barbara Blanchard Garsoe

Nicholas Humphrey's house, 282 Main Street, is the parsonage of the Congregational Church today. Building at right, where he had a store, later became the village blacksmith shop, run for many years by Fred Adams. The old horse sheds for the church show further to the right.

Packing Association, with C. E. Merrill as manager. Other crops such as beans and tomatoes were also canned there.

Other industries near the railroad station were the warehouse, down the tracks toward Portland, of the Paris Flouring Co., and during the 1920s it was a grain, feed, and flour store run by Allan P. Corey. There was also the Farmers' Union across the tracks from the station, run by Samuel Ross, and from 1924–55, run by Garsoe Brothers to sell grain, fertilizer, and coal. At the approximate location of the old corn shop was (1973–74) a large grain storage plant run by Humphrey's Poultry Farms of Gray.

Ray Hill had a butcher shop at the stable of the present parsonage. Other larger butcher shops were run by F. R. Sweetser & Son at 15 Blanchard Road and one by Edward B. Osgood at 318 Main Street. During many years in the 1920s and '30s a blacksmith shop was run by Fred Adams two houses south of the Congregational Church.

Farming had always been the mainstay of the economy of Cumberland, and until recent years there were many farms, large and small. Church deacon Edward B. Osgood (1860–1944) had a large produce farm as well as his butchering business. In a small store beside his butcher shop the deacon sold his products, among them his famous sausages made by his own secret recipe, hams and bacon smoked on the premises, and country cheese aged especially for him by a company in New Hampshire. For years people came from far and near for his fine products, and his grandson Fred continued the business for some years after the deacon's death. Another farmer, Victor Burnell, grew seed corn on his farm in Pleasant Valley and developed a special strain.

Samuel R. Sweetser with his brother Amasa were pioneers in apple orcharding. In the 1830s they began the grafting of trees to produce true varieties and develop new strains. Samuel's son, Frederick R., continued the orchard started on the farmstead at 15 Blanchard Road. He was an early member of the Maine Pomological Society. His son Herman, a professor of horticulture at University of Maine in Orono, came back to Cumberland in 1926 to carry on and enlarge the orcharding enterprise, and his grandson, Greg, still carries on the family tradition at the "Sweetser's Apple Barrel and Orchards."

Other orchards have been those belonging to George Emery in West Cumberland and to Arthur Blanchard at his Broadmoor Farm. The other large orchard still in operation in Pierce's on Orchard Road.

Although Cumberland is now largely residential, the Maine Register for 1974–75 gave the following statistics:

Population of Cumberland in 1970 was 4,096

Service stations—Brown's Texaco, Ron's Getty, Christensen's, Budd's Chevron in West Cumberland

Other industries in West Cumberland were:
Copp Motors and Cumberland Auto Salvage—Snowmobiles
Allen's Farm & Garden Center
B. J. Stratton & Son—Hardware Dealers
Kinney's American Grocery Store & Service Station
Portland Sand & Gravel Co.

Blue Rock Industries—Cumberland Division

In other parts of town:
Cabinetmaker—Dale Butterworth
Restaurants—Raven's Lunch, Howard Johnson on Turnpike
Grocery Stores—Penny's Place, Hardings
Auto Repairs—Rocky's Garage, Green's Body Shop
Fence Mfrs. —Main Line Fence
R. C. Hazelton & Co. Inc.—Contractors' equipment, road machinery, snowplows, and tractors
Wells and Farwell, Inc.—Real Estate
Bank—Federal Loan and Building Assn.

Poultry Farming and Processing

The poultry business has always played an important part in the economy of the town. Every farm included a small flock of chickens. In the 1920s with the increase of the tourist trade a great demand from hotels for chicken broilers brought a big change in poultry farming.

One of the first large houses was started by Mel and Mabel Wilson; other farms were owned by the Morrill brothers, Lenville Hawkes, and Herm Hulit of West Cumberland, to mention just a few.

At the Center there were Oscar Kemp, Ernest Frye, Walter and Willis Thurston, Walter Nelson, William Senior, the Hansons, and Marston Sweetser, whose house and buildings burned. Later on the same site George Burgess built a large henhouse which finally was torn down to make way for the Mabel I. Wilson School. Chester Verrill raised turkeys for a time on the corner of Main Street and Greely Road.

Before World War I Harvey Blanchard had a processing plant behind his home where the now vacant Shell station now stands. Gilbert Strout, who had worked for Harvey, bought the business from his widow and soon moved to a new location at 310 Main Street where he built a modern plant and continued a successful business until his retirement about 1950.

New York Times *photo, November 1931*

Potatoes for President Hoover.

The Florist Business

The Chase Brothers

About 1892, the Chase brothers, Frank and Arno, had a greenhouse on the Tuttle Road farm of their father, Heber Chase, who had died in Salisbury Prison during the Civil War. They first sold plants from a wagon with the name Chase Brothers painted on it, delivering to customers. In 1896 Arno moved to the Center and built his own greenhouse on the southerly corner of Main Street and Tuttle Road. Frank added to the original buildings on Tuttle Road and was in business there until 1915, when his home and business were destroyed by fire. He then moved his family to

327 Main Street and built a new greenhouse. He continued to do business until his death, when Harold Bragg became manager. It is now vacant.

On a night in March, 1933, a large crowd had gathered at the Congregational Church to hear Donald McMillan lecture and show slides of his trip to the Arctic. The fire alarm blew, and the male members of the audience disappeared to help fight a fire at Arno Chase's barn and greenhouse. Miraculously the home and greenhouse were saved. Arno repaired the damage and continued in business, selling his carnations for 1/2 to 1 cent apiece until about 1940.[1]

Jenkins's Greenhouse

Charles Jenkins, after graduating from Gray's Business College, decided to build a greenhouse at his home on 23 Blanchard Road, building his first house in 1913. In 1928, he enlarged and improved his buildings and dealt in wholesale only until his retirement in 1945.

Maurice Small then bought the business, which he later sold to Charles Haynes. It then became the business of his son, Norman, who finally sold it in 1996. It is now a housing development. Maurice Small moved and built a home and small greenhouse at 267 Tuttle Road on the same site of the first business of the Chase Brothers.[2] The greenhouse was dismantled in 1984 and sold to Reinhard Farms in Naples.

Sunnyside Greenhouses

Two small greenhouses were built in 1914 by Howard C. Blanchard as the expansion of operations of Sunnyside Farms on 70 Blanchard Road. Later structures of 30,000 square feet were built in two stages in 1921 and 1927 by Howard Blanchard. Carnations which were shipped to markets in New Jersey and New York were the principal crop.

In 1949 the business was purchased by Mr. Blanchard's son-in-law, William J. Garsoe. At that time, local markets were expanded, and by 1960, the entire crop was distributed in Maine and New Hampshire. With the advent of low-cost production of carnations from foreign markets, it became unprofitable to produce them in this climate. Sunnyside Greenhouses closed operations in December 1972, and the buildings are now dismantled.[3]

Sources

1. Information supplied by Kenneth Chase, Laura Chase Whitney, and Harold Bragg.
2. Information from Maurice Small.
3. Information from Barbara Blanchard Garsoe.

Sawmills

On the Mill Brook, which runs out of Forest Lake at West Cumberland, there have been at least six mills at one time or another.

Wilson's Mill, on the Skillins Road, was started by James Leighton and Lorenzo H. Wilson about 1874. James later sold his share to Lorenzo, and the business has been in the Wilson family, coming down from father to son through Willis and Henry until 1961, when they sold the property to Mr. B. J. Stratton. He continued it for a while, but due

Courtesy of Dan Dow

Mountford's Mill.

to economic conditions, soon closed the mill. It was sold to Alan and Katrina Rich, who have converted it to a private residence. A unique feature incorporated into the home is the brook running over a section of ledge through the northwest corner of the living room.

On the brook below is the Mountford Mill, built before 1860, by Edward Roberts. This mill burned, as did another built on the same site. In 1865, it was rebuilt by Hollis Mountford, whose son Samuel later took it over. His sons, Walter and Charles, continued the business until after Charles's death, when Walter retired. Mr. Pierre Dumaine purchased the property in 1958 and made it into a charming summer home. It is a great attraction when the Dumaines open it for various occasions.

Old-time mills were:

A shook mill in operation around 1780.

A carding mill run by James Leighton in 1800.

A shingle and clapboard mill operated by Joseph Nash in 1817.

A gristmill run by Adam Purvis.[1]

Other sawmills were Thomes Mill, south of 42 Blanchard Road, which burned in 1913, and the Dew Drop Mill on the brook behind the Thomes property, in operation between 1860 and 1870.

Sources

1. Information supplied by Mrs. Melville Wilson, Mr. Brad Hawkes, and Mr. Pierre Dumaine.

Dairy Farming and Beef Cattle

The two oldest dairy farms begun and carried on by their descendants are Broadmoor Farm and Springbrook Farm, both belonging to members of the Blanchard family.

Nathaniel Blanchard purchased land and buildings at the easterly corner of Main Street and Tuttle Road from Joel Prince in 1829. His son, Captain Enos Blanchard, with help from his wife, Joanna, who ran it while he was still at sea, took over the farm in 1833. Their son George started a dairy farm of purebred Jersey cattle in 1874. His cattle became famous and were shipped to every state in the Union. Many earned highest honors in the American Jersey Cattle Club, among them the "Duke of Cumberland" and the "Belle of Cumberland." In an advertisement in the *Cumberland Globe* of June 1, 1878, some of his cattle were listed, one of which sold for $1,500 ($24,308.95 in 2016 dollars). In 1935, Arthur, George's son, became the owner and continued the high quality of the herd until his death in 1972. In 1974, Broadmoor Farm went out of the Blanchard family.

Springbrook Farm is located on the southwest side of Greely Road, about two and a half miles from Cumberland Center. It has been owned and operated by the Blanchard family for some 150 years and involves seven generations. In 1820, the farm of 110 acres with house and barn belonged to Beza Blanchard, who was born in 1765. His son was Captain Reuben Blanchard, born in 1794, who came into possession of the farm in 1825. He made it his home, when not going to sea, and raised his family here. One of his sons, Frank, born in 1838, was next to own and operate the farm. After returning from the Civil War, he started operating the farm as a commercial business. He purchased some Jersey cows and proceeded to make butter, which he sold locally, as well as developing a route in Portland, expanding his farm operations and adding more cows to his herd.

His son Fred, born in 1875, was the next to carry on. He worked with his father to further increase the productivity of the farm. The butter business was increasing, more cows were added to the herd, and more attention given to the development of better cattle. In the 1920s about 100 pounds of butter a week was being made and sold, but soon the butter market began to drop, and in 1931, Springbrook Farm changed to selling wholesale milk. In 1934, one of Fred's sons, Stanley, bom in 1911, joined his father on the farm and would be the next operator, working as a partnership for about thirty years. By 1960 Stanley's son, Lawrence, born in 1937, went into business with his father. This arrangement lasted for ten years, when Lawrence chose to go into other fields. In 1971, one of Stanley's daughters, Katherine, born in 1940, and her husband, Gregory Fowler, came into the partnership to fill the position vacated by Lawrence. Their son Dennis, born in 1972, is the seventh generation on Springbrook Farm. Each generation operating the farm has been blessed to have as his partner a very special kind of woman. Each wife did a great deal to contribute to the success of the business and shared in the setbacks and heartaches that were bound to happen.

Through the years improvement of the Jersey herd has gone on continually, with the newest methods in breeding, the use of modern machinery, and the latest information used to build up a fine herd of 170 head of cattle, 100 of which were milkers. The original house still appears much as it did 200 years ago, with the most modern conveniences added to its old-world charm. The old barn is gone, being replaced by various modern structures, and a second dwelling has been built. The farm is now under the management of Jeffrey Storey.

James S. Wilson, of 32 Mill Road in West Cumberland, ran a dairy farm of registered Holsteins with at least 120 head of cattle, 50 of them being milkers. In August 1974, a disastrous fire that burned his numerous barns and large crop of hay was a serious loss. He continued farming for a short period of time after the fire, then turned the business over to his son, Steven. Steven consequently discontinued the business after a couple of years.

Originally owned by the Allen family, the Oulton Farm at 8 Winn Road has been run by the Oulton family since 1928, when E. Albert Oulton and his family came from Prides Corner. He ran it for a few years, then his son Frank E. Oulton Sr. operated it until 1958. His sons, Frank E. Jr. and Edward B., took over. Oulton Brothers raised Holsteins and dealt in the wholesale milk business with 150 head of cattle, 85 of which were milkers and 65 young stock. Part of the farm was sold to developers and is part of Falmouth Country Club.

The former A. P. Corey farm at 232 Main Street was sold in 1940 to Benedict and Elva Stockholm. They raised Holsteins for the wholesale milk business and for some years made and sold delicious ice cream. They went out of business in 1968. Their daughter Karen Birthisel and her family live there.

There were two farms in the business of raising beef cattle. One belonged to Herman D. Ruhm Jr. (now Ayres and Catherine Stockly) of 97 Greely Road. Mr. Ruhm was formerly president of Bates Fabrics Inc. of New York with the Bates Mills in Lewiston, around the 1950s.

The other is Sunrise Acres Farm, which belonged to Paul E. Merrill at 42 Winn Road, and is now owned and operated (on a much smaller scale) by his daughter, Sally Merrill, the fourth generation of the family to run the farm. The operation was begun in 1948 when the original homestead was obtained from his father's estate in order to develop the raising of beef cattle. The amount of land was approximately 150 acres. After taking several years to rehabilitate the land, in 1952 ten head of Hereford cattle were obtained and a herd of registered stock built up, until by 1974 the farm had over 300 head of cattle and comprised about 500 acres of land. During the last year a herd of about 70 Holstein milking cows for the dairy trade has been developed. These freshening heifers were marketed throughout the Maine dairy industry and the polled Hereford beef cattle through New England and Nova Scotia. The Hereford cattle comprised some of the outstanding bloodlines of their type in the country, and the enterprise had proved that beef can be raised profitably in this area. Also on the farm were twelve registered Belgian draft horses, which were a great attraction and were used frequently in parades all over the state of Maine. Two of these animals, bred mares, came from Amish farms in Indiana. They had produced outstanding offspring, and sales of both stallions and mares have been recorded in the New England states and Canada.

Chapter Sixteen

Cumberland Libraries

by Grace Trappan

From "A Short History of Cumberland Libraries," published for the sixtieth anniversary of Prince Memorial Library, April 1983.

The Second Social Library in North Yarmouth

When the Prince Memorial Library opened its doors in January 1923, for the first time Cumberland had a library with a permanent home. Over the years it had others, but information about those earlier libraries is scarce.

Cumberland's library history actually begins with the library history of Ancient North Yarmouth, since Cumberland was a part of North Yarmouth until 1821. William Hutchinson Rowe, in his book *Ancient North Yarmouth and Yarmouth, Maine 1636–1936*, tells us that thirty pounds for "the purchase of books to be placed in the care of the pastor of the First Church and lent by him to the people . . . in 1805 a second library, the Social Library, was organized and maintained for nearly fifty years. A second Social Library was maintained later by people in that portion of the town now Cumberland Foreside."

A record book in the possession of the Prince Memorial Library confirms that a group of men from the northwest section of Old North Yarmouth, which was in 1821 to become the Town of Cumberland, founded the Second Social Library in North Yarmouth in 1793, and incorporated it in 1817. These men lived, not on the Foreside, but rather in that small community in the center of which was the church in the process of being built, and which is now known as Cumberland Center. They were joined by men living in the section known as Walnut Hill, North Yarmouth, according to Phyllis Sturdivant Sweetser and Elizabeth Sweetser Baxter, descendants of early settlers in this section, who have been shown the list of the proprietors of the library.

The community that has grown up here was so far removed from the old parent community of Old North Yarmouth that the residents found it very difficult to go back and forth in all weathers to attend the only church, the First Church of North Yarmouth. In 1973 the men in these two sections, Cumberland Center and Walnut Hill, organized a society and either began or continued to build (the records vary) a church. On being refused a dismissal from the First Church, which felt it needed their financial support, in 1794 these men petitioned the Legislature of Massachusetts to be allowed to incorporate as a separate parish to be called the North West Congregational Society of North Yarmouth. The petition being granted, the church was organized as the Second Church of North Yarmouth, and now is known as the Congregational Church in Cumberland.

It was probably the very same feeling of wishing to be independent of a parent community so far removed from them that moved the proprietors of the Second Social Library of North Yarmouth to organize their society at this same time. Of the fifty-three early proprietors of this library, more than half of them were listed among the petitioners to the Legislature for a separate church.

There is but one record book of this library in existence and it has many gaps. The title page reads "Records of the Second Social Library in North Yarmouth—Founded 1793—Incorporated 1817." But it records only the years 1817–23 and 1844–45.

The lengthy preamble seems to assure that most of the books are to be of a religious nature, verified by the list of books in the back of the volume, as among the early titles are *Owen on Sin, Owen on the Spirit, Owen of the Supper, Owen on Communion*. There are books of history, such as volumes of Josephus, Goldsmith's *England*, and *Cook's Voyages* scattered among the sermons, and it seems likely that the early church pastors had a great deal to do with the selection of the books, and probably provided some from their personal libraries.

The laws state that a right to a library shall stand at two dollars (these rights are later referred to as "proprietors' shares"), and that all taxes, the amount taxed each share annually to buy books and supplies and which we should call annual dues, are to be raised at the annual meeting. The annual meeting seems to be the only meeting held unless some special problem arises. Each proprietor was to be allowed to take out one book at a time for a period of two months, and overdue books were to be paid for at a charge of one cent a day. If a delinquent proprietor did not pay his debt (taxes or overdues) within a certain time of having been notified, his share was to be advertised and sold at "public vendue [sic]." The taxes for the years recorded in this book, 1817–1823, varied from none at all to 6 1/4 cents, 8 cents, and 12 1/2 cents, and the fines never seem to have amounted to very much, but a twenty-five-cent fine reported at the annual meeting meant the sale of the share unless it was paid within a certain length of time. Since this was the money relied on for the purchase of books, not many books were added each year.

The annual meeting was originally to be held at the house of the librarian on the third Monday in October, but this had been crossed out and "some convenient place Christmas evening unless it should fall on Saturday or Sunday then the Monday Meeting succeeding" substituted. No meeting in this book is held on Christmas evening—probably something the men dreamed up and the wives canceled. Not that any women belonged to the Society. It was strictly a gentlemen's library.

At the annual meeting a moderator, a proprietor's clerk, a librarian, a treasurer, and a standing committee of three to manage the affairs of the library were to be chosen. The duties of each were spelled out in the bylaws. During the period covered by these records the Reverend Amasa Smith, who served the Second Church of North Yarmouth as its second pastor from 1806 to 1820, was the first moderator listed, followed by Jeremiah Blanchard, Beza Blanchard, John Blanchard, Joseph Smith, son of Amasa Smith, Samuel Fisher, and Charles Kent seem to have held this office at various times. As for the office of librarian, Joseph Smith evidently held this office until November 1820, when Charles Kent was elected to succeed him. At this time Joseph Smith turned over to the new librarian ninety-three bound volumes, one pamphlet, one slate, Washington's maps, a bookcase, and an account of nine volumes in trust, together with the books of records.

The office of treasurer was held by Jeremiah Blanchard until October 1822, when Charles Kent was elected to that office, and again elected in October 1823. As for the three members elected annually to serve as a standing committee, the following men served in that capacity for one or more years during this period: David Buxton, Moses Stubbs, Beza Blanchard, John Blanchard, Levi Blanchard, Jeremiah Blanchard, Asa Greely, Benjamin Sweetser Jr., Joseph Smith, and Solomon L. Blanchard. Many of the surnames listed here are familiar ones to those people living in and around Cumberland.

The book collection was almost certainly kept in the home of the librarian, and in spite of the fact that the by-laws, which had originally said that all meetings were to be held at the home of the librarian had been corrected to "some convenient place," there is no way of knowing when this change took place. The first two meetings recorded, those of January 13 and April 14, 1817, were held in the home of the Reverend Amasa Smith, who had built the house at 340 Main Street where Dr. Stephen B. Paulding now lives. Since Joseph Smith, his son, also resides there, the meetings during the period in which he held the office of librarian were also held at his home. It was not until the annual meeting on October 20, 1823, that a change was made, and this and the meeting of October 30, 1823, were held at School House No. 3, the redbrick schoolhouse in the Center, now the home of the Cumberland Historical Society. The October 30th meeting was the last one recorded in the book.

The next item in the record book is the account of books taken out by the proprietors in 1844 and 1845. Since the books are recorded by number rather than by title, one would have to refer to the numerical list of books in the library in order to discover what books a particular individual was reading. Some of the early proprietors are listed here, and others have the same surnames, but Asa Greely Jr. and some of the Blanchards, Merrills, Princes, Sweetsers, and Buxtons are probably of a later generation.

This completes the information in the record book except for "An Index of the Books in the First Social Library in Cumberland" numbering 1–143, and "A Report of the Names of the Proprietors of the Second Social Library of North Yarmouth," with a record of taxes paid by each member from 1817 through 1823, except for a few jottings of financial transactions, of taxes paid and books bought, on the last three pages.

During the period covered by thee records a number of important actions were taken at the meetings. Cumberland having been incorporated as a town on March 19,1821, on October 15, 1821, the proprietors voted "that the Corporation be hereafter known by the name of 'The First Social Library of Cumberland.' " And at the annual meeting of October 29, 1823, it was voted "that Beza Blanchard, Jeremiah Blanchard and Charles Kent be a committee to confer with the committee of the Second Social Library in town to see if a union can be affected between the two libraries." This is the first time such a library has been mentioned. Could it be the library Mr. Rowe mentions in his book as being on the Foreside? On October 30, 1823, the committee reported that in their opinion "it is expedient to receive the members of the Second Social Library on their paying into the Treasury twenty-five cents on each share together with their books." It was then voted that the members of the Second Social Library be received as members of the First Social Library, their names recorded in rotation on the books belonging to the First Social Library, beginning with number 53 on its books.

Slipped into the book are a few additional papers, of which one is a transfer of a share from Paul Prince to Isaac Pearson. Others are calls for annual meetings for February 6, 1844, February 16, 1844, and for March 30, 1855. This last one interests us the most, as the fourth item, not appearing in any other calls for meetings, is "To see what disposition shall be made of the books and to manage the concerns of said Library." This is signed by Reuben Rideout, Israel True, Asa Greely, J. B. Morse, and Benjamin Sweetser, and dated on March 20, 1855. All held at the vestry of the Congregational meetinghouse.

This was evidently an important meeting, as with the call is a note from Benjamin Sweetser dated March 30, 1855, in which William D. Sweetser is authorized to act as proxy for him at the meetings. Does the "disposition of books" mean an end to the library as it seems to imply, or is it a way of saying that a new home in someone's house must be found for the book collection?

What about the great gap in these records? What happened between the founding of the Society? And at the same meeting Amasa Smith, Jeremiah Blanchard, and Asa Greely were appointed to revise the constitution and adopt by-laws. Obviously the record book in the possession of Prince Memorial Library contains the new constitution and the new by-laws, but when Joseph Smith turned the books and other items in his care over to his successor as librarian, Charles Kent, on November 20, 1820, he is given a receipt for the other items "together with the Books of Records." Where are these earlier records?

There is an additional item to prove that the library was active throughout this period. In volume 3, number 3 of *Old Times in North Yarmouth* (July 1879) among the Notes and Queries is the following: "Who can give information of the Second Library of North Yarmouth? I have a transfer of a share, date 1805. C. E. B."

What about the periods from 1823 to 1844 to 1855, and from 1855 to 1897, when the Cumberland Library was founded? Is it too much to hope that in some of the old houses in Cumberland there are records stored away and forgotten that at some time may reappear to fill some of these gaps?

The Cumberland Library

There is no way of telling whether Cumberland had any type of library between the years of 1855 and 1897, but we do know that from 1897 to the preparations for the opening of the Prince Memorial Library in 1923, when its book collection was turned over to the new library to be added to that collection, there was a library, housed in various homes around town and managed by women of the community who served as volunteer librarians, called the Cumberland Library.

The library was originally organized through the efforts of the Reverend Frank Davis, who served as pastor of the Congregational Church of Cumberland from 1892 to 1899, and his wife, Helen. It had a catalog, printed on heavy 4 1/4 by 5 3/4 inch, punched cards, on which titles were numbered in order of their acquisition by the library. As new books were ordered, new cards were printed and tied to earlier cards.

And as each borrower evidently had a set of these cards, each borrower had a complete catalog at home to consult at leisure. The Prince Memorial Library owns three sets of these cards, one set originally owned by Carrie Wilson, who lived and did dressmaking in rooms in the second story (since removed) of the ell at the house at 3 Blanchard Road. She had penciled her name and "1897," the date of the beginning of the library on the first card, and on the two others "Get more of these." She had also added additional titles beyond the 675 printed on the cards.

As one looks over the list of titles, it is evident that the women have come into their own. No longer are they excluded from the library, as they were from the First Social Library. They have organized a library to which both men and women are welcome, but in which the greater number of titles appeal to women. Taking the year 1920 in the last accessions book, we find that five men read 95 books that year, an average of 19 books per borrower, while seventeen women read 289 books, an average of 17 books per borrower. Although many of the books would have been read by both men and women, and many by the older children, in this library there is nothing for the very young child who enjoys picture books and must be read to. Nor of course are there any reference books. As for the quality of the book collection—the great majority of the books in the collection were fiction of the late 1800s and early 1900s—of course that was when the library was started. But very few of these have any appeal today. There were books which have a lasting appeal—a set of Walter Scott, Kipling's *Jungle Book*, *Kidnapped* by Stevenson, and *The Mill on the Floss* by George Eliot, but Myrtle Read, Clara L. Burnham, Amelia E. Barr, and Alice Hegan Rice have none for present-day readers.

There is no better description of those years during which the Cumberland Library provided service to the community and of the early years of the Prince Memorial Library than that given in a speech at the twenty-fifth anniversary of the Prince Memorial on October 6, 1948, by the librarian, Mildred Wyman Doane. She speaks from her own knowledge, having lived through the latter part of this period and having been able to ask those of an earlier generation about the earlier years. I shall only be able to fill certain gaps, such as the several locations of the library, which her audience already knew and did not need to be told.

There is no record of just when the library was located in each home, but it is known that the last location was at the home of Mrs. Olive Hall a 283 Main Street. It is in this house that it is best remembered by the longtime residents living in Cumberland at the present time. According to Harold Bragg, Mrs. Hall was the widow of Dr. Frank Hall, who had started to erect a stable back in from Main Street at the time of his death. His widow moved it forward to Main Street and made it into a two-family house for herself and her daughter and son-in-law, Mr. and Mrs. Arno Chase. He remembers it being said that the two kitchen sinks faced each other on either side of the dining wall and a window was cut through at that point so that mother and daughter could visit while "washing up." His most vivid memory of this library, which had begun with a few books in someone's living room, available a few hours each week, is of two rooms of shelves filled with books, each with a number on the spine. To find a book one had to select a title from the printed catalog, note the number, and then find that book on the shelf. No colored jackets to attract readers, but he assured me that each book was in new condition within the paper cover no matter how long it had been in the library. Mildred Doane said of this same library "and keen is the remembered smell of old books and a kerosene lamp at Mrs. Hall's . . . It was a great event when we heard that new books were in."

The library immediately preceding the one at Mrs. Hall's was probably in the home of Mrs. Esther Hill at 282 Main Street, and just across the street from Mrs. Hall's. Both Margaret Wyman and Phyllis Sweetser remember it there. Mildred Doane mentions another librarian, Mrs. Coral Adams, who, she had been told, served the longest. She, too, had lived at 282 Main Street, and her husband, Fred Adams, had had his blacksmith shop between the house and the church. She later lived at 3 Blanchard Road, but it was when she lived at the earlier address that she housed the library. The last librarian whom she mentions and whom she herself did not know was Mrs. Annie Small. She was the daughter of the Buxtons who lived in the old Buxton house at 363 Main Street and was the wife of Charles Small. Both Harold Bragg and Phyllis Sweetser think she lived in that section of Main Street near her parents, although they did not know that she had housed the library at one time.

No matter where the library was located it was evidently a community affair. Money was raised for books through library suppers, plays, and other entertainments, most of which were put on in the old Union Hall, still standing in back of 299 Main Street, on school property and now used by the School Department. The women put on these affairs and the entire community looked forward to them.

When the Prince Memorial Library opened in 1923, over six hundred books from Cumberland Library were transferred to its shelves, "as good as new," as Harold Bragg would say, but without paper covers, I'm sure. Does it matter that as the Prince Memorial Library book collection grew, these books were probably found to have outlived their usefulness and were discarded. For years they had brought pleasure to the readers of Cumberland.

One other library is mentioned by the earlier residents. That is the Sunday School library housed in the right-hand little room near the front of the church and containing Dotty Dimple and Little Pepper books, as well as books by Ralph Connor and others. So there were some books for small children in the community.

Bibliography

Corliss, Augustus W., Editor. *Old Times of North Yarmouth, Maine.* Somersworth, New Hampshire, New Hampshire Publishing Company, 1977. (Facsimile of *Old Times of North Yarmouth, Maine,* a periodical, Yarmouth, Maine 1877–1884, now published in one volume.)

Cumberland, Maine. Cumberland Library. Catalog of Cumberland Library. Cards listing the holdings of the Cumberland Library, numbered 1–681 in order of addition to the library. New cards were printed and added as the new books were received. In possession of the Prince Memorial Library.

Cumberland, Maine. Cumberland Library. Register of borrowers. 1913–March 1921. In possession of the Prince Memorial Library.

Cumberland, Maine. Prince Memorial Library. Assession book, November 8, 1922–August 3, 1927. In possession of the Prince Memorial Library.

Cumberland, Maine. Prince Memorial Library. Catalogue—1936. Printed, classed catalog evidently financed by the advertising in the booklet. In possession of the Prince Memorial Library.

Cumberland, Maine. Prince Memorial Library. Guest register at the Dedication of the Addition to the Library given by Mr. and Mrs. Paul Emery Merrill in memory of his parents, Mr. and Mrs. Wallace L. Merrill in 1959. In possession of the Prince Memorial Library.

Cumberland, Maine. Prince Memorial Library. Register of borrowers, 1923, 1928, 1934, 1939, 1945, 1951. In possession of the Prince Memorial Library.

Cumberland, Maine. Prince Memorial Library. Register of borrowers, 1958. In possession of the Prince Memorial Library.

Doane, Mildred Wyman. History of the Prince Memorial Library with recollections of some earlier Cumberland libraries. A speech delivered at the 25th Anniversary of the Prince Memorial Library, October 6, 1948. Manuscript in the possession of her sister, Margaret Wyman.

Merrill, Harriet C. (Mrs. Wallace L.) Diaries, January 1, 1921–December 31, 1925. Manuscript in the possession of her granddaughter, Sally Merrill.

North Yarmouth, Maine. Second Social Library in North Yarmouth. Records of the Second Social Library in North Yarmouth, founded 1793. Incorporated January 13, 1817. Includes records of December 31, 1817–October 30, 1823; 1844–1845. Manuscript in the possession of the Prince Memorial Library.

Rowe, William Hutchinson. *Ancient North Yarmouth and Yarmouth, Maine, 1636–1936*. Portland, Maine, Southworth Press, 1937.

Sweetser, Phyllis Sturdivant, Editor. *Cumberland, Maine in Four Centuries*. Cumberland, Maine, Town of Cumberland, 1976.

With additional information from the following present or former residents of Cumberland:

Elizabeth Sweetser Baxter
Harold M. Bragg
Hope N. Dillaway
Floyd Wilson Norton
Phyllis Sturdivant Sweetser
Margaret Wyman

Prince Memorial Library

By Phyllis S. Sweetser

The Prince Memorial Library Corporation came into being in November 1921, in consequence of the bequest of Carroll D. and Annie L. Prince, of money to erect and maintain a library in Cumberland. Mr. Prince was a native of Cumberland, the only son of Captain Meaubec and Susan Buxton Prince. He was one of the earliest students at Greely Institute.

Courtesy of Dan Dow

Prince Coat of Arms

By their joint will, the sum of $35,000 was left to the town for a library to be known as Prince Memorial Library: $20,000 to be used for the erection and equipment of the building, and the remaining $15,000 to be kept as a maintenance fund. The architect was Mr. George C. Emery of Boston. A building of Georgian Colonial style was erected. The front doorway was copied from one in Old Hempstead, England.

Dedication of the library took place on January 7, 1923. Professor Wilmot B. Mitchell of Bowdoin College offered a prayer at the library and gave an address at the Congregational Church.

In 1959, Mr. and Mrs. Paul Emery Merrill built an addition to the original building, in memory of his parents, Mr. and Mrs. Wallace L. Merrill. His mother was one of the original incorporators of the library and a devoted worker who gave much able and unstinted service for

Courtesy of Dan Dow, 1975

Front entrance of Prince Memorial Library.

many years. Mr. Merrill also enlarged the lot on which the library is located by the purchase of land back of the building, to be kept as an open space for the benefit of the people of the town of Cumberland.

Until this time there had been only three presidents: Dr. Henry Moulton, Frank Chase, and Harlan H. Sweetser. Mr. Sweetser served from 1931 to 1968. He was a most capable and devoted head of the library and many fine improvements occurred during his presidency. There had also been only three librarians:

Mrs. Cecil Wilson Adams (1923–1930)
Mrs. Mildred Wyman Doane (1931–1950)
Mrs. Phyllis Sturdivant Sweetser (1951–1970)

Since that time, Robert L. Cram has been president till Mrs. Cynthia Murdock took office in 1973. Mrs. Robert Pawle was librarian from 1970–1995. Beth Hoffer was librarian from 1996 through October 1997, followed by interim librarian Anne Dixon from October 1997 through April 1998. Thomas Bennett, the present library director, has served since April 1998.

An item of great interest is a cavalry saber which belonged to President Andrew Jackson. The blade which is half black is embellished with gold leaves and insignia of the cavalry. The hilt is of carved ivory and ornate brass, and at the base on either side is a shield-shaped insignia bearing an eagle with stars and stripes. The brass scabbard is ornamented with oak leaves and flowers. The gift was accompanied by the following note:

Courtesy of Dan Dow, 1975

Prince Memorial Library.

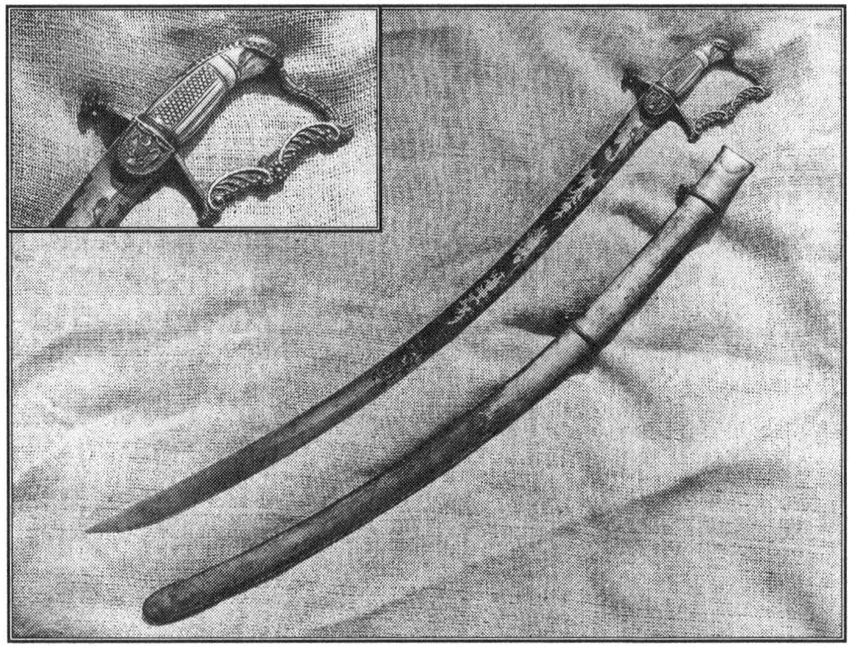

Photograph by Daniel Dow, 1975

Andrew Jackson's saber and scabbard; ivory and silver hilt of saber.

> *When in Congress the late Governor Fairfield of Maine and President Andrew Jackson became fast friends. On one occasion the President came to Maine to attend the "last muster" and to visit the Fairfields at their home in Biddeford. "Well, Governor," he remarked, "I guess I've seen enough blood and fighting and I'll leave you my sword as a token of my esteem." The Governor gave it to his grandson, the late Frank Emery of Gorham, who in turn gave it to the undersigned.*
>
> *It is my desire that the Prince Memorial Library Association of Cumberland, Maine, accept this rare trophy and keep it on display for this and coming generations . . . Signed, Robert Scott Thomes.*[1]

It is interesting to note that on the library site stood the home of one of the first ministers of the Congregational Church, Mr. Rufus Anderson. Mr. Anderson planted two elm trees in 1753, the first to be planted along Main Street. They became the largest and tallest in the village, till due to old age and disease they had to be removed in 1963.[2] The house burned and about 1808 the land was purchased by Benjamin Sweetser, who built a two-family house of bricks. These bricks were made in a brickyard on the rear of his property. Benjamin Sweetser's daughter Elizabeth married Captain David Wilson, and they lived in this house for many years. This house burned down about 1906. The land was purchased by a niece of Captain Wilson, Mrs. Maude Merrill Thomes, who gave it as the site for the Prince Memorial Library.

Portland Evening Express and Advertiser, *July 2, 1921*

Cumberland's first two elm trees, planted in 1794 by Rev. Rufus Anderson.

Endnotes:

1. A native of Cumberland and one of the original incorporators.
2. Two young maple trees were planted at that time by Herman P. Sweetser, a trustee of Prince Memorial Library.

Chapter Seventeen

Old Houses

By Phyllis S. Sweetser and Hazel McGoff

This chapter on old houses could include many others equally worthy of note, but space does not permit.

Old Shaw Houses at West Cumberland

The first recorded history of West Cumberland began when three Shaw brothers made their way up there from Cumberland Foreside after the French and Indian Wars ended in 1763.

Joseph Shaw built his home about 1769 where the late Joseph William "Jo Bill" Shaw lived, at 473 Range Road. The address has changed to 42 Shaw Farm Road and the property is now owned by Robert and Megan Waterhouse.

Daniel Shaw had built a Cape Cod house about 1756 (destroyed by fire in July 1964) at the location near the house now lived in by Claude and Jill Guyot, now 284 Range Road.

Nehemiah settled at what is now 91 Bruce Hill Road.

It was the family tradition that when two of the brothers had to return to the Foreside for additional supplies, the third was to stay and guard the materials already brought to the new site. He kept the fires

Courtesy of Daniel Dow, 1975

"Jo Bill" Shaw house.

burning and fought the wolves away during the night. This part of the town has always been called Shawtown because of the number of inhabitants by that name.

Mrs. Raymond Shaw, 1973

> The Orrin Whitney homestead at 549 Range Road in West Cumberland can be traced back for over a century and a half. It was constructed around 1820. It was later owned by Walter Morrill, who was a veteran of the Civil War. The property comprised 110 acres and extended from the Gray Road to the Cumberland Fairgrounds.[1]

On the present site of Prince Memorial Library there once stood a small house where Rev. Rufus Anderson, the first minister of the Congregational Church, lived until 1804, in front of which he planted the first elm trees in the village. This house burned and the land extending some distance behind it was purchased by Master Benjamin Sweetser. He built a two-family house of bricks, which were made in a brickyard

Hutchinson photograph, 1964

Whitney Homestead.

Photograph by Floyd Wilson Norton, 1902

Benjamin Sweetser's old brick house which stood on present site of Prince Memorial Library. Capt. David Wilson stands on left. Note old well sweep still in use in 1906.

in the field in the rear of his property.[2] He and his wife Aunt Dolly lived in one side and Capt. David Wilson, married to his daughter Elizabeth Sweetser, lived in the other. This house burned about 1906 and the land was acquired by Maude Merrill (Mrs. John Thomes), a niece of Capt. Wilson, who gave it for the site of Prince Memorial Library. Picture taken in 1902 shows Capt. Wilson at left of group.

Endnote:

1. *Evening Express*, Friday, May 8, 1964.
2. Bricks from this old yard were used to build the schoolhouse for District No. 3, later the town office and present quarters of the Cumberland Historical Society, at present 306 Main Street.

Sturdivant Houses

The first house was built in Westcustago (North Yarmouth, Massachusetts, now Cumberland, Maine) in the mid-1600s on what was reported to be a land grant on Sturdivant Road. It was of double-walled brick with one-inch-thick bull's-eye glass for its few windows and triple-thick plank doors. The windows were barred for further protection

Courtesy of Helen Dunn Maxim

Second Sturdivant house on Route 88.

Courtesy of Cumberland Historical Society

Ephraim Sturdivant's House.

against the Indians, many of whom were not friendly. A spring coming up through sandy soil and feeding a stream running through a gully beside the house supplied water, and was reached by a shored-up tunnel, used for safety. Below the house, going down into the gully, was a path made by the Indians to water their horses. This path was still in existence until the 1950s when the land was sold to Dr. Nicholas Fish. Pieces of the bull's-eye glass still exist.

The second Sturdivant house was built in 1700, a yellow-painted Cape with an ell. Excerpt from a newspaper dated September 1902 says, "The first house was built and had its day and the second house was built in 1700, a small, unpretentious affair but comfortable and cozy for those days." The cellar hole is still visible on Rt. 88, across the road from Wildwood Park, a little to the south. Next to it, but with all traces now removed, was the old cattle pound. The house was unlived in at the time the trolley line, Portland to Yarmouth, was built and was demolished to make way for the track.

The third house, next door and still standing at 114 Foreside Road, was built by Capt. Ephraim Sturdivant in 1810 of wood cut and milled on the place. The bricks for the large center chimney came from the remains of

Photograph by Daniel Dow, 1975

Another Sturdivant House, 28 Foreside Road.

the blockhouse, built on an adjoining piece of land by Capt. Nathaniel Blanchard, for the protection of the settlers from the Indians, during the French and Indian Wars. For its time, the woodwork in the interior is considered lavish and was done by a relative, Mr. Joseph Collins. The "best parlor" has ribbon carving around the fireplace, the chair rail, and the cornice. Little has been changed in the house and most of the outbuildings still stand, including the seventy-five-foot barn by the road. On the hill behind the house and known as "Ephraim's Mount," there once stood a group of twelve tall pine trees that were the second "sighting" for ships coming into Portland Harbor and known as the Twelve Apostles (the first "sighting" was Two Lights). The last lone tree fell in 1935.

Two other Sturdivant houses very like this one were built along present Rt. 88: one, two houses to the south and the present 106 Foreside

Road, was built for Ephraim's sister in 1812, and a second one, a half-mile to the south, was built by a brother, Greely Sturdivant, in 1807—now 28 Foreside Road. A third brother, David, in 1800 built the house at present 52 Foreside Road. Among other enterprises he was a drover and kept cattle pastured in the fields behind his home.

—Janet Lowe Palmer

Three Blanchard Road was built about 1827 by Deacon Jeremiah Blanchard who owned the land, part of original lot #71, and sold it to the Congregational Church for a parsonage in 1828. Rev. Samuel Stone was the first minister to live there; he was a distant relative of Grace Stone Lincoln, who moved into it on November 14, 1960—132 years to the day after Jeremiah Blanchard sold the land. In 1835 Rev. Stone sold the house to Capt. John Wilson, who lived there with his family for many years.

Photograph by Daniel Dow, 1975

3 Blanchard Road.

Photograph by W. Chester Rideout, c. 1875

15 Blanchard Road.

Courtesy of Mr. and Mrs. Philip Dana

Old Buxton house on early town lot #100 (Main Street).

Fifteen Blanchard Road also was built by Jeremiah Blanchard about 1810 for Widow Pittee, whose daughter married Samuel R. Sweetser and whose descendants, Greg Sweetser and Debbie Freeman, still own it. In 1849 Samuel Sweetser purchased the dwelling and about ten acres of land from the estate of Jeremiah Blanchard for the sum of $190—he being the highest bidder.

The house now belonging to Richard and Christine Bucsko at 363 Main Street, built by David Buxton, has a tile with the date 1799 in the center of the huge chimney.

The Tuttle House, for which Tuttle Road was named, was originally owned by Libeus Tuttle. There is an old story that he was tarred and feathered and ridden on a rail for keeping another woman upstairs in his house. His wife detected her presence by hearing a noise made by the dropping of scissors. It was later the home of Ezra Knight Sweetser and his wife Clara Sturdivant Sweetser, who presented the land to the town

Collection of Jeannette Sturdivant Edwards

Old Tuttle House.

Photograph by Daniel Dow, 1975

Capt. David Loring house.

for the E. K. Sweetser School. The house stood on the location of the pond at the Mabel I. Wilson School.

The fine old brick house at 97 Greely Road, now owned by Ayres and Catherine Stockly, is recorded in a deed dated 1790 and completed in 1820 by Capt. David Loring, in whose family it remained for many generations.

Records supplied by a relative, Loring Farwell of Northfield, Illinois, show the following:

> February 12, 1825—Solomon Loring gave his farm and all things on it to David Loring to be managed jointly until Solomon's death, and then to be David's. This deed has no specific reference to place, boundaries, or acreage, but is the first reference to a "farm."

> April 3, 1826—Solomon Loring Jr. conveyed to David Loring 27 acres in Cumberland. This is the first reference to the town of Cumberland and to the State of Maine, in the family records.

Photograph by W. Chester Rideout, c. 1875, courtesy of W. Scott Fox, Jr.

Doughty homestead.

This old photograph of the property at 198 Tuttle Road shows the "new" house built by Benjamin Franklin Doughty in 1850, as well as the small older dwelling near the barn. This was an original 100-acre lot as laid out in Ancient North Yarmouth, and had been in the Doughty family until purchased by W. Scott Fox Jr. in 1968. It is now owned by Joseph Reynolds.

Records show that this ancient house, now 6 Foreside Road and owned by Mrs. Kathleen Sawyer, was built for Samuel York by John York in 1729. From the Registry of Deeds Book 9, p. 264, is the following excerpt:

> I, Samuel York of North Yarmouth, for the sum of 14 pounds—paid by Joseph York of Falmouth, Mariner, sell to same a piece of land—being my part of the home estate—also my part of the pews in the Meeting House, dwelling house and barn. Signed February 26, 1773, in the 13th year of the reign of George III.
>
> Samuel York and Margery York

Courtesy of Mrs. Willard Wormwood

Old York house as it looked in the 1800s.

Photograph by Dan Dow, 1975

The York house in 1975.

The former Drinkwater Homestead at 154 Foreside Road, directly opposite Wildwood, was built by a sea captain about 1800. It is built along classical colonial lines, has artistic interior carved woodwork, with corner posts and Indian shutters remaining in some rooms. At one time it was used as a summer residence by Mr. John B. Keating, the British vice consul for the Port of Portland and all ports of entry in Maine from 1895 to 1915, and older residents can remember seeing the British flag flying from a tall flagpole still there at the time it was purchased by then owners, Mr. and Mrs. John M. Kimball, in 1935. Since 1993, it has been owned by his niece, Sally W. Means Kirkpatrick, and her husband, William. They continue to paint the chimney with black at the top to designate the house as a safe haven for the Loyalists.

Courtesy of Cumberland Historical Society, 1964

The Drinkwater homestead.

Chapter Eighteen

Architectural Styles in Cumberland

By Ursula Baier and Shirley George
of Greater Portland Landmarks Advisory Service

Like so many other small towns in this part of New England, Cumberland has its share of attractive old houses of many periods displaying the careful craftsmanship of local builders. Most have been well maintained by generations of successive owners, many of whom have made their own additions and alterations so that one house may portray a series of architectural styles.

There are some that are still outwardly fairly typical of one particular period, and we show here a few examples from the many lovely houses throughout the town that can be seen by the careful observer.

Eighteenth-century examples dating from the earliest period of the town's settlement no longer exist today in a recognizable form. However, pictures of houses now destroyed or much altered, such as the old Sturdivant house (page 244), and the John York house on Rt. 88 (page 252), give one a good idea of what many of the first houses might have looked like. They were very simple, functional dwellings, lacking in the elegant details that became possible later when more settled, comfortable living conditions prevailed.

Photo by Shirley George, 1975

Doorway at 212 Greely Road.

Around 1800 much land was being settled inland along the range roads, and many houses admired today date from this period.

The two-and-a-half-story foursquare center chimney house, often set on a slight rise of ground with attached outbuildings and barn, can be seen all around Cumberland. The windows originally would have been small-paned and had no blinds (outside shutters), although there might have been interior sliding shutters to keep out the cold.

They had an attractive simplicity, with interest centering on the carefully made, narrow doorway. There were usually glass panes over the door lighting the small hallway and its winding staircase.

This house at 212 Greely Road was originally a one-and-a-half-story "Cape Cod," raised to its present height to provide more living space. The present side door and the large-paned windows are a later alteration.

Photograph by Shirley George, 1975

212 Greely Road.

Photograph by Daniel Dow, 1975

Federal fan doorway at 3 Blanchard Road.

During the *Federal Period* of the early nineteenth century, the architectural trim, even in the smaller houses, became more elaborate. Cumberland has several examples of a particularly lovely local version of the Federal fan doorway.

We do not know who actually made these doorways, although Jeremiah Blanchard (born 1771) is thought to have built these three houses, among others.

The doors themselves are most unusual; seventy-two angles in the molding are required to produce these pleasing notched corners, instead of the twenty-four needed for a normal six-panel door.

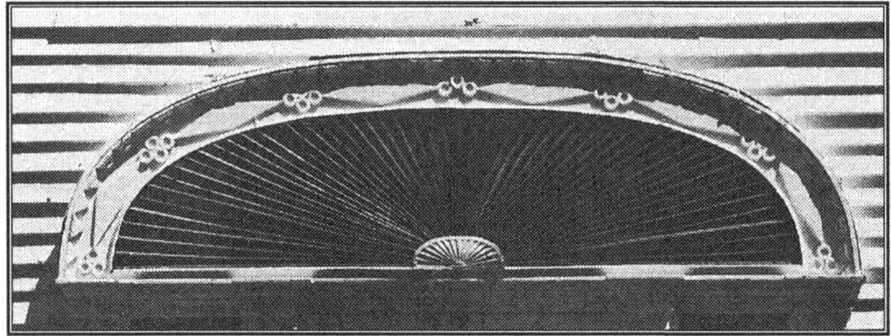

Photograph by Shirley George, 1975

Detail of fanlight at 371 Tuttle Road.

Photograph by Shirley George, 1975

Doorway at 15 Blanchard Road.

Photograph by Daniel Dow, 1975

Federal-style Loring Homestead at 97 Greely Road.

Federal-style building was sometimes of locally made brick, with granite lintels over the windows.

Another example of the lovely doorways mentioned earlier is found on this house.

Courtesy of Shirley George, 1975

Former Capt. Pinkham House at 40 Blanchard Road.

Courtesy of Shirley George, 1975

Doorway at 40 Blanchard Road.

The *Greek Revival Period* of 1840–60 is well represented by one-and-a-half-story houses with a wing or an ell attached. The main door is often in the gable end, as it is here.

The corner boards of this house are wide and flat, as are also the surrounds to the doorway, shown here.

Photograph by Shirley George, 1975

Window at 40 Blanchard Road.

We often see windows like this, with attractive, slightly pointed caps over them. Louvered wooden blinds and 2/2 glass panes are also typical of the period, although they may also be 6/6.

This is another rather more elaborate, and probably later, version of a Greek Revival doorway that is frequently found.

Photograph by Shirley George, 1975

Detail of Greek Revival doorway at 70 Blanchard Road.

Photo by Shirley George, 1975

Detail of cornice at 70 Blanchard Road.

Detail becomes more elaborate and boldly projecting around the 1860s.

Overhanging eaves, stove chimneys, bay windows, and porches characterize the *Victorian Period.* This example has an unusual rope-like detail and dentils under its eaves.

Photograph by Daniel Dow, 1975

Victorian-style house at 16 Blanchard Road.

Photo by Shirley George, 1975

Doorway at 283 Main Street.

A Victorian doorway—double doors with glass insets, approached by outside steps above high foundations. This bold machine-carved hood over the door was often also put onto earlier houses to modernize them. These often form an interesting feature and should be preserved.

This house is late Victorian style, built in 1891 by William E. Wilson. It is delightfully ornate and adds greatly to the interesting variety of architectural styles on Main Street.

Photograph by Daniel Dow, 1975

Wilson House at 268 Main Street.

Barns

No old home was complete without its barn and outbuildings to house the stock which most householders kept. Many fine examples which now have disappeared are shown in the old plates and photos in this book; each year another one goes, a victim of the changing economy or of fire. But many are still in use and carefully maintained, each one adding greatly to the interest of the landscape, the village street, and the house to which it belongs.

Photograph by Daniel Dow, 1975

Corncrib at Top Knot Farm, 100 Middle Road.

Photograph by Daniel Dow, 1975

Farmstead at 198 Tuttle Road.

Photograph by Daniel Dow, 1975

Another hilltop barn at 224 Tuttle Road.

Courtesy of H. D. Ruhm Jr. (c. 1970)

Barn at 97 Greely Road.

Chapter Nineteen

Clubs and Organizations

Cumberland Center Brass Band

Courtesy of Cumberland Historical Society

In existence in 1854 until 1880 at least. One costume, complete with epaulets and hat with plume, a tuba, and the drum are in the Cumberland Historical Society collection.

Cumberland Farmers Club

The Cumberland Fair, presented by the Cumberland Farmers Club, takes place the last week of September. Rating high among the fairs each fall in Maine, Cumberland's is complete with a midway that each night for a week is ablaze with lighted Ferris wheels, merry-go-rounds, and other fantastic, exciting, breathtaking rides that delight young and old alike, and lined with booths full of items to be obtained by games of chance.

Hot dogs, hamburgers, onions, popcorn, fried dough, and cotton candy fill the air with a perfume found only on fairgrounds. The Exhibition Hall is filled with the choicest products of local farms and kitchens all vying for the coveted "blue ribbon." A few commercial booths add color, but the Extension Groups and the Grange exhibits bring back memories to the older fairgoers of tales told by their elders of the days when it was known as the Cumberland Center Fair.

What now is pari-mutuel harness racing was once a race held on Main Street, then a wheel-rutted highway extending from the junction of the Blanchard Road, Tuttle Road, and Main Street to what was known as the head of the Greely Road. The same highway served for the ox-pulling contests. Lacking a building, tents were used and families brought picnic lunches and spent a day filled with thrills and memories for the whole family.

After two years of racing on the highway a circular track was laid out in the pasture owned by the Blanchard brothers and adjoining Greely Institute.

The following is a description of Cumberland Center Fair, October 10 and 11, 1871, as written by Solomon Loring Blanchard to his brother George.

> Tuesday was a real summer's day. About 9 o'clock people began to come and by noon Cumberland Center seemed like Tremont Street, Boston. It was the largest assembly of people Cumberland ever had. The Town House was filled with articles of agriculture and fancy work and was a splendid sight to behold.
>
> The Meeting House sheds were filled with hogs, colts, sheep, etc. Back of the Meeting House was the stock, two rows of splendid oxen, steers, cows, and young cattle. There was an oxen pulling contest at 10 o'clock. From 12 to 2 o'clock, dinner was served in a

> tent in Miss Frothingham's yard with food prepared in her kitchen and that of S. M. Rideout. At 2 o'clock was the display of young colts on the track which had been prepared as a trotting park of 1/3 mile behind Capt. Enos Blanchard's home. At 3 o'clock the races were held on the racetrack. There were horses from Portland, Yarmouth, and North Yarmouth. Wednesday afternoon a large crowd came to see the "trot-out." First came the gentlemen's driving horses and family horses and matched horses. Following that the crowd went to see the exhibits at the Town House, which was so crowded with people one could hardly get around. This year's Fair was a huge success.[1]

The need of an exhibition hall became apparent but the location of the hall was a touchy subject. West Cumberland residents pressured for it to be located in their section of the town, but Enos Blanchard, who owned the pasture and raised high-blooded Jersey cattle imported from the Island of Jersey, England, deeded the now used land to the "Agriculture Hall Company" on October 19, 1874, for the sum of thirty-five dollars.

Despite many meetings with tempers flaring and Fair time near at hand, neither side would give in as to location. The men of Cumberland Center vowed they would have a hall, now and on their own land. Plotting for a night of a full moon a select group of men and older boys, quietly working with pick and shovels, staked out the location of the new hall and as if by magic the necessary lumber began arriving. At daylight the walls became evident as hammers and saws rang out. The opposition made a valiant attempt to reroute some of the lumber to West Cumberland; however, lacking in numbers they lost out, but being staunch with town spirit they turned to and helped erect a hall complete with shingled roof. A dirt floor served for the first year of the building that was to be known as "Union Hall," signifying the union of the labors of two groups.

In 1875 the West Cumberland farmers erected a two-story building and held their fair for two days with an attendance of four thousand. The first floor of the hall was utilized for exhibits. Dinners were served on long tables, laden with food prepared by the best cooks in town.

A copy of a local paper dated September 30, 1875, mentions a large number of quilts on display, one made by a lady eighty-two years old and another made "expressly for the fair by a very small girl." The very small girl has been replaced by numerous 4-H clubs; the eighty-two-year-old lady, by scores of what are now called senior citizens, and their handicraft is unlimited, including paintings, rugs, knitting, crocheting, woodworking, and the products of their kitchens and gardens.

The Cumberland Fair of the 1800s has left a spirit of neighborliness that permeates the atmosphere today. Inflation reared its ugly head in those days too, as we look back and observe that in 1872 it became necessary to charge a ten-cent admission for adults.

The two groups had merged and located at West Cumberland, and the Cumberland Farmers Club, with the combined efforts of all working together, draws people from many states and Canada each year. In recent years the International Ox Pulling for the International Trophy and an exhibition of Head Yoke Pulling with International Rules has become an event that attracts thousands.

Due to the many improvements of the exhibits of handicrafts, agricultural products and farm animals, the Pari-Mutuel racing program, and the International Oxen and Horse Pulling, great sums of money are poured into the running of the Cumberland Fair Association.

Sources

Compiled by editor from material by Velma L. Merrill and Ruth Blanchard Norton

1. This letter is in the possession of George's son, Robert G. Blanchard.

Cumberland Fair Corrections

The current Cumberland County Fair is held in West Cumberland and is sponsored by the Cumberland Farmers Club. As a member of this organization, I have done additional research, and the history of the fair is somewhat different than reported in the original printing. The following is an attempt to bring new perspective to the origin of this annual tradition and draws from the *Portland Daily Press* and *Eastern Argus* newspapers.

The Cumberland Farmers Club was formed in 1869 and held the first fair on October 7, 1869 in Cumberland Center. It was referred to as the Cumberland Town Fair. The Fair used the grounds of Captain Enos Blanchard, the old Town Hall for exhibitions (where the fire department is located), and the horse sheds at the Congregational Church for animals. There was a large crowd in attendance. Amos J. Osgood was the marshal, and featured events were a foot race, pulling, and trotting.

An article in the *Daily Press* on October 9 praised the event and said it was important to have because of the ability of individuals "to get the merits recognized and articles of local interest can have their just desserts"; and "The honorable emulation it awakens can but prove a powerful stimulus to intelligence and enterprise in farming."

In 1870 the fair was held October 5 in the same place. It rained but the crowd was large. One hundred boxes of different apple varieties were on display, and it was alleged to be one of the largest apple displays ever in Maine.

A track was built in 1871 for the trotting horses. Edward Beals of North Yarmouth exhibited the best herd of cows, and Silas Skillins of North Yarmouth had the best sheep. Working cattle pulled in the afternoon.

In 1872, the fair was extended to two days, October 8 and 9. The *Daily Press* said the Town of Cumberland will hold their annual fair "in connection with North Yarmouth and Yarmouth." The fair is listed as being held behind Greely Institute. There was a carriage parade on the new track with twenty entries, and all the livestock paraded as well. This tradition continues on Saturday at Cumberland Fair. Greely Institute students assisted in serving a fund-raising dinner, with the money going to buy a bell for the school. Sixty dollars was raised.

Due to the large crowds coming to the fair, in 1873 they advertised that patrons might want to ride out on the Maine Central Railroad and then take a carriage ride from the station to the grounds. The Farmers Club exhibited a Shorthorn bull that they owned for the benefit of the members. Forty-one oxen were exhibited.

In the year 1874, conflict tore the Cumberland Fair apart and the story is different than printed. It is not clear what caused the split. The Farmers Club announced that they were moving the fair to their newly purchased grounds in West Cumberland. A fenced-in trotting park of half a mile had been built and the club membership tripled. However, "a few disaffected members of the old club" were determined not to move and instead decided to hold the first Cumberland Centre Fair of two days' length on October 6 and 7, which overlapped with the West Cumberland Fair that ran October 7 and 8. They adopted the name Cumberland Centre Farmers Club.

Bitter feelings were evident. Each group claimed that they had most of the original members so they were the true Cumberland Fair. West Cumberland announced that this was the Sixth Annual Fair. Newspaper advertisements from the Cumberland Centre Club stated "WE STILL LIVE." Members from each club went to the others' fair and tried to lure patrons away by announcing their event from the judge's stand. Confrontation resulted. Some patrons were observed attending both fairs. The *Daily Press* said that if the two fairs had been united in their efforts they would have had the best show in the state.

The ill will continued after the fairs, with each group petitioning the Maine Legislature to be allowed to incorporate. Both were granted corporate status in early 1875. The petition documents signed by the members provide an interesting look at the membership. The Cumberland Centre Club was comprised almost entirely of Cumberland residents, while the Cumberland Farmers Club had almost as many members from North Yarmouth as from Cumberland.

The two groups ran competing fairs for five years, although it appears the public did not record any ongoing competition between them. It is not clear why the Centre Club gave up after their 1878 event. Attendance was not known to be a problem, so perhaps it was due to the death of a key member or the loss of their fairground, as they did not own much of the property they used.

Due to the ongoing conflict between the groups, it is unlikely that the story of how Union Hall at the Centre Fairground was named can be accurate. It is more plausible that the intense sense of patriotism that swept the Northern states after their Civil War victory in 1865 held the country together was the reason for the choice of this name. It was a common practice at that time to call buildings Union, and numerous examples can be found throughout Maine. Cumberland Centre also had a baseball team for several years in the 1870s that was called the Unions, indicating that this name was one the Centre residents were proud of.

The Cumberland Farmers Club has purchased additional properties to expand the grounds over the years and is now substantially larger than in 1874. The fair has gone from two days to seven. It has been held every year except a few at the end of World War I when fire destroyed the exhibition hall. Many events are held on the grounds each year, and the September fair continues to signal the arrival of fall in southern Maine.

—*Lincoln J. Merrill Jr.*

Red Men

Sawga Tribe #20—Improved Order of Red Men—is a benevolent and social organization which held its first meeting in Union Hall on October 18, 1889. For many years there was an active sister organization called Indianola Council 44, Daughters of Pocahontas. When ground was broken on April 27, 1914, for the new hall on Blanchard Road, between the Congregational Church and present Cumberland Historical Society, the first shovels full of dirt were removed by members of Pocahontas: Mrs. Bessie Powell Burnell and Mrs. Florence Merrill Blanchard, wife of Sachem Harvey Blanchard. The new Red Men's hall became a real community center, with a fine dance floor, large stage for amateur theatricals, and large space for parties and all kinds of meetings. Later it was used for some years to house three grades of Cumberland schools due to overcrowding of the schools, caused by the rapid growth of the town.

It was sold in 1974 to the town for $1.00, to be renovated and used for town offices, with a five-year privilege to the Order of Red Men to continue holding their meetings in the upstairs council rooms. It is now the home of the Cumberland Historical Society.

—*Wayne H. Merrill*

We Neighbors

"We Neighbors" began meeting in 1894, as a gathering of neighborhood ladies for the purpose of study and enjoyment. It was formally organized in 1904 by a pastor's wife, Mrs. Frank Davis, and became a Women's Literary Club, with eighteen members. The accompanying picture shows a group at a Field Day in Old Orchard on June 23, 1908. Back row: Mrs. Philip Sturdivant, Mrs. Fred Adams, Mrs. Archie Wyman, Mrs. Howard Buxton, Mrs. James Sawyer, Mrs. Frank Doughty. Middle row: Mrs. Oren Thomes, Mrs. J. L. Dunn, Mrs. Albert Sweetser, and Mrs. Frederick Sweetser. Front row: Mrs. Edith Whiting, Mrs. Fen Blanchard.

Collection of Phyllis Sweetser

"We Neighbors" Field Day, 1908.

"We Neighbors" has grown through the years and is a very active club today.

Cumberland Fire Department

Cumberland did not always have the well-organized volunteer fire department that it has today. During the town's early days citizens had to rely on the "bucket brigade" if a fire broke out. This was not a very efficient means to fight fires, as the houses were far apart and men and water were frequently scarce.

The first evidence that Cumberland residents were concerned about organized fire protection came in 1906 with the appropriation of money to buy hydrants for the Foreside Road. In 1910 an article appeared in the town warrant to buy one or more fire engines and to raise $1,000, but the article was defeated. The people of Cumberland seemed reluctant to commit themselves to an organized fire department. The residents of Cumberland Foreside joined the people of Falmouth Foreside, forming the Foreside Fire Department. Cumberland gave this company 300 feet of hose in 1911.

Cumberland's first fire warden was elected in 1913. (Before this, men had gone to fires doing the best they could with no one officially in charge.) Merle F. Willis was the first to serve in that capacity. It was also voted to purchase some hand fire extinguishers, which were placed around Cumberland Center. In 1914 the townspeople voted to fix the price of labor for those fighting fires, but the amount was not specified.

The first elected fire chief in Cumberland was Lester Bragg, who served from 1914 until his death in 1921. During the first few years, Bragg was fire chief in name only, as there was very little equipment, no budget, and no organization of men to head! Then Cumberland finally made a commitment and bought a fire engine. It was an American LaFrance Fire Equipment Company, Model T Ford, with two thirty-five-gallon chemical tanks. The truck had 100 feet of hose and a short ladder, all for $1,400. This truck was housed in a stable at 279 Main Street.

The town meeting in 1921 brought the appropriation of $100 for the fire department. The first fire station was built that year. It was a metal building, built beside the old blacksmith shop, near the present Congregational Church parsonage. This one-car garage cost $340 to construct. The fire chief was given a salary of $50/year in 1922, but there was no organized fire department in the Center or West Cumberland.

The year 1928 was a landmark for the cause of fire protection in Cumberland. Eighteen men met in the kitchen of the Cumberland Congregational Church vestry. They voted to form a volunteer company, drew up by-laws, and elected officers. The chief, Gilbert Strout, had been elected at town meeting, so the men chose Gerald Packard, first assistant, T. R. Jordan, second assistant, Edward Bragg, third assistant, Harold Bragg, clerk/treasurer. The people of Middle Road and Tuttle Road disbanded their private hose company organized in 1923 and joined with the new organization. A new truck was bought in 1928 at a cost of $2,500. The truck bought in 1921 was sent to Chebeague. Until this time Chebeague only had access to a portable fire pump, which was given to the Island in 1922. This truck was housed near the present Island Hall. It was a welcome addition to Chebeague, for like the mainland, nearly every major fire had been a total loss before the advent of modern firefighting equipment. In 1928 half of the old Cumberland Town Hall was converted into a fire station, and the Cumberland Center Water Company was formed, placing small hydrants in strategic positions in the Center.

The Cumberland Fire Department, finally organized, began to grow every year. Plans were developed for firefighting in various sections of the town.

Prior to this time, the Foreside had the only water system in town. In the early days, the rest of the town relied on water from wells and cisterns in their cellars, which were not very reliable in the event of a very large fire. Former chief "Cap" Bragg remembers one such fire. "The fire department had a plan 'A,' which was to go into action should a fire break out in the Center. The plan was to make use of a large cistern full of water, under the workshop in Arno Chase's greenhouse. As soon as the fire started, a pump was to be hooked up to the cistern-well. You can guess where the first fire was—in Arno Chase's greenhouse. There wasn't anybody putting a pump in there, I'll tell you! That was the first one to burn in that area, but we saved the rest of the village. They were 'bout ready to vacate the post office, and the telephone operators thought for sure that they would be burned out."

In 1936 there were thirty-six alarms. The fire department saw the need for a better water supply in the Center, so a fire pond was built off Main Street. That same year a combination pumper and hose wagon was added, so the town sent the 1928 truck to Chebeague.

The West Cumberland section of town felt that they needed better fire protection than a central fire station could provide. The people of this area built their own fire station with volunteer labor, and raised money to purchase a truck, all at no cost to the town. West Cumberland also acquired a resuscitator that year. This was an important addition for West Cumberland because of many near drownings at Forest Lake in that area of the town.

The year 1947 was the year of the fire crises in Maine. In many communities every able-bodied man was needed to fight these fires. Cumberland bought two government-surplus fire engines for about $2,500 each. Mainland Cumberland was spared any major fires that year, but Chebeague was not as lucky. A fire started on the end of Deer Point; government barracks quickly burned, and the fire spread through the dry evergreens and headed for the settlement on the West End. Luckily, the town meeting in 1946 had passed a warrant providing for the purchase of engine #6 for Chebeague, which was a great help in fighting the blaze. The fire was out of control for two days. Nearly every man on Chebeague battled the blaze, saving the occupied houses from certain destruction. Two and a half acres burned, but no real damage to personal property occurred. Another fire truck was bought for Chebeague in 1949. After the fire in 1947 the town realized that the Island must have adequate equipment, as there were no other companies available to help in a major disaster. The Island firehouse had been moved (several years before) to a renovated building on what is now Firehouse Avenue. With the purchase of these new trucks, an addition had to be made to the existing structure.

Until 1952 the mainland alarm system had been sounded by the telephone operator in town. When there was a fire she would have a continuous ring-ring-ring on each party line to alert the people to a fire. They would all answer, she would give the location of the fire, and continue with the same system on the rest of the lines. Extra power was needed to

Photograph by Daniel Dow, 1974

Cumberland Fire Department.

keep up the constant ring. "Cap" Bragg remembers, as a boy, turning a hand generator to get enough power for the alarm. Even after a siren was added, the telephone operator still provided this important service. The dial telephone came to Cumberland in 1952, replacing the operator, so the Red Network system was started. This rang the alarm in the homes of several firemen, and their wives would call the other men, giving the location of the fire. Today, Cumberland has a dispatcher, Janet Bragg, who goes on the air and transmits to radios placed in the homes of many firemen the location of the fire. An air horn is also used to alert those firemen who are not at home when a fire breaks out.

Cumberland got its first real standard type fire truck in 1956. In 1957 West Cumberland got a new fire engine. The property adjoining the old town hall (the Central Fire Station) was bought in 1962. Construction was then begun on the present firehouse. It was several years before the old building was completely demolished, and the project completed. The West Cumberland Fire Station on the Blackstrap Road was constructed in 1963, and the Central Fire Station received a new fire engine. That year the Cumberland Water District merged with Portland, which lowered Cumberland's fire insurance.

Chebeague got a new fire truck in 1972. This engine was purchased at a cost of $19,000, a far cry from the early days of rejects. The Island firehouse houses two fire trucks and a rescue unit. A new public safety building was built in 1983.

Cumberland residents have continued to support better fire equipment for the town. The town's three fire stations are in good shape. The volunteer firemen meet frequently to practice and keep the equipment in A-l condition.

The fire department serves a social function as well as being a necessary part of municipal government. The once-a-month suppers are still held at all firehouses, although the price has increased somewhat from the thirty cents "Cap" Bragg remembered in the early days. Greely High School still has an auxiliary that has aided in many a fire. Few towns are lucky enough to have such skilled young adults in their high schools.

—Written by Donna L. Miller, from an interview with Harold M. Bragg

Cumberland Fire Department (1977–2015)

The membership of the Cumberland Fire Department (CFD) consists of many diverse and multitalented individuals who volunteer in Cumberland, with several having made it their career in nearby cities.

Over the last thirty years the Cumberland Fire Department has experienced significant change in many areas. This is a brief summary of those changes.

The number of annual calls the CFD responds to has increased dramatically. In the 1970s the average number of calls the department responded to was well under 100. Since 2000, the department routinely responds to 500 to 600 emergency calls annually. The responses aren't just to building fires, but a wide variety of emergencies, including: car accidents, fire alarms, sledding accidents, hazardous material incidents, wildland fires, electrical problems, mutual aid, and others.

While the number of fire apparatus hasn't really changed in thirty years, the type and capability of the apparatus has improved significantly. This is a brief summary by company:

- Engine 1 became the first truck to seat six, with three inside and three outside in "jump" seats. This truck also was the first 1,000-gallon engine. Engine 1 has recently been replaced with a fully enclosed cab that seats six. This engine also has a Class A and B foam system.
- Engine 2 changed from mini-pumper to a full-size Class A pumper carrying 500 gallons of water. It was later replaced with a refurbished engine/tank truck carrying 2,000 gallons of water. This truck was refurbished from the original Ladder 7. A new engine/tank truck is being purchased.
- Forestry 2 was created from a military truck to deal specifically with wildland fires.
- Tank 2 moved from the West Station to Chebeague Island and replaced Tank 1.
- Engine 3 was upgraded to a Class A pumper that sat three people in the cab. Recently this truck was upgraded to a six-person fully enclosed cab; it holds 1,000 gallons of water and has a Class A and B foam system.
- Enginc 5 was replaced with the town's first five-person fully enclosed cab. This type of cab became necessary in the 1980s as firefighters were no longer allowed to ride on the rear step over fire trucks. This truck carries 1,000 gallons of water and has a Class A and B foam system.
- Engine 7 became Ladder 7, a used 100-foot ladder and pumper truck also known as a "quint." Having a dedicated ladder truck provides safer roof access and clearly defines who performs the ventilation function at fires. Ladder 7 was then later replaced with a new 75-foot quint with a six-person fully enclosed cab.
- Squad 1 was added to the fleet as an equipment truck with tools to help people who need extrication from cars or other places they may be trapped. There have been four different vehicles used as Squad 1: one van, one ambulance, one rescue truck, and today, an eight-person fully enclosed cab with a heavy rescue body. The squad now car-

ries an even wider variety of equipment, including air packs, air cylinders, hazmat, rope rescue, saws, torches, hand tools, rapid intervention team (RIT) equipment, ice rescue boat, etc.
- Marine 1 is a 16-foot Avon with a 50-horsepower motor and was donated to the CFD for water rescue.
- Snow Emergency Rescue Vehicle (SERV1) is a Polaris snowmobile built for towing, and is used for off-road snow rescue.

The fire department has received many grants in the last several years. These grants have provided personal protective equipment, a Plymovent vehicle exhaust system, breathing air refill system, and gear washing and drying equipment.

A town-wide fund-raiser led to the purchase of two Thermal Imaging Cameras (TICs), one for the mainland and one for Chebeague Island. The TIC adds a whole new dimension of visibility for interior fire attack and search and rescue by allowing firefighters to see in zero visibility. Additional grant money has allowed for the purchase of three more cameras.

An Explorer Post program was created to train and support high school student volunteers in the fire service. This program allows young people to explore the fire service while learning the importance of volunteering. The Cumberland Fire Academy program was created to support the Explorer program. The Fire Academy is structured to have post members stay at the fire station around the clock while participating in training and responding on calls. Students from surrounding communities also participate in the academy, which creates stronger relationships between departments.

Recently the CFD started a fire police division to assist with traffic control. These members provide timely traffic control that helps to ensure emergency worker safety and assists the public with knowledge of the options they have for reaching their destination.

The CFD currently has a per diem program to help with daytime coverage while volunteers are away at their jobs. These firefighters provide not just fire suppression coverage, but also building, apparatus, and SCBA (Self-Contained Breathing Apparatus) maintenance, as well as performing fire prevention, inspections, and medical emergency response.

The CFD is fortunate to have a fire community service liaison program servicing the department, the Town of Cumberland, and surrounding communities. Fire community service liaison K. C. Putnam provides emergency-response counseling to those in our communities in the middle of a crisis.

Fire chiefs over the last thirty years:

Ralph J. Brown	1971–1982
Kenneth C. Wagner	1982–1990
George B. Small	1990–1992
William I. Fischer	1992–1999
Daniel R. Small	1999–present

—Submitted by Deputy Chief Daryl Rawnsley

Rescue Unit

Cumberland Rescue Unit was formed in 1958 with a first-year total of 36 calls. Its new vehicle pictured on the cover of the Town Report for 1971 had 158 calls that year. It is an integral part of the Cumberland Fire Department, with three squads having made up its wholly volunteer operational group: one at the Central Station, one at West Cumberland, and one on Chebeague Island. Now it is back to two with the secession of Chebeague in 2007.

—Richard W. Sweetser

The vehicle represents a tremendous effort by all concerned and is a tribute to each and every citizen of the town and the several community-spirited organizations who contributed toward its purchase.

At the present time the Rescue Squad has returned to being part of the fire department, after a few years of being a separate department, headed by Rescue Chief Chris Bolduc. The per diem program is incorporated into the Rescue Squad. The entire Fire Department and Rescue Squad is headed by Fire Chief Dan Small. There are three deputy chiefs: Chris Copp, Daryl Rawnsley, and Evariste Bernier.

26 Portland, Me., Evening Express, Friday, July 23, 1971

AT YOUR SERVICE — Cumberland's new rescue vehicle is now ready for use. Rescue Captain Richard W. Sweetser, left, here examines the white, International ambulance together with Fire Chief Ralph Brown, Dr. William E. Wyatt, and Selectman Harold M. Bragg. Sweetser led the fund-raising drive which led to purchase of the vehicle. The patient compartment is 55 inches high, providing plenty of room for attendants to give medical assistance. It can carry four patients if necessary. (Hutchinson Photo)

July 23, 1971, Evening Express, *Portland, Maine*

Cumberland Rescue Unit.

Cumberland Historical Society

The Cumberland Historical Society was founded on March 25, 1939. Its possessions were housed at Prince Memorial Library, where most of its meetings were held until 1989. The Town of Cumberland sold the 1853 schoolhouse to the Historical Society, which restored it. The building was sold back to the town in 2014. Meetings and programs are held in the council chambers at the town office. There are also artifacts to view, research resources available, and education programs presented. All residents are welcome and urged to attend.

Cumberland Garden Club

The Cumberland Garden Club was organized in February 1956, and joined the Federation of Maine Garden Clubs in June 1956, but is no longer a member of it. The objective of the club is to study horticulture and allied subjects, encourage environmental projects, and strive for community betterment in accordance with state and national plans. Yearly programs, workshops, and field trips are varied and informative. Club projects include placing arrangements in the library year-round, planting and maintaining present plantings around schools, filling and maintaining window boxes at the Town Hall and urns at the cemetery, involving juniors in environmental improvement through the schools, decorating the monuments, public buildings, and schools at Christmas, sponsoring a Cadet Girl Scout troop, financing the landscaping of the new town garage, maintaining and decorating the Merrill monument in the center and at Prince Memorial Library. Each year members exhibit at the Cumberland Fair. One of the greatest accomplishments was involving the citizens in creating a sanitary landfill, for which the club won $1,300, to use for environmental improvement in Cumberland.

—*Rebecca S. Hilton*

Mill Pond Garden Club

The Mill Pond Garden Club of West Cumberland was organized in February 1973, by Mrs. Robert Allen. The name was chosen because of the mills at this end of town. The club tries to keep its major projects restricted to the West Cumberland area. To earn money to promote the projects, the club has maintained a booth at the Cumberland Fair for the past three years, where they sell articles members have made at special workshops. The club sponsors a Brownie troop from West Cumberland and donates to the Girl Scout Council to send a needy girl to camp. At Christmastime there is a door-decorating contest offering cash prizes; wreaths and lights are placed on the West Cumberland fire station and wreaths on the church doors. Each year $25 is donated to the Bruce Roberts Christmas fund. In the spring, flowers are planted in the flower boxes of these buildings. The club has donated a check for $500 to the town to be used for fencing the ball park next to the West Cumberland fire station, and will be working with the recreation committee of the town to get the recreation area organized and beautified in the spring. It has disbanded.

—Roberta Violette, Secretary

Cumberland Lions Club

The Cumberland Lions Club was organized in 1961. The Charter was issued June 12, 1961. There were twenty-five charter members.

In addition to the support of sight conservation by supplying glasses to persons in need, some other services of the Club are listed below:

Sponsor of Little League Team
Sponsor of Boy Scout Troop
Sponsor of the Ernest Rand Scholarship
Sponsor of holiday baskets to needy and floral arrangements to shut-ins
Sponsor of Diabetes and Glaucoma Clinic
Annual cleaning of village library
International Foundation—Relief for disaster areas
Donation to Neighborhood Youth Corps of Cumberland County
Christmas gifts to South Portland Training Center
Purchase of National Safety Council material for local schools

The Club has fifty-two members at present.

—Russell Ross

Nu-Cumbers Club

The Nu-Cumbers Club of Cumberland was founded in 1962 to provide new residents in the town a chance to know one another and to learn more about the town. The club was responsible for the story hour at Prince Memorial Library, and each year presented a gift to some organization or town project. This club has disbanded.

Country Club

Val Halla Country Club originated as a corporation in 1964 with a eighteen-hole golf course on about 80 acres, part of 150 acres of beautiful woods and open space in the geographical center of Cumberland. In January, 1975, it was purchased by the town for developing more diversified recreational use, as well as for future environmental protection. The name now is Val Halla Golf and Recreation Center.

—*Myron M. Hilton*

Chapter Twenty

Some Citizens of Note

Rev. Amasa Smith

When the Second Congregational Church in North Yarmouth, the church at Cumberland Center, decided to invite a fifty-year-old man, plain, tall, with more than a hint of military bearing, to become its second minister, they were not sure they had made a good choice. Amasa Smith was their third choice. He was born in Belchertown, Massachusetts, in 1756. He had an unusual background for a minister, and up in Turner where he came from, they had been having a hassle in the church over Unitarianism, and his parish there had dwindled. Moreover, he had a large family, his wife, Sophia, and ten children, some of them grown, but a number who would need a good-size house to live in and a fair income, too. He had "commenced his ministry somewhat late in life."[1] Indeed, he had helped fight the Revolution as a Minuteman in Massachusetts, and had commanded artillery with the rank of major. In 1785, according to an old account book, he had kept a tavern in Belchertown, Massachusetts, for some years, a respected occupation, but hardly what one might expect for a minister.

Since the church had invited two other men before the Rev. Smith and they had refused, there did not seem to be much choice left. However, he turned out to be a good choice. His successor, Rev. Isaac Weston, wrote that during his ministry the church "was visited by a

Courtesy of Cumberland Historical Society

Home of Amasa Smith, 340 Main Street.

refreshing shower," and that "an extensive revival accompanied his labors among our people in 1808." An installation service in 1806 included a sermon by Rev. John Smith, brother of the new minister and minister of the church in Salem, New Hampshire, and soon to become one of the original faculty members of Bangor Theological Seminary.

Amasa built his home at the present Mary J. Walker home at 340 Main Street. Amasa was a solemn, impressive man completely dedicated to God. In the pulpit he dwelt much on biblical doctrine, especially on the prophecies. The early 1880s were a period of great challenge for a minister, and he was expected to settle problems both in and out of the church. A paper has been in existence in the Sweetser family indicating that at least once he encountered and tried to settle an argument which developed among several women of the community when one accused another of theft, and the entire population was upset.

It was also the period when churches were confronted with the Halfway Covenant. Among other aspects, this doctrine allowed church membership by less strict rules of faith. Amasa Smith was convinced that this was weakening to the church and did not accept the belief. In 1820 he requested to be dismissed from the Cumberland pastorate.

Then, when he was sixty-four years old, the Rev. Amasa Smith started a new career. He undertook what he called his "Missionary Labors."

Starting out on horseback, he traveled from Cumberland to most points of the compass. Stopping usually in small villages lacking a minister, he went west to Vermont, south to York and Boston, and beyond to Fall River and New Bedford and to Rhode Island. From Boston he also went "home" to Northampton and Belchertown and west to the Connecticut valley. He made trips to Bangor and Bath. And in the town of Brooks, Maine, when he was seventy-eight, he recorded in his journal that he was "unwell and very weary."

This was his last missionary labor, and his influence in towns where he preached throughout New England cannot be measured. He was one of the founders of the Maine Missionary Society. According to his own journal he often recorded periods of "religious excitement" in the places he visited. There is no doubt that he helped keep a spark of religion alive in many places during his travels.

Photograph by Daniel Dow, 1975

Amasa Smith's gravestone.

He returned to Cumberland where he died in 1849 at the age of ninety-one. His stone in the old cemetery in the Center records a few facts of his life, but gives no clue as to the tremendous influence he must have had upon Cumberland and New England.

One of his sons, Col. Joseph Smith, was the master builder of the four Cumberland Churches: the Foreside Community, Tuttle Road Methodist,

Cumberland Congregational, and the West Cumberland Methodist, as well as the first Town House on Tuttle Road. He was inspector of customs at the US Customs office in Portland.

—*Elizabeth Sweetser Baxter*

Source

1. Weston, I., *History of the Congregational Church and Society in Cumberland, Me.*, Brown Thurston, 1861, p. 30.

Oren Scott Thomes

Oren Scott Thomes was born in Cumberland, May 24, 1837, the only child of Capt. Ebenezer and Dolly Rideout Thomes. He married Abbie Eveleth of New Gloucester in 1861. In his youth he attended Cumberland schools. At eighteen he went to Boston where he served as an apprentice for three years, learning the carpenter and builders' trade, and later attended Lowell Institute. He returned to Cumberland and had a store for general merchandise by the name of Thomes & Blanchard. This store was located at the present 299 Main Street in front of old Union Hall.

From 1880 History of Cumberland County
Photo by Conant, Portland

O. S. Thomes.

In 1877 Mr. Thomes was called to California to take charge of the estate of his uncle, Robert H. Thomes. The ranch of over 26,000 acres of land was one of the largest land grants by the Spanish government, then part of Mexico, and Mr. Thomes had

Evarts and Peck, 1880

Oren S. Thomes and his early homes at 53 (top) and 42 Blanchard Road.

the original deed. The ranch had 4,000 head of cattle, 500 horses, and 400 hogs, with over 200 Indians living and working on the land. His uncle was one of the first persons to undertake the hazardous journey to California in 1841, and a member of the first party to discover gold. His land was rich and he was the fortunate person to take out the largest run of gold, when one shovelful was valued at $300. After settling this vast estate Mr. and Mrs.

Courtesy of Cumberland Historical Society

Thomes mansion.

Photograph by W. Chester Rideout, courtesy of Mary Webb Richardson

Mr. and Mrs. Oren Thomes and their son Robert and his family at the mansion built in 1882.

Thomes and their sons Robert and John returned to Cumberland and lived in their home at 42 Blanchard Road, where he engaged in agriculture, ran a modern stock farm, and carried on a grist- and sawmill business. In 1882 he built the fine mansion across the street (shown on page 291).

"Daddy Thomes," so called by everybody in town, liked to recall that he cast his first vote for Abraham Lincoln as president. He was the carpenter who did the woodwork on Greely Institute and who remodeled the Congregational Church in 1907. He was a spry little man and even in his eighties the only person in town who could climb to the weather vane of the church. He and his wife celebrated their fiftieth wedding anniversary in August 1911, at the spacious mansion which burned in 1913. Even at his advanced age he rebuilt the house, but not on such a grand scale. For some years he served as town treasurer, and was a member and deacon in the Congregational Church. He died in 1931.

Source

Compiled by editor from *History of Cumberland Co.*, Evarts & Peck, 1880, and from item in *Portland Press Herald*, March 5, 1923.

Judge Scott Wilson

Courtesy of his granddaughter, Martha McCullum

Judge Scott Wilson (c. 1940).

Judge Scott Wilson was born in West Cumberland in January 1870, the son of Nathaniel and Loemma Leighton Wilson. They lived at the present address of 150 Gray Road at the top of Morrison's Hill. The annual report of the Town of Cumberland for the year ending February 22, 1889, shows "Mr. Scott Wilson as the teacher in District No. 2, who seems to be a favorite with his pupils, which enables him to mould and direct them with ease. His efforts to awaken in the minds of his pupils a desire 'to be somebody' will not soon be forgotten." He graduated from Bates College in 1893, and the University of Maine Law School in 1894. He became a member of the Maine Bar in 1895 and practiced law in Portland. He was the Attorney General of Maine in 1913 and a Justice of the Maine Superior Court from 1918–25 and Chief Justice from 1925–29. At this time he lived in Portland, but was always interested in his native town, and for many years was a trustee of Greely Institute.

He was appointed Judge of the US Circuit Court of Appeals where he served until he retired in 1940. He died in 1942.

Horace A. Hildreth

Horace A. Hildreth was born December 2, 1902, in Gardiner, Maine. He is a graduate of Gardiner High School, Bowdoin College, and Harvard Law School, with honorary degrees from University of Maine, Bowdoin, Temple University, Suffolk University, Bucknell University, and Peshawar University of Pakistan.

During his student days he was active in athletics and debating, and during the summers worked as dishwasher and counselor in boys' camps, as seaman on a Swedish tramp steamer, and as US Ranger in Yellowstone Park. In 1929 he married Katherine Wing of Boston, Massachusetts, and Northport, Maine, and practiced law in Boston with Ropes & Gray. In 1935 the Hildreths purchased the Spaulding Bisbee estate on Cumberland Foreside, and he became a partner in the Portland firm of Cook, Hutchinson, Pierce & Connell. He is a life member of the American Bar Association.

He served in the 89th Maine legislature as representative from Cumberland and Falmouth, in the 90th and 91st as senator from Cumberland County. He became president of the Maine Senate and then served two terms as governor of the State of Maine from 1945 to 1949—during which time he served as head of the National Governors Association and president of the Council of State Government. In 1949 he became president of Bucknell University in Lewisburg, Pennsylvania. In May of 1953 he was appointed United States Ambassador to Pakistan, the fifth most populous nation in the world, which post he resigned in May 1957, to return to Maine.

He was a member of the Congregational Church and was frequently the preacher on Laymen's Sunday in the Church in Cumberland. He served as a member of the Board of Trustees of Bucknell University and of the Board of Overseers of Bowdoin College. He was the founder and first president of Mount Washington TV and a director of the Colby-Bates-Bowdoin Educational Telecasting Corporation. His chief business activity at present is serving as chairman of the Board of Diversified Communications Inc., which runs a radio and television network in Maine, and a publishing business. He was a director of other Maine business companies.

Photograph by Franklin Grant (c. 1945)

The Honorable Horace A. Hildreth.

In an interview, Governor and Ambassador Hildreth told of many unusual and varied experiences and felt very fortunate that he and his family had led such interesting lives. His most harrowing experience as governor was when forest fires swept the State of Maine and destroyed much of Bar Harbor and other areas.

Being ambassador to Pakistan proved to be a great adventure and contained more interesting experiences than any other four-year period in his life. One exciting event for him and Mrs. Hildreth was a roundup of wild elephants to which they were invited by the brother of the Shah of Iran, who presented them with a baby elephant which weighed 750 pounds. It became quite a pet and with its mahout (person who works with, rides, and tends elephants) was flown home to Cumberland, where it was of interest to their friends and neighbors and finally ended up in the Stoneham, Massachusetts, Zoo.

Back in Cumberland, Governor Hildreth started the first television station in the State of Maine and owns the oldest radio station in the state. Starting Mount Washington TV on the top of Mount Washington was most exciting and an engineering marvel at the time.

Although the Hildreth family has traveled far and wide they have always kept Cumberland as their legal residence and home base, and three of their four children and their families still live in the area. Hildreth died on June 2, 1988.

—Interview by editor

Paul Emery Merrill

Paul Emery Merrill was born in Cumberland, September 1, 1913, the son of Wallace L. and Harriet Cutter Merrill. He attended Cumberland schools and graduated from Greely Institute in 1931. As a sophomore he took his savings and purchased a used truck for $150, thus starting the trucking business which has now become Merrill Transport Co. In 1932 he started Merrill's Express, serving the towns of Falmouth, Cumberland, North Yarmouth, and Pownal daily from Portland. The Merrill Transport Co. is now the largest petroleum carrier in New England.

Photograph by Roger Paul Jordan (c. 1970)

Paul E. Merrill.

From 1933 when he started Maine Lumber Co. and in 1935 when he took over the R. A. Linneken Moving Co. of Portland, he has been engaged in the following business and industrial developments: president of Cook Concrete

Co., president of Norway Laundry, Inc., president of Commercial Leasing, Inc., president of Merrill's Rental Service, Inc., president of Chase Transfer Corp., president of Maine Fidelity Life Ins. Co., President of Merrill Industries, Inc., president of Merrill Warehouses, Inc., treasurer of Washington Storage & Distribution Center, director of Maine Fidelity Life Ins., director of No. Central Co., St. Paul, Minnesota, director of Canal National Bank, director of National Tank Truck Carriers, Inc., president of Maine Truck Owners, Inc.

His affiliation with civic and other organizations consisted of: member and president of Portland Lions Club, member and president of Maine State Chamber of Commerce, member and chairman of Salvation Army Board, member of Portland Club, Woodfords Club, Portland Country Club, Cumberland Club, member and deacon of Woodfords Congregational Church, member Vermont Society of Engineers, member Portland Chamber of Commerce, member Marco Polo Club of New York City, member Mark Mainers, Department of Commerce and Industry, member of Northeastern Lumber Manufacturing Association, member of American Polled Hereford Association, member of New England Hereford Association, and member of American Belgian Draft Horse Association.

In 1973 he was appointed by Governor Curtis to be chairman of the delegation from Maine and went to Japan representing the Department of Commerce and Industry, cooperating with the United States movement for better commerce and trade between the two countries.

In 1936 he married Virginia C. Sweetser, and they resided in Portland until 1972, when a new home was built on the old homestead site in Cumberland. He died in April of 1982.

—Interview by editor

Owen Farwell

Owen Farwell was born on November 26, 1913, and has lived in Cumberland, his native town, most of his life. In 1946, having sold several small businesses in the town and surrounding areas, he went into the real estate business and developed the first subdivision in Cumberland Center. This came about because at this time, land which had belonged to his family for years became available to him. This plot of land of seventeen acres and the house at the corner of Main Street and Farwell Avenue, built by his grandfather Simeon Farwell, was ideal for such a purpose. This development of forty-one lots and two streets was surveyed and laid out by Harlan H. Sweetser, a registered civil engineer. The first lot on Farwell Avenue was planned for a new post office building, built in 1947, a second for a store with an apartment, a lot across the street sold to Chase's Greenhouse, and an acre of land donated to Moss Side Cemetery. Four homes were built for speculation and sold so well that more and more were built, until the area of Farwell Avenue and Prince Street was filled. This development was named Cumberland Center Terrace.

Photograph by Jackson Studios (c. 1970)

Owen Farwell.

By 1957 he needed to expand his building activities and was able to purchase twenty-seven acres of land off Main Street and northeast of Cumberland Center Terrace. This development became Pinewood Acres and contained forty-five lots.

He was also in the real estate brokerage business under the name of Wells and Farwell, Inc., in Portland, until he built a new home and office at 215 Main Street in Cumberland. In 1964 he took in a partner, William C. Reynolds, who ran the business for several years after 1982. William's son Craig joined him in 1982. Mr. Farwell thought Cumberland had many years of growth ahead. He died in 1995. His wife Dorothy died in 1997.

—Interview by editor

Chapter Twenty-One

Tales and Legends

When Colonel Samuel True became postmaster in 1849, the office was in a corner room in a house situated on the site of the present Gulf station. A sheltered doorway was where the patrons called for their mail. A hanging cord was used to ring a bell in the post office room. Col. True would open a shutter in the wall and say, "You want your mail, I suppose." A bare table in the room was sufficient to hold all the letters in any mail. He would smile as he peeked out to see who it was, and allow them to enter the room. He would then read the postcards aloud, or he might comment, "Your sister is coming next week and bringing her boy," or "Here is a letter and I would be glad to know who it is from and what it contains for news."

A paper pad hung on the wall and each person receiving mail signed the sheet and took time to see who else had signed for any mail that day.

The colonel always bowed and shook hands with his patrons. He was postmaster for nearly thirty years.

—By Herman P. Sweetser

The unusual name *Meaubec* is due to the fact that at the time of the French Revolution, which began in 1789, a skilled physician who was about to be executed was smuggled out of France by a Yarmouth sea captain. Out of gratitude the doctor settled in Yarmouth and was a greatly beloved man. He delivered many babies, over twenty of whom were named for him. Hence, Capt. Meaubec Prince, the father of Carroll D. Prince, who gave Prince Memorial Library to the town.

—Related by Harlan H. Sweetser

The Witch of Cumberland, "Granny Banks"

The only sources we have for this story are a newspaper clipping found in a scrapbook, kept by Herman Sweetser's mother, and called "An Evening at Master Ben's," and the following account which I took down as my uncle, Horatio Herrick, told it. I had heard it many, many times for it was one of his favorite stories.

Her name was Banks. We don't know who her parents were nor her given name, but we do know that in 1807 a Lucretia Banks and a Dr. Elias Banks joined the old Congregational Church at Cumberland Center.

Granny is said to have lived in a tumbled-down shack near the southwest corner of the lot where Prince Memorial Library now stands.

From the first that we can hear, she was decidedly peculiar. Unlike the pictures of most witches that we see with their noses and chins touching, toothless, and with disheveled gray hair, she was tall and straight as an arrow with piercing black eyes, jet-black hair, and a set of teeth she could have sold to a princess for their weight in diamonds. These teeth she preserved by occasionally catching a snake, holding his head firmly between her fingers, biting through his body close to his head, and drawing through her teeth the rest of his body. Her toothpicks were always the splinters from a lightning-riven tree.

When displeased with the neighbors, she had a way of solemnly shaking her forefinger, and repeating several times, "You'll be sorry! You'll be sorry!" She feared no one and cared for no one with the exception of Parson Amasa Smith's wife.

Captain Nicholas Blanchard, who displeased her, had the following experience. Jogging along the road, as he passed her house, the harness dropped from his trembling horse. Not a buckle was unfastened. Not a strap was broken. It was some time before Captain Nicholas could move to harness the animal, for he too was under a spell.

Again she asked Bill Batchelder to take a small grist of grain to the mill for her. Since the going was icy and he had a heavy load, he refused. As he started up Morse's Hill, the road was suddenly full of hogs. When he turned back, and after a while started out again, the hogs were there in greater numbers. After many attempts to get along the road he had to put up his team for the day. As he passed Granny's house on his way back home, she stood in the door shaking her fist at him and saying "I told you you'd be sorry!"

When Deacon Hamilton of North Yarmouth refused to do a little errand for her on his way to the market, he also "was sorry." Two or three nights later his house was surrounded by dogs, leaping and putting their paws on the windowsills. The cattle bellowed in their stanchions, the sheep bleated in terror, but not a yelp nor a bark from the dogs. They were the Spook Dogs of the Shakers, for our great-grandmother Herrick saw them come down the old Gray Road.

One young lady, against whom Granny had a grudge, tried to cross a brook on her way to a party, but every time she thought she crossed she found herself on the same side.

One night after dark, Olive Porter was walking home from a friend's house when she almost ran onto a skunk. She ran away as fast as she could but the critter kept following her. She picked up a stick and hit it on the head and left it for dead—but when she tried to find it the next morning it was gone. That day Granny's face was all scratched up and she was so lame she could just hobble around. Olive declared that Granny had a grudge against her and turned herself into a skunk to torment her, but if she did she got the worst of it.

Master Ben's wife, Aunt Dolly, was making soap and it wouldn't form as it should and kept coming and going all afternoon. Just at sunset Bill Batchelder happened in. "Perhaps Granny has bewitched it," says he, and seizing a horseshoe, he threw it into the boiling lye. The soap formed in two minutes and Aunt Dolly had a kettle full of soap so thick you could cut it with a knife. The next morning Bill Smith, who was keeping the Tavern down the road from Master Ben's, came in and said that Granny had been taken real sick about sunset the night before, with terrible pains and cramps. Bill said, "I guess that dose of horseshoe fixed the old lady this time." In those days, which weren't too far distant in time from the Salem Witchcraft Trials, and when most people were very superstitious and governed by stern religious beliefs, Granny must have been a source of fearful—and at times, pleasurable—excitement to the people of Cumberland.

—*Margaret Wyman*

Memories of the 1880s

I remember arguing heatedly some ninety years ago with my playmate, Geneva Blanchard, as to who was older, she or I. I believe we wouldn't argue about it now. However, it is true that with age one has the advantage of being able to recall things that happened long ago. I enjoy my memories of being a child in the 1880s in Cumberland Center, Maine.

First of all I remember living in the brick house that stood where the Cumberland Library now stands. It was built with an apartment on each side, quite a modern arrangement for that day. My grandparents, David and Elizabeth (Sweetser) Wilson, lived on one side and my parents, Will and Emily (Norton) Wilson, lived on the other. I remember the old brick oven on my grandfather's side, and upstairs the wealth of old magazines that were stored under the eaves of the house.

A few steps from our back door was a building my father used as a carpenter shop. This he had had moved down from where it had stood as a blacksmith shop opposite the cemetery, and though it was full of workbenches and builder's equipment, it still contained an interesting assortment of odd horseshoes, spikes, and nails.

Then I have memories of the year or so my father kept the Cumberland Center store, and all the activity that went on there. We lived in the apartment over the store, 277 Main Street, with the long stairway to the ground. I remember the Fourth-of-July morning my father cautioned me and my small sister Cecil to be sure not to set off snapping crackers if there were any horses near the loading platform at the front of the store. We tried to be very obedient, but just as Cecil had sent one flying and sizzling, up drove somebody, and, sure enough, there was a rearing and snorting that brought parental wrath down upon us.

What else do I remember? Well, I remember going up to Martha Blanchard's house. She and her brothers and sisters, children of Solomon, George Blanchard's brother, were playing circus in the barn there, when they lived opposite the store at the Center.

I remember going down to Aunt Mary Herrick's after buttermilk, and being invited down with Florence Merrill to pick mustard greens in Mrs. Oliver Collins's backyard. Those errands took me just down over Morse's Hill where we used to slide in winter. My father had won quite a reputation there some years before as a boy, for his sled that would go so remarkably fast and far. I remember, too, the miniature sled models that he constructed, one of which was like the Flexible Flyer later on the market.

Speaking of going for milk recalls a time when I was given six cents to go for a quart of milk up to George Blanchard's. Five cents was for the milk, the penny for me. This was a treasured possession. Aunt Joan Blanchard, George's mother, who was doubtless much younger than I am now, seemed impossibly old to me. I have since heard that this lady, as a girl, was the much-sought-after sweetheart of my crusty old uncle John Wilson, who, then a handsome and dashing suitor, came back to the hometown, after a spell away, only to find her married to his rival, Enos Blanchard.

Other glimpses of elderly neighbors were of interest to me. There was Sarah Blanchard Buxton, the venerable grandmother at the old Buxton place "over the road." I told my grandfather how she looked at me with her snapping bright eyes. He said, "You didn't know, did you, Rita, that she was once the belle of the town?" My mother added, "She was a very popular young lady because of her lively wit."

She was the mother of Howard Buxton, who won some fame as a singer. He went on tour as one of a quartet giving concerts in many places in Maine. He conducted a singing school in Cumberland Center, which my mother attended one winter when I was small, and on Christmas Eve I was allowed to accompany her.

Then I remember Aunt Julia Sweetser, who was our next-door neighbor, at 270 Main Street. She was the widow of Uncle Amasa, who had died about the time I was born. Uncle Amasa always interested me because he had made for my father, as a boy, a big military drum and drumsticks. George and Nell, his son and daughter, were good to us children, and I remember when Nell first took us over to the Mill Brook. She showed us the spot where the Dew Drop Mill used to stand, by a high rock down which fell a rushing waterfall. It was at this old mill that Uncle Amasa had lost a leg, after which he had to stick to his trade as shoemaker. On the way to the Mill Brook we were shown the hollow where had stood the house of Betsy Baker. She it was who was chased by the bear, on a Sunday as she was returning from church.

Along with my father's drum, I prized my violin. It was made by 'Liphe Reed, who was skilled in this craft. My father used to play a game of chess with him now and again. He lived in the old Reed place at 224 Tuttle Road and was a nephew of Eliphalet Greely, the donor of Greely Institute. Incidentally, in that day the Institute was quite a new school, built less than a dozen years before I was born. My father had attended its opening classes as a young man of eighteen.

But in the 1880s I was concerned only with the little red schoolhouse, certainly never to be forgotten, with its double seats and desks, the two stoves for warmth in winter, the teacher's ready bell, and that pail of water with the old familiar dipper shared by all. I always thought it interesting that the water came from "the old oaken bucket, the iron-bound bucket, the moss-covered bucket that hung in the well." It was indeed a real old-timer, that well across the road, probably the same that served the original schoolhouse that also stood across the road in the real old days. I never drank that water, however, after my grandfather remarked one day, "The water in that well drains right down from the graveyard across the road!"

I guess I wasn't a very cooperative pupil in those days. I remember crying on my first day in school, at the age of four, and having to be taken home. Later I remember refusing to let my red silk parasol be used as a toadstool for the school entertainment. I hope I soon became more helpful. Anyway, I enjoyed school and sometimes being allowed to erase the blackboards.

One morning I remember in particular. The teacher let us stand outside in the schoolyard and watch the Joab Black house burn to the

Photo collection of Herman Sweetser

School District No. 3, with teacher, Ezra Knight Sweetser (c. 1893).

ground. It stood on higher land "over the road," and we could see it plainly. It made a great impression on me. That must have been one of the old-time houses, as I have been told that my great-grandmother lived there for a time when quite a young woman.

One of my first teachers in the little school was Ezra Sweetser. He had us sing hymns every morning, which we all did with enthusiasm. He always had us say the Lord's Prayer in the morning, and always made a special prayer for us on Mondays. The scholars all liked him, though they were amused at the way he blinked his eyes in the middle of the prayer. I suspect he was just taking a peek himself to see who was being disorderly. But he was very fond of the children and kind to them on all occasions. One incident I well remember. My little sister Cecil suddenly burst into tears in the midst of the morning. Mr. Sweetser comforted her and asked the trouble. I recall his kindly yet amused smile as her answer came: "Earle Jackson kissed me!"

Well, years go by and times change, but children are always the same. We cherish our memories of early days in Cumberland.

—*Rita Wilson McCloskey*

The Dash—*The Ghost Ship of Casco Bay*

The Porter brothers had been shipbuilders in their native Freeport until "Mr. Madison's War" had disrupted shipping. Now there was no foreign trade, and sloops and schooners engaged in coastwise trade were taken and plundered. Shipbuilding was at a low ebb, for shipping in the Province of Maine had been cut in half. In 1813 the Porters had engaged

Sketch by Alicia Stonebreaker, courtesy of Miriam Stover Thomas

Hermaphrodite brig Dash, *which became known as the "Ghost Ship of Casco Bay."*

Portland Press Herald, *1974*

The brig Dash *above the entrance of W. T. Grant's store at 512 Congress Street, Portland, Maine.*

Master James Brewer to build a 222-ton merchant ship at Porter's Landing in Freeport. It would be surprising, however, if she should dare venture out of the harbor, for fear of looting, so they outfitted her as a privateer with sixteen guns. When she sprung her foremast on her first voyage, this now famous topsail schooner, the *Dash*, was converted to a hermaphrodite brig, which was a two-master, square-rigged forward and schooner-rigged aft. The *Dash* was now the speediest vessel afloat in the Province of Maine. No British vessel could catch her. Indeed, in less than two years cruising from Portland to Bermuda, Port-au-Prince, and North Carolina, the privateer *Dash* had captured fifteen prizes. She was the first privateer to be commissioned by the United States in the War of 1812. In the fireproof vault of the Maine Historical Society are four logbooks of the hermaphrodite brig *Dash* and her commission papers signed by

James Madison. In November 1814 Capt. John Porter in command of the *Dash*, with his crew of sixty men, sailed out of Portland harbor and captured three schooners, one sloop, and three brigs. One member of this crew was Job Bennett of Chebeague Island. Others were two Leighton brothers, Joshua and Robert from West Cumberland.

In January 1815 the *Dash* sailed out of Portland harbor in company with a new privateer, the *Champlain*, and no trace of her captain and crew was ever found. The captain of the *Champlain* said they lost sight of the *Dash* six hours out that first night. A nor'west gale and snow came up and he thinks it drove the *Dash* onto George's Bank, where a strong tide sent her to her grave. But the ghostly brig has been seen again and again, so it is claimed. Capt. David Johnson of Bailey Island saw her sail up Merrucoonegan Sound the very day that he learned of the death of his son. The ghost ship sailed straight up the sound but just before she hit the T-Ledge, she turned and went out past Jaquish Island. Capt. Johnson viewed her with his glass and saw no living man aboard. The parents of Job Bennett and of other men who had been members of the crew have also seen the Ship of Death. John Greenleaf Whittier said of it in his poem "The Dead Ship of Harpswell":

She rounds the headland's bristling pines;
She threads the isle-set bay;
No spur of breeze can speed her on,
Nor ebb of tide delay
Never comes the ship to port,
Howe'er the breeze may be;
Just when she nears the waiting shore
She drifts again to sea.
Old men still walk the Isle of Orr
Who tell her date and name,
Old shipwrights sit in Freeport yards
who hewed her oaken frame.
From Wolf Neck and from Flying Point,
From island and from main [she sails]
In vain for her the lamps are lit
Within thy tower, Seguin.

Have you seen her as she winds her way from island to island? If you have, you had an ancestor lost on the *Dash*. If you have not seen the ghost ship, then look at the stone half-model on the upper facade of the W. T. Grant store at 512 Congress Street, Portland, for there rests the only known reproduction of the *Dash* in existence.

—Excerpt from "Come Hell or High Water," Copyright 1970, used by permission of the author, Miriam Stover

Armistice Day for World War I

In 1910, the local central office of the telephone company was under the management of Lester B. Bragg and his wife, Gertrude Merrill Bragg. An ell was built on their home, now 279 Main Street, formerly the residence of Silas Rideout.

At five o'clock in the morning of November 11, 1918, word came through of the Armistice for World War I. Their young son, Harold, rushed to the Congregational Church across the street to announce the happy event by ringing the church bell. To his surprise, he was joined by an eighty-year-old neighbor, Harriet Humphrey, the daughter of Nicholas Humphrey, who had once run a store in what is now the stable of the church parsonage.

They were joyously ringing the bell, when Ozro Huston, the first selectman, appeared and demanded that they stop that racket. Miss Humphrey, a lady of strong character, said, "Mr. Huston, I rang this bell when Lee surrendered, and this boy and I are going to ring it now—so you might as well go home."

—as told by Harold M. Bragg

Chapter Twenty-Two

Government and Politics as They Developed in Cumberland

By Grace E. Hutchinson

Ancient North Yarmouth was an extensive block of land which began at the seacoast adjoining Falmouth and ran to the Kennebec River. In 1739 Mere Point was set off to Brunswick and in 1741, Small Point to Georgetown. Merriconeag and the adjacent islands became Harpswell in 1758; and Harraseeket, which included the present towns of Freeport and Pownal, was incorporated as a town in 1789.

In the northwest portion of what was left of ancient North Yarmouth in the early 1800s, sizable villages had sprung up around the stage routes which passed through the center of what is now Cumberland. Main Street was laid out by the Massachusetts Court of General Sessions in 1796. The stage route to Lewiston and other inland parts of the territory ran through Shawtown, the western section of the territory.

That these sections had become heavily populated is supported by the fact that new churches were built in these areas. In 1792 the Tuttle Road meetinghouse was erected at the crossroads in the Center, and in September 1793, it was incorporated as the Northwest Congregational Society of North Yarmouth, the third church to be organized in the territory. In 1812 a meetinghouse was built in the Shawtown section; it was known as Union Meeting House and was occupied by various church organizations until in 1826, the present Methodist Society was organized. Although the Foreside church was not built on the Cumberland-Falmouth line until 1831, there were many households built on the coast and along the lower stage route in the early 1800s.

With these centers of population developing rapidly in the northwest section of old North Yarmouth, it is not surprising that the inhabitants should begin to feel inconvenienced at being so far removed from the town offices and the place where town meetings were held. Seeing other sections become separate towns made these inhabitants decide that they, too, should be set off as a new town.

Town records which prosaically set down the votes at town meetings do not include the political issues which very likely helped precipitate the separation; nor do they explain why the name "Cumberland" was chosen for the new town. However, in 1818 the North Yarmouth town meeting warrant included an article asking that the northwestern section be set aside as a separate town for the convenience of its residents. The motion was summarily dismissed, but the urge to become an independent town persisted in the minds of Tuttle Road and Shawtown residents.

As soon as this Massachusetts territory became the State of Maine in 1820, these discontented North Yarmouth residents decided to appeal to the new Legislature for separation. In the spring of 1820 a petition to the Legislature was drawn up and signed by 176 men asking that all lands lying to the westward of a line beginning at the seashore of the dividing line of the farms then occupied by Alexander Barr and Reuben Loring and extending northerly to the bounds of the territory, together with all islands belonging to North Yarmouth except Cousins, Little John's, Lane's, and Great and Little Moses (Mosiers), be set aside as a separate town to be known as Cumberland.

Matters moved slowly through the Legislature even in those days, and it was on January 8, 1821, when a petition signed by nineteen residents was sent to the Legislature, protesting the separation. There were thirty-eight men who were taxed in the territory to be set off who neither signed the petition to be set off nor the one remonstrating against separation. Because most citizens were in favor of separation, an Act of Incorporation for the Town of Cumberland was granted by the

Legislature in 1821. Although North Yarmouth fought vigorously against it, the act of incorporation was approved on March 19, 1821, by William King, Maine's first governor.[1]

The Act of Incorporation spelled out the terms of separation. Among them were included the provisions that all paupers chargeable to the town when the division took effect would be divided one-third to Cumberland and two-thirds to North Yarmouth; Cumberland residents would be expected to perform one-third of the labor on the County Road from New Gloucester to the meetinghouse; Cumberland residents were to pay to North Yarmouth any back taxes which were in arrears; school funds from common lands were to be divided between the towns; the stock of powder, guns, balls, flints, and camp equipage should be divided in proportion to the number of men carried on the rolls of militia in the respective towns; use of the several burial grounds and privileges of obtaining clams and "muscle" mud from the flats in said towns would continue in common for time immemorial; and people living on the dividing line between Cumberland and North Yarmouth would have the right to choose in which of the two towns they wanted to live. The last provision accounts for the irregular boundary line on the northeast side of Greely Road where one house is in Cumberland and the next in North Yarmouth or Yarmouth.

The first town meeting was held on April 9, 1821, at the church, renamed as the Congregational Church of Cumberland at the time of separation. David Prince was moderator; James Prince, town clerk; David Prince, William Buxton, and Beza Blanchard, selectmen and assessors; and Ephraim Sturdivant, treasurer. There were two tax collectors, Ambrose Hamilton for the Islands and Nathaniel Sweetser for the mainland. Other town officers included thirteen surveyors of highways, three fence viewers on the mainland and three on Chebeague Island, sixteen tithing men, nineteen field drivers and hog reaves, a sealer of leather, a pound keeper, and two harbormasters. The new town had a population of 1,368.

Relations between the two towns were strained for the first few years. Disputes of such serious nature arose that they were not settled until the fall of 1823 when a board of referees negotiated a settlement at a meeting held in the third-floor ballroom of the Seth Mitchell tavern.

Future town meetings were held at one or another of the churches in town, alternating from the Center to Shawtown and, when it was completed, to the Foreside church. By 1832 Cumberland residents were ready to build their town house for meetings and elections. The only problem was that they could not agree on its location. Every few weeks there would be another town meeting to reconsider the vote taken at the last meeting. Several locations were proposed, agreed upon, and subsequently changed. More than a year after the first vote to build a town house on May 13, 1833, town records include the vote "that the Nov. 11, 1832 vote for building the town house on Lot 65 be reconsidered and that the committee procure a deed from Isaac Merrill of 15 square rods to set the town house on."

The story passed down from generation to generation is that some of the town fathers grew tired of the indecision as to where the building was to be located. In the middle of the night they hauled in the lumber and set to work framing up the building on the Isaac Merrill property where the present fire station stands. When the sun rose, the framework of the town house was up—and the location of the town house was settled.[2]

The town house was finally built and the first of many town meetings to be held there was on September 9, 1833, for the state election for governor. The hall was also used for social events. The doors of the building opened from Dunn's Alley, the now-extinct road running from behind Dunn's Store on Main Street (the present apartment house) to Tuttle Road by the present fire station. Inside the door was the selectmen's office on the left and a pile of stove wood on the right. A raised platform at the further end of the building supported the speaker's lectern and the ballot box. A removable railing kept voters moving around the perimeter of the building for casting their ballots during elections. For town meetings the floor was covered with a six-inch layer of sawdust for the convenience of tobacco-chewing citizens. Only the men attended town meetings in early days. Small boys watched and listened from perches on the woodpile at the back of the building. Discussions were often hot and sprinkled with personal opinions. One moderator, Frank Merrill, is remembered to have run a pretty good meeting without benefit of Robert's Rules. If someone talked too long or became repetitive, Merrill would say, "You sit down and shut up; give someone else a chance to talk!"[3]

Cumberland continued to be a rural town through the 1800s, with agriculture the leading business. Other local occupations were operating saw mills, lumber mills, gristmills, brickyards, blacksmith shops, or stores where both groceries and hardware were sold. There were also some shipbuilders, sea captains, mariners, and fishermen here.

The most pressing problems brought before town meetings in those days were season to season maintenance of the roads, deciding whether or not businesses were to be allowed to "sell spiritous liquors to be drank in their stores or shops," and support of education. From the very earliest days when $550 was appropriated for schools in 1821 to the present, the major part of Cumberland's tax dollar has been spent for education. Government was a very personal business. If someone had a problem, he called it to the attention of the selectman who was his neighbor. The number of "surveyors of highways" dwindled to a road commissioner for each of the various sections of town—three on the mainland and one on Chebeague. Otherwise few changes in government evolved.

Courtesy of Cumberland Historical Society

Centennial Parade, 1921, included Herman and Phyllis Sweetser on horseback, and Deacon and Mrs. Edward B. Osgood in their carriage. High-wheeled bicycle followed as they passed the Congregational Church.

The town held a gala centennial celebration on July 4, 1921. Many houses and other buildings were professionally decorated with US flags, bunting, and streamers, and telephone poles had two or more small flags high above the lines. Festivities included a ball, Fantastics (talent show), a parade for which the Yarmouth Band played and received in payment $210, a dinner put on by the Ladies' Circle, baseball games, and fireworks. The sum of $235 was deposited in the savings department of the Casco Mercantile Trust Co.—probably to pay for the monument the town authorized the Centennial Committee to erect on the lot directly in front of the Arno S. Chase property commemorating the celebration of the 100th anniversary of the town. This was a native boulder marked with a brass plaque containing the appropriate dates and jokingly called "Barter's Reef" because it was done largely through the efforts of Walter Barter, a member of the Centennial Committee. This rock has since been moved to the park-like triangle at the junction of Main Street and Blanchard Road and has been replaced by the William Merrill monument.[4]

Having celebrated the town's first hundred years, the townspeople apparently turned their attention to the workings of town government and plans for improving the town in the next hundred years. Although government in Cumberland had changed very little, many changes came into being during the next half-century, culminating in 1972 in a vote to adopt a council-manager form of government. After World War I automobiles brought greater mobility to rural townspeople and the radio further expanded their spheres of interest. Citizens began to expect more from their town government than education for their children and suitably maintained roads.

One of the first moves toward a more-sophisticated town government came in 1923 when the town voted to "constitute and appoint a budget committee of eight members."[5] In this year the town also voted to purchase from the Milliken-Tomlinson Co. the stone wharf known as Hamilton's Landing at Chebeague for a town landing. Although these items of business may not seem to be interrelated, the amount of time future budget committees have had to spend considering maintenance, dredging the approaches to the Stone Pier, and providing parking space for people traveling to the mainland from the pier would convince anyone the vote had financial significance for the town as well as social significance for Island residents.

The need for an additional group of representatives to review the proposed town appropriations and try to keep a check on the rising tax rate was felt to be urgent. In 1923 the total tax commitment for the town was $44,322. That sum included $11,215, town schools; $3,211, Greely Institute; $7,707, town highways; $2,955, state highways; $300, the first of three equal payments for the Stone Pier; and $200 for dredging the channel at Hamilton's Wharf to be matched by subscription. Although the commitment seems low by present standards, the tax rate was not. The rate was $31.60 per thousand based on a total valuation of $1,360,200. Fifty years later in 1973 the town's total valuation was $41,040,050; the commitment was $1,162,400, and the tax rate was $28 per thousand.

The budget committee grew in authority and political power until it became a major part of town government. Serving on the town budget committee was considered good training for anyone who aspired to being elected selectman or member of the school board. The 1932 Town Report first printed the report of the budget committee; voters depended so heavily on that report that within a few years the budget committee's recommendation for each money-raising article was printed in the warrant directly beneath the request. In 1945 the budget committee was expanded to twelve members with the notation that one from each section of the town was to be elected yearly for a three-year term.

By the 1950s the power of the budget committee had grown to the extent that town by-laws were amended to put some control over the committee. In addition to recommending such sums of money to be raised or borrowed at the annual town meeting, the committee was required to hold at least one public hearing before February 20 and to post notices for the meeting. The chairman of the committee was to be elected by members on the day of town meeting, and it was required to meet at least five days before a special town meeting. Elected or appointed town officials who handled expenditures of town money were excluded from membership. In 1957 the town voted to elect budget committee members by Australian (secret) ballot with other elected town officials.

Town government had become so complex that selectmen began to doubt the ability of budget committee members to make sensible recommendations on the budget they had been working under all year after only one or two briefing sessions before the annual town meeting. In the 1960s budget committee members themselves recognized their limited understanding of town departments and began a process of becoming more involved with the day-to-day operation of the various departments. They met with town officials during the year and sent a representative to attend selectmen's weekly meetings. In spite of occasional political maneuvers, the committee served the townspeople well as a check on town spending until the town changed its form of government. Cumberland's charter for council-manager government does not provide for a citizen budget committee; members of the council serve on a finance committee to review the budget prior to its presentation to the full council.

Another modern concept initiated in Cumberland in the 1920s was conservation. This town had the first town forest in the State of Maine because of the interest of Ernest A. Rand, who was instrumental in founding the forestry project at Greely Institute of planting coniferous trees on town-owned land at the Drowne Farm and having the area established as the town forest. The forest was to be managed under a program of systematic cutting and the proceeds used to benefit education. Rand was a forester employed by the Oxford Paper Company who served on the board of selectmen from 1932 to 1947. His habit of looking toward the future resulted in many of the programs developed during that period.

The town house was becoming crowded; not only was the selectmen's office cramped, but the meeting hall just wasn't big enough for town meetings. In 1928 the annual town meeting was held in Red Men's Hall. By 1930 there was a proposal to purchase Red Men's Hall for a town hall and convert the meeting room of the old town house to a town garage for fire engines and road equipment. The budget committee did not recommend its purchase, and the voters followed the recommendation of the committee. However, the proposal was only postponed by this vote. In 1936, in spite of the negative recommendation of the budget committee, the town voted to purchase the building from Sawga Tribe #20 of Red Men for $3,500. The purchase was also opposed by Rand, who embarrassed his family by grumbling in open town meeting, "All right! You've got the goddamned thing. What are you going to do with it?"[6]

The town office, except for the vault, was moved to a second-floor room of Red Men's Hall, and town meetings were held in the hall until 1947, when Gyger Gymnasium became the location for town meetings. The new office did nothing, however, to relieve the burden of clerical work required for handling town business by the three selectmen. The 1947 Town Report prepared by Glendon B. Doane, Philip A. Seabury, and Sumner S. Lowe included a plea for authorizing selectmen to establish a modern system of accounting, to purchase necessary filing and office equipment, and to hire a clerk to do the office work. The report said, "Selectmen are elected on the basis of their judgment and integrity, and not on their ability to do clerical work . . . Good men would be attracted to the job if the clerical work were eliminated."[7] These selectmen pointed out that as assessors they were unable to do their work competently unless something was done to improve the records pertaining to description and valuation of properties. They urged the town to acquire assessing maps where each lot is plotted on a map having a scale of 250 feet to the inch. The town authorized clerical help for the selectmen, but this did not solve the problem.

In 1949 the number of selectmen was increased from three to five; a selectman was to be elected as representative from each of the town's four geographical districts and one man was to represent the town at large. To relieve selectmen from clerical work and to keep the town office open five days a week, voters agreed to appropriate $1,000 for a clerk in the town office. This clerk would also be elected as town clerk and town treasurer and would work regular hours in the town office; fees from his clerk position and a $500 stipend for work as treasurer would fill out his salary.

Herbert S. Foster was elected to this position in March 1949. A few years later he added the job of tax collector to his other duties. He was without opposition for election to these offices until 1973, when the new council-manager form of government was instituted. The first Saturday in March, which would have been town meeting day, was proclaimed as "Herb Foster Day," and townspeople honored him at a reception and presented him with tickets for a trip to Hawaii in appreciation for his many years of service.

Photograph by Wendall White, 1961, courtesy of Lena G. Foster

Herbert S. Foster.

In 1951 the town voted to sell Red Men's Hall back to the Red Men for one dollar and appropriated $500 to repair the Cumberland Center redbrick school building beside the hall for a town office building. On October first of that year the town office was moved into the renovated brick building, which at that time provided ample space for all town officers and their respective accumulated records. The new quarters also proved to be more accessible for the public and provided greater comfort for town officials with respect to heat, lights, and general maintenance. A fire in the new town office building on December 26, 1955, prompted renovations for the town office. Since it was necessary to redecorate, town officials were authorized by vote at the March 1956 town meeting to spend $7,500 to have an addition built on the back of the town office. A fireproof vault, two flush toilets, and a furnace room were added. Until that time the only vault was in the old town house, then being used as the town garage; it was overcrowded, damp, and not easily accessible.

Long-range planning is another concept that Cumberland began to develop early. This town had grown little in population since its separation from North Yarmouth until the 1940s. At that time agricultural land had diminished in value, but easily accessible land bordering highways was increasing in value for building lots. In the decade from 1940 to 1950 the population in Cumberland increased from 1,491 to 2,030, and had jumped to 2,765 by 1960. During those twenty years more than three hundred new dwellings were recorded; summer cottages in Wildwood Park and on Forest Lake were being converted to year-round homes. Witnessing the horde of new settlers coming to their little town, townspeople started to look for ways "to preserve the rural character of the town." In March 1948, the town elected a zoning committee in lieu of a planning board, and charged it with writing a zoning ordinance. Preparation of a town map was also in progress. For the next few years various building codes and zone changes were considered and adopted in hopes of controlling new housing construction. The first housing development, Farwell Avenue, had been started in 1947 with construction of the new post office.

A true planning board appointed by selectmen in accordance with state statutes was authorized in 1955, along with membership in the Regional Planning Commission and appropriation of dues of $500. First members of the planning board were Henry Steinfeld, chairman, Lenville L. Hawkes, Wayne E. Ball, Silas K. Baker, and Harlan H. Sweetser, a county engineer who seemed to know the soil structure of every section of town and who served the town well on the board for many years. In 1957 the town voted to adopt a comprehensive planning program to be conducted by the Regional Planning Commission, financed in part by the federal government. The town appropriated $1,250 the first year and $500 the next year for its share in this planning venture, which surveyed the character of the town, made projections for future growth, and made recommendations for future development of the town. By 1959 the official map of the town, the subdivision ordinance, a revised zoning ordinance, a building code, and a trailer ordinance which prohibited maintaining house trailers outside trailer parks, were all ready for adoption by the town. Although some of the townspeople did not take too kindly to the idea that an ordinance could tell them what they could or could not do with their land, all proposals were approved by the voters.

In 1961 the second part of the Federal 701 Comprehensive Plan, the recommendations for future development, was submitted to selectmen. The plan called for a ten-year development program which would cost more than a million dollars in capital improvements. School construction would include a twelve-room high school to be used as an elementary school until future additions to the elementary schools were completed. Other proposals were to establish a new town center near the school, with a new town road to be built along the old railroad bed from Greely Road across Tuttle Road to Lower Main Street connecting to Winn Road; building a new central fire station by 1970, a Foreside fire station by 1968, and having a full-time professional fire department by the '70s; developing the police department in such a manner that the proposed 1970 police budget would be $15,500

Photograph by Daniel Dow, 1975

Town Office (1951–1975), once School District No. 3.

instead of the current $600 appropriation in 1961; and developing Chandler's Cove on Chebeague for a public landing, utilizing land already under tax lien there. The report estimated that the tax rate would increase from $35 per thousand to $45 per thousand in the next five years.

Local reaction to the report was dismay. Henry Steinfeld, former planning board chairman who was serving in 1961 as chairman of the selectmen, said, "That survey is a planners' pipe dream. As far as I am concerned, it can stay right where it is—buried. Reaction has been horrible because of taxes. Naturally we would do it all if we had the money, but we are still a little town of 2,400. We can't even see when these things are going to be done; so therefore we don't see any need for any great upsurge in taxes."[8]

Robert M. Ewing, Regional Planning Commission planner who did most of the work on Cumberland's Comprehensive Plan, said, "So far as I know, Cumberland is the only town in the State of Maine which has had this sort of developmental study made. Other towns' taxes will go up too; that is inescapable."[9]

And James H. Palmer, Cumberland planning board member, characteristically said, "No comment!" Palmer was appointed to the planning board in 1958 and continued to serve locally and regionally until 1970. He came to represent the planning board in the minds of the townspeople. His eyes looked far into the future and his proposals usually received heated opposition from townspeople who kept their attention on the present. Many of his more radical projections proved to be on the conservative side as time proved him to have been right. He never betrayed his principles to curry public favor, but he preferred not to be quoted. He often cautioned the news correspondent that his words were "Off the record," and then a few minutes later would add, "And this is *strictly* off the record!"

Some of the proposals in the comprehensive survey were implemented. The high school was built. The trailer ordinance was tested in court and proved to be valid. The town actually voted to "set aside and designate town lots 5 and 6 as shown on the map of Chebeague Island properties at Chandler's Cove as a town beach for use of its residents."[10] Although it is shown as town property on the official town map, through some mistake the property owner was allowed to repossess his land and the town owns no beach on Chandler's Cove.

Through the years the planning board has written some excellent ordinances. Unless gravel pit owners had been required to operate according to requirements of the Board of Appeals as to restoring the land to a grade and reseeding it after removal of gravel, West Cumberland might well have become a gaping hole. That planners in 1975 are still working to "preserve the rural character of the town" testifies to the success of early planners.

The police department did grow according to the comprehensive plan forecast; in fact, the 1970 police budget was $26,500. The Cumberland Police Department was first organized in 1954 with Earle A. Woodbury as part-time officer and chief. In 1964 Richard J. C. Andersen was elected police chief; the following year he requested $5,900 for providing twenty-four-hour on-call service to the townspeople. Voters approved his budget proposal against the recommendation of the budget committee. Andersen developed his department in spite of attempts by the budget committee and selectmen to cut down on police costs, as he knew the people were behind his attempts to provide better police protection. By 1972 when the form of government changed, Andersen had a second full-time officer, twelve special officers who worked relief shifts and special assignments, two town-owned cruisers, and a budget of $50,668. List of Police Chiefs in Appendix **XX**.

The fire department also built its two stations according to the proposed plan, but the area station was located in West Cumberland instead of Cumberland Foreside. Before the 1964 town meeting Fire Chief Harold M. Bragg worked for political support for building a West Cumberland fire station because the majority of his volunteer firemen available during the day lived there. Fixing up the old station on Blackstrap Road would be "like fixing up old shoes after you have outgrown them," Bragg said. The budget committee and town officials opposed the West Cumberland construction because they wanted to cut out all but the most necessary expenditures to hold down the tax rate, and because they felt a central station would soon be needed. The town was so evenly split on the issue that the moderator could not tell the result of the vote by show of hands. Count of the written ballot showed a one-vote majority for construction of the West Cumberland station at a cost of $13,500.

The new central station with quarters for police and fire departments was harder to come by. The town voted against construction three times, but by 1969 the old fire station was found unsafe by the state fire inspector. The new fire horn had to be mounted on the end of the building because the center of the roof would not support it. An engineering firm said the building could be repaired, but it would cost as much as the first payment on a new station. On March 10, 1969, voters approved a $10,000 appropriation and authorized borrowing $75,000 for construction of a new four-bay fire station to replace the old station built for a town house 127 years before. The thrifty town officials moved the old building to the site of the town garage and dump and used it for a storage building. Groundwork has been established to add to or build new, a central fire station.

The history of the school system is told elsewhere in this book (see Chapter 13); however, no chapter on town government would be complete without some discussion of the formation of a School Administrative District, which tore the town apart politically for nearly ten years.

With the passage of the Sinclair Act in Legislature towns joined in school administrative districts received more financial aid than those towns operating their school systems independently. A study committee of Cumberland and North Yarmouth residents began looking into the question of district formation in 1958. Discussions with various towns continued until 1960, when it was decided that a three-town district of Cumberland, North Yarmouth, and Pownal would be logical. These towns were already sending their high school students to Cumberland on a tuition basis. Because the three towns would not have 300 high school students, the towns had to get special permission from the Legislature to authorize the district. Authorization was given, and the three towns were to vote on district formation on November 8, 1962. School officials who carried the proposal to the voters were Superintendent Vaughn A. Lacombe, Frederick M. Logan, Clifton R. Turner, and William H. Chandler; leading the opposition were Selectman Robert G. Dillenback, James H. Palmer, and Philip J. Murdock, both members of the planning board.

Proponents argued that the small towns would bring additional state funds to the district because the subsidy was based on the valuation of member towns; as a further incentive proponents stressed the fact that the State would pay 32 percent of construction costs for towns in districts. Cumberland was facing construction of school buildings whether or not it joined a district. Opponents claimed that Cumberland, as the largest town, would pay the lion's share of the district's costs. Furthermore, because Cumberland was growing at a rate faster than the other towns, its proportionate share would also increase. The planning board issued a four-page report opposing district formation, which included school enrollment projection figures so much higher than those issued in projections by the school committee that Palmer was ridiculed. (The planning board projections proved to be under the actual enrollment figures; Cumberland's population doubled between 1950 and 1970—2,030 to 4,096.) Letters to the editor in the newspaper kept the issue hot. Voting day in the three towns finally arrived. North Yarmouth and Pownal approved district formation by large majorities, but Cumberland voted 396 to 360 against joining the district—killing the proposal for the time being.

Because the vote was so close, school officials from the three towns decided to try again. North Yarmouth and Pownal had already approved the question, so those towns decided to wait until Cumberland voted on May 10, 1963, before going to the expense of having another vote. In Cumberland ranks were solidly formed on both sides of the issue once more. This time one of the most vocal opponents was Leroy Hill, selectman from Chebeague Island. At a public hearing on Chebeague when town officials went to the Island to explain the issue, Hill said he was surprised to see "the battery of people Cumberland had sent down to brainwash the Islanders. If Cumberland can't run its own town affairs it deserves to go bankrupt. Chebeague opposition defeated the district when it came to a vote in November. I have been accused of influencing votes in the past when I haven't done so, but I intend to in the future."[11]

On the night of May 10 town clerk Herbert Foster announced that a double-check of the vote showed 500 for approval and 494 against; the decisive margin was provided by Chebeague Islanders who favored the plan 73 to 62, while the mainland rejected it, 432 to 427.

The next morning Hill, who had not yet sent the ballots to the mainland, made an unofficial recount and found that the Island vote was 70 to 65, thereby creating a tie vote—497 to 497. A recount made by the State on June 3, 1963, resulted in another tie vote; 491 to 491 was the official count. District formation was defeated a second time. More people voted than ever before in Cumberland, 55 percent of the town's 1,800 registered voters. The following year a proposal was made for a two-town district, Cumberland and North Yarmouth; special legislative approval was obtained and the vote on January 14, 1966, was 283 to 108 in favor of membership in a school administrative district. Then, after nearly ten years of fighting to become a school administrative district, twenty-five members of the District Building Committee in a unanimous vote declared that it should NEVER be referred to as School Administrative District 51, but instead, the Cumberland-North Yarmouth School System, in order to avoid being called in headlines SAD 51.

With all the problems arising from the rapid growth of the town during the 1940s and 1950s, selectmen began to realize they did not have time to conduct the town business as well as it should have been done and earn a living at the same time. In the late 1940s there was an article in the warrant asking that a committee be appointed to study the town manager form of government. However, with the addition of two selectmen to the board and a full-time clerk in the town office, pressure on town officials was relieved to the point that little thought was given to changing the town's form of government until the 1960s.

The 1960 Town Report included this message from Selectmen William J. Garsoe, Robert G. Dillenback, Henry Steinfeld, Leroy H. Hill, and Earle A. Woodbury. "The town officers' account is overdrawn this year. The biggest part of the overdraft is due to the fact that Selectmen drew more pay than during the previous year. This circumstance reflects the increasing demands that town government is placing on the individuals who serve it . . . There is the feeling in some quarters that it is now time to take a look at the structure and functioning of our town government."[12]

A few years later the town voted to appoint a committee to study the town manager form of government. Members were Harold M. Bragg, chairman; Maynard W. Robinson, Gordon E. Robie, Raymond J. Koshliek, and William Garsoe. The committee recognized the fact that the town had changed from an agricultural town to a commuter community with the average householder who earned his living elsewhere showing characteristic lack of interest in and knowledge of town affairs.

> Public apathy is shown by the lack of attendance at budget meetings and town meetings and by the lack of informed debate on the part of the few who do attend. Only when some highly controversial proposal is made do we see any widespread interest in town affairs, and much of this well-intentioned interest is confused because of a lack of background information against which to judge the claims and counterclaims of opposing factions . . . The fact that each selectman is primarily concerned with earning his own livelihood, coupled with the increasing complexity in operations of the various departments of government, has gradually isolated the selectman to the point where he can no longer be an effective force in the direction of these activities. . . All our town officials have been practicing economy while achieving progress in the best interests of the Town. If the change were to burst on us suddenly, it would be easy to demonstrate the necessity for changes in our government. Rather, the changes will occur gradually and it

> will be years before we become aware of the price we have paid in excessive costs and reduced efficiency by not instituting a businesslike administration of town affairs.[13]

The committee did not recommend that selectmen hire a manager and put him to work immediately, lest inserting a manager into the current system would merely increase costs and confusion. The committee did recommend that further study be given to developing a charter for a council-manager form of government for the town.

The following year that committee (with Joseph J. Jordan and David G. Stanley replacing Bragg and Hill as members) reported that further study reinforced their opinion that the council-manager form of government was best suited for Cumberland. In March 1965, town meeting voters approved appointment of a charter committee and appropriated $500 to cover the cost of legal fees that might be necessary in drawing up and presenting the charter, and for printing copies of the charter for distribution. Selectmen appointed the following to this committee: Richard F. Blanchard, Mrs. Rita V. Skillin, David P. Snow, Archibald M. Dodge, Maynard W. Robinson, Chauncey L. Somes, and Robinson Verrill. This group of citizens drew up a fine charter which transferred the powers of the traditional town meeting to a council of seven members to be elected at large from the town; the council would hire a professional town manager. Rights of the citizens would be protected by initiative and referendum procedures. The committee recommended that the proposed charter be accepted by the town in the March 1966 town meeting, and that a bill for the enactment of the charter be introduced at the regular session of the 103rd Legislature in 1967, as was required by law. If enacted by the Legislature, the proposal would still have to be submitted to town voters for adoption.

The charter was approved at the March town meeting by a vote of 84 to 66, although there was some discontent because town meetings were to be abolished, and from Chebeague residents who wanted area representation. The charter was enacted by Legislature and submitted to the townspeople for enactment by a referendum vote on November 7, 1967. The charter was rejected 423 to 358. This was another instance when strong opposition on Chebeague, because of their lack of guaranteed representation on the council, decided a question which was controversial on the mainland. The Island vote was 90 to 22 against the charter, whereas the mainland approved making the change by a 336 to 333 majority.

It was fortunate for the town that its affairs were being administered during this time by some of its most able town officials. Robert C. Robinson, an attorney, and Robert G. Dillenback, a business executive with considerable knowledge of building construction and engineering, were adept at reshaping town government within the framework available. Selectmen got more control over town departments with appointment of department heads. Other issues of major importance to the future of the town demanded their supervision; the most important were the merger of Cumberland Water District with Portland Water District, getting the town to appropriate funds for a Cumberland Sewer Survey to be made by the E. C. Jordan Engineering Company, and the subsequent merger with the Portland Water District's Regional Sewer Plan.

In 1971 another committee was appointed to look into establishing a council-manager form of government. This committee—Harold M. Bragg, Ottie T. McCullum Jr., Louis B. Dennett, Norman Fortin, and Conrad Bernier—conceded that a manager would be desirable, but because they could find no substantial economic savings for the town, voted four to one against recommending adoption of the council-manager form of government at that time.

The negative report at the 1972 town meeting brought out the League of Women Voters to champion the cause of council-manager government. The Cumberland Unit LWV issued a statement to the selectmen criticizing the five-member manager-study committee for deciding the issue without holding any public meetings and for basing its report solely on economic considerations. They asked town officials to establish another charter committee.

Procedures for changing the town's form of government had changed between 1967 and 1972. Under the Legislature's new policy of allowing "Home Rule," towns no longer had to submit their proposed charters to the Legislature. However, the charter committee had to be elected rather than appointed.

Selectman chairman Harland Storey told Mrs. Helen Loose, who was spokesman for the League, that selectmen were ready to look into the council-manager form of government. Conrad Bernier, new planning board chairman who had been the dissenting vote on the last manager-study committee, recommended that a true charter commission should be elected according to state law, because the question had been researched enough. To give townspeople time to decide to run for election to the charter commission, the election was scheduled for June 19, the State Primary Election. The vote was nearly two to one in favor of establishing a charter commission, 767–397; elected to the commission were Richard F. Blanchard, Robert C. Robinson, David P. Snow, Richard J. C. Andersen, John E. Mitchell, and Mrs. Joan O'Toole. According to the law selectmen appointed three members: Gordon Evans and Milton Tibbetts, who had been candidates for the commission and Louis B. Dennett to represent Chebeague Island.

Selectmen had received no report from the commission; they called the commission together in October and asked them to get the charter before the people by the end of the year because they could no longer handle the business of the growing town efficiently. These selectmen were Harland E. Storey, Earle E. Doughty, Earle A. Woodbury, David R. Higgins, and Mrs. Mary Louise Smith, Cumberland's first woman selectman. They told the commission they would be forced to hire a manager under the selectmen form of government if the charter were not ready for adoption.

The charter commission was unanimous in endorsing the concept of council-manager government and had completed the first draft of a proposed charter, which differed from the first only in that area representation would be authorized. There would be one council member elected from each of the four districts of town, and three council members elected to represent the town at large. Public hearings were scheduled and December 13 set as the date for voting on acceptance of the charter and December 28, the date for election of the council members.

Selectmen and the charter commission gave their full attention to getting the proposed charter before the people. At the hearings there were complaints that town officials were trying to "ram this down the throats of the voters in less than a month," but officials responded that the concept had been before the people for the past ten years, and had been thoroughly discussed many times in the past. The new charter avoided the pitfall of failing to provide area representation which had caused the earlier charter to be rejected. The charter spelled out the fact that the council would have all powers formerly vested in the people at town meetings; there was no compromise by having a public vote on the budget or any proposed large expenditures. The charter provided for a strong manager and a strong council; the people would have the opportunity to overrule actions of the council by petitioning for a referendum vote within twenty days following an unpopular vote. The charter also spelled out procedures for the people to initiate action on a subject they petitioned the council to consider. The vote was 418–365 in favor of adopting council-manager government for Cumberland. Chebeague Island still opposed the action by a 74–41 majority against the change.

Strong public interest in the new form of government was evidenced by the fact that seventeen residents filed nomination papers for election to the council. Citizens had a wide choice in candidates who had experience in many fields as lawyers, bankers, business executives, dentists, housewives, schoolteachers, truck drivers, grocers, or farmers. Many candidates had had former experience in town government. From the seventeen candidates voters chose three immediate past selectmen: Storey, Higgins, and Mrs. Smith; one former selectman and former town manager in another town, Richard F. Blanchard; two immediate past budget committee members: Dr. Kenneth M. Partyka and Richard Walker; and Kenneth Hamilton, Chebeague schoolteacher. Higgins was elected by the council as its first chairman, and Walker, vice chairman.

The council named former selectman Earle A. Woodbury to the position of acting town manager. Woodbury had served as selectman, overseer of the poor, and assessor for more than twenty years, and had no desire to be a town manager any longer than it took the council to find a suitable man to employ as Cumberland's first manager.

From fifty-eight applicants the council hired Jared S. A. Clark, municipal administrator for the borough of Lincoln Park, New Jersey, as the town's first manager. Clark was young, personable, intelligent, and extremely expert in the role of administrator. In his first year as manager he introduced a new budget format and accounting system, reorganized the police department, and with a full-time assessor and building inspector, began to build coordination among the town's inspection services. Under his leadership the transition from selectmen to a council-manager form of government moved very smoothly, and seems strong and likely to endure.

Town managers since 1975 have been Jared Clarke, Robert Benson, and William Shane.

Endnotes

1. Lists of the petitioners may be found in *Town Register, Cumberland, North Yarmouth, 1904*.
2. Harold M. Bragg, interview.
3. Ibid.
4. *Cumberland Town Report*, 1921, p. 66. Account of the Cumberland Centennial Committee; Mrs. Bessie Burnell, chairman; Mrs. Mary Brackett, Mrs. Gertrude Brewer, Miss Helen Lewis, Walter H. Barter, Henry W. Bowen, Urban E. Carter, and Charles E. Lewis.
5. *Cumberland Town Report*, 1922.
6. Elizabeth Rand Surgi, interview.
7. *Cumberland Town Report*, 1947, pp. 12–13.
8. *Portland Press Herald*, April 24, 1961.
9. Ibid.
10. *Cumberland Town Report*, 1960.
11. Personal notes taken as news correspondent.
12. *Cumberland Town Report*, 1960, p. 8.
13. *Cumberland Town Report*, 1963, p. 41.

Bibliography

Abbott, John S. C. *The History of Maine*. Portland: Russell Press, 1875.

Hutchinson, Grace E. Notes taken as news correspondent for Gannett Newspapers since 1963.

Mitchell, Russell, and Strout. *The Cumberland-North Yarmouth Register 1904*. Brunswick, Maine: H. E. Mitchell Publishing Co., 1904.

Official Town Records. Cumberland Town Office, 1821–1975.

Rowe, William H. *Ancient North Yarmouth*. Yarmouth, ME: Southworth-Anthoensen, 1937.

Sweetser, Mary E. *History of the Town of Cumberland*. Printed for the Centennial Celebration, 1921.

Chapter Twenty-Three

Cumberland Up to 2009

By Mary Louise Smith
Updated 2009 by Carolyn Small

The first year of the council-manager form of government was a thrill to all involved. Needless to say, many of the old-time residents of Cumberland who had voted against the change sat back to see "What that new manager from out-of-state, and the new council would do to our town." Actually, they moved very slowly. The new manager, Jared S. A. Clark, spent many hours acquainting himself with the people of the town as well as the problems.

Photograph by Patriquin, 1975
Town Manager Jared S. A. Clark.

Under the new charter all boards had to be set up. The council introduced an appointments committee within the council which interviewed all possible candidates, choosing the most qualified, in turn recommending their choice to the entire council for approval.

This system worked very well, and the many committees in the town had well-qualified and dedicated members.

One of the first projects of the new form of government was to continue a project set up by the last board of selectmen. This was a pressing need for a new town garage. A committee had been appointed and had spent many long hours investigating all phases of this project. This committee had much foresight, with thought for the future growth of the town. Located on Drowne Road, near the landfill operation, it was officially opened in March of 1974.

The reorganized Cumberland Police Department has grown to an eleven-man force with a full-time secretary. With two police cruisers and a police boat, the residents of Cumberland are aware that their town is well protected. The police department has gained the respect of law enforcement officers throughout the state. The Cumberland reserve officers are a valuable, well-trained group of men who capably assist the full-time department.

The seven-member planning board has worked diligently with the council for three years on a new zoning ordinance. The purpose of this ordinance, made as part of a comprehensive plan for the development of the town, is to encourage the most appropriate use of land throughout the town; to promote traffic safety; to provide safety from fire and other elements; to provide adequate light and air; to prevent overcrowding of real estate; to promote a wholesome home environment; to prevent housing development in unsanitary areas; to provide a street system; to promote the coordinated development of undeveloped areas; to encourage the formation of community units; and to provide an allotment of land area in new developments sufficient for all public services.[1] The ordinance was passed in July of 1975 after many public hearings.

Besides the zoning ordinance, the planning board has worked on such problems as shoreline zoning, new street construction, and many development areas. The members are to be commended for their many hours of dedication to the welfare of their town.

Another issue inherited from the selectmen, still of prime concern to the council, is the necessity of a sewer system on the Foreside and in parts of Cumberland Center. Some of these areas have been overly developed and the septic systems had been a constant problem. Some of the newer streets with small lots were in trouble. A sewer plan had been completed by E. C. Jordan, and the Town of Cumberland was placed on a priority list at the state level. The year 1984 saw the completion of the construction phase of the sewer system. Due to new state environmental laws, the Wildwood area, which has a septic system opening into Casco Bay, was threatened with no sewerage, or a new system which was not economically possible. Once again, this work could not have been accomplished without the valuable help of a special sewer study committee.

With the newly appointed full-time assessor the tax records of the town became better organized. The building inspector, the plumbing inspector, and the electrical inspector are available during regular hours at the Town Office. The Cumberland Farmers Club and other properties within the town were found to have areas that could add to our tax revenue.

Surprisingly enough, the area most opposed to the council-manager form of government derived many benefits. Mr. Clark visited Chebeague Island, and in no time realized the Island and its problems were different from those of the mainland. Transportation to and from the island posed no problem, but the parking situation at Cousins Island in Yarmouth suddenly became a very hot issue. The residents of Cousins Island wanted a halt to the parking. The Blanchard parking lot at Cousins was restricted to only enough parking places for year-round residents. The towns of Cumberland and Yarmouth formed a committee to work out this problem. While these meetings were going on, the Chebeague Island Transportation Company was able to rent the old outdoor theater area in Yarmouth to provide temporary parking for the summer residents. A small bus transported the many people and their belongings to the boat at Cousins. The issue was not easily resolved. Bills were entered into the 106th and 107th Legislature by the Town of Cumberland. Both times they were withdrawn with promises from Yarmouth to resolve the problem. This has not been done, and summer residents continue to be transported to meet the boat. Finally, a parking lot was built on a parcel of land owned by the State of Maine. It is located on Route One, just at the Cumberland-Yarmouth town line. It is hoped that the day may come when the people from Chebeague may meet their boat on the shores of their own town. Chebeague now has a mini town office. The residents can meet the town manager at this office to discuss any problem they may have. At various times of the year the town clerk goes to the Island to be available to them, a system much better than having to come to the mainland to pay taxes, obtain dog licenses, and excise taxes. Fire Chief Daniel Small meets with the Island firefighters at their monthly meeting. True, the islanders are a removed part of the town, but the new form of government has shortened the gap. Police service on the Island has improved, with a full-time officer in residence during the busy summer months. The Island is actively represented on the planning board and the recreation committee.

In the fall of 1973 the council voted to have the town manager investigate the possibility of purchasing Val Halla Country Club. The club was for sale and the council felt the area would serve better as an open-space recreation area for the town rather than have it become a large housing development. The town would apply for federal subsidy, have open space planned for the townspeople, and hopefully have an income that would support the operation. Hearings were held, plans were developed, and the project was accepted by the state for federal funding. In the spring of 1974 the town council made a formal offer to purchase the club. Some residents of the town objected to the council making a decision on their own involving so much of the taxpayers' money. Thanks to the new charter those people were able to petition the council to have a referendum vote. In January of 1975 the townspeople voted two to one to support the council's decision to purchase the club. The town changed the name to the Cumberland Golf and Recreation Center, and hired a golf pro and added double tennis courts to the recreation facility. The name has changed once again to Val Halla Golf and Recreation Center. The recreation committee acts as advisors to the manager and council. A part-time recreational director has been hired by the manager and helps manage the club as well as the year-round swim program, made possible through a contract with MSAD 51. An active summer recreational program, combined with the winter recreation program which has been in effect for many years, rounds out the needs of all age groups in the town.

In 1974 the town council voted to repurchase Red Men's Hall for the sum of $1.00, and other considerations. Due to the added full-time bookkeeper, the assessor, town clerk, two secretaries, and the town manager, the town office was bulging at the seams. Rather than build a new municipal building, it was decided the central location of Red Men's Hall was most desirable. In 1975, after twenty-four years, the town office

Courtesy of Cumberland Historical Society

The new Cumberland Town Hall.

returned to the place it had been before. Income was derived from the lower level of the building, which was leased as offices of MSAD 51. The much-needed space allowed the employees of the town to work under comfortable conditions, with conference rooms and a council chamber where the council and other boards hold public hearings. Elections were held in this building, eliminating using Gyger Gymnasium where classes had to be rescheduled. The renovated building, after many years of disrepair, added beauty to the Center. The little brick schoolhouse, used for twenty-four years as the town office, housed the Cumberland Police Department. Formerly this department was in one room at the Cumberland Fire Station. The schoolhouse now belongs to the Cumberland Historical Society. The town office moved once again after renovating the vacated school on Drowne Road. It occupied that building from 1988–1998. Now, at last, Cumberland has a town office that was built specifically for that purpose, opening its doors for business on March 2, 1998. This state-of-the-art structure is located at 290 Tuttle Road.

The loss of many elm trees throughout the town made the council aware of the need to plant trees for the future. Many varieties have replaced the elms, and new streets have been planted with shade trees. As new streets are developed, more trees will be planted.

The Conservation Commission became aware of the need to evaluate the open space in the entire town, along with town-owned property. Since

Patriquin photo, 1975

Town Council, back l–r: Kenneth H. Hamilton, David R. Higgins, Harland E. Storey, Richard Walker. Front l–r: Richard F. Blanchard, Mary Louise Smith, Dr. Kenneth M. Partyka.

word-of-mouth knowledge of ownership in today's world is no longer acceptable, all so-called town-owned property has to be proven. The Ford Foundation awarded the commission a $750 grant to assist in title searches.

The council could not accomplish the many things it has without the help of the devoted people who serve on the many boards and committees. Besides the seven-member council, there are sixty-two men and women serving the Town of Cumberland in many capacities. These people work without pay for the betterment of their town. They have been well chosen, and the council and manager would not have been able to accomplish so much without them. These people spend many hours planning Memorial Day parades, managing trust funds, devising a town health code, studying shellfish conservation, planning for town communications, protecting the citizens through Civil Defense, as well as serving on the board of adjustment and appeals and the board of assessment and review.

With a population of over 7,000 in the Town of Cumberland, the needs of the citizens have increased with the population. Town government has strived to make the citizens proud to live in the town. People of all walks of life live in this suburban community, with very few making their livelihood within the area. As people go to their jobs in surrounding towns and cities, they are confident that they leave well-protected homes, and that they will be able to return home even in the worst storms of the winter months, thanks to the efficient work of the town and state highway departments.

All government costs money. The Town of Cumberland strives to keep the tax dollar within the means of the taxpayers. Eighty-two percent of the taxpayers' dollar supports the schools in the town, leaving 18 percent to be spent on other services. The future of the town is in maintaining and improving the public services, as its forefathers have done.

The selectman form of government served the town for a great many years. It did a fine job; it built the town to what it is today. But the need for a full-time manager was long overdue. Selectmen could no longer on a part-time basis accomplish the many needs of the citizens. Having three former selectmen on the council helped the transition period run smoothly, and all three have served as chairmen of the council. In 1973 David Higgins served as chairman, 1974, Mary Louise Smith, followed by Harland Storey in 1975. These people with the remaining members of the council have served the town well.

Time does not erase the memory of the days when one walked into the town office to ask the well-known town clerk, Herb Foster, for assistance.

Courtesy of Dan Dow

Main Street from Prince Memorial Library.

He is a part of the history of the town. Now, as one walks into the new town office, one wonders how Herb did the many things that he did.

Town management is a business in this modern world. Cumberland has a business to be proud of. The office is open to all citizens. It is their office; they must use it. It is their obligation to the future. Apathy in one's town government should not exist.

The future goals for the town with its new zoning plans is simple: to maintain what we have; to have well-planned growth with the aesthetic beauty that was a part of Cumberland always; to have each and every citizen of Cumberland—young and old—retain the spirit given to us by our forefathers to pass on to future generations.

Just a little country town,
No resort and no renown,
Nothing great and nothing grand,
Cumberland.
All its well-remembered ways,
Traversed from our childhood days,
Dearer far than cities grand,
Cumberland.
Home is more than house can be
Broader than a family;
Native town long may it stand,
Cumberland.

—*Nellie L. Sweetser, written for the Cumberland Centennial Celebration,* 1921

In July 2007, Chebeague Island was officially declared a town in its own right, having seceded from the Town of Cumberland.

Sources:

1. Zoning Ordinance; Cumberland, Maine 1975, p. 1.

Chapter Twenty-Four

A History of Wildwood Park

By Cumberland Historical Society

From an illustrated pamphlet published in 1913 by the Concord Realty Co. of Portland, Maine, the brand-new Wildwood Park Beach is described as a "tract of about 50 acres covered with fragrant sweet-smelling pine trees extending from the newly built state Foreside Road down to the smooth sandy beach at the water's edge." It also points out the shore park, the tennis courts, rustic summer houses, a reserve with a gazebo, the ravine, the bathhouses, and a 600-foot-long dock providing opportunities for fishing and boating. There were streets, electric lights, and telephones installed, as well as sewer and water systems, and the ability to reach the area from Portland by trolley or auto "in about 30 minutes."

Today the Foreside Road (Route 88), park, reserve, tennis courts, sandy beach, and utilities remain. The rustic summer houses have, for the most part, been converted to permanent homes, the bathhouses and gazebo on the reserve are gone, the trolley no longer exists, and the 600-foot dock has disappeared. The ravine, though still there, is filled in with bushes.

This property was purchased in 1909 from Sumner Sturdivant, son of Captain Ephraim Sturdivant, a veteran of the War of 1812, and the person designated to give the Town of Cumberland its name when it seceded from North Yarmouth in 1821. Captain Sturdivant died in

1868, and Sumner inherited the Wildwood property, which he sold in 1909 to Herman Rausch and Concord Realty. The first house was built by Mr. Rausch at 21 Pine Lane. Water was supplied to the first houses by a natural spring in the park. Later, sewer and water was provided.

The Sturdivant family had used this area for family outings, and Mr. Rausch continued the practice of outings after he developed it. The Wildwood Inn and Teahouse, later shortened to the Wildwood Inn, was an "all the rage" trolley stop, providing celebrated shore dinners for folks who came from near and far to enjoy. According to the "History of Wildwood" by Wendy Joy, "The customers would enter the Inn on the left, pay for their dinner, pass through the Japanese room noted for its oriental design, and then proceed to the porch for their meals. The porch accommodated eight large tables seating ten people at a table, with soda fountain chairs."

At the beach there was a raft, pier, a diving chute, and at least three beach houses. The Wildwood Pier could accommodate the island steamers which provided people another mode of transportation from the Portland area. The pier was a two-part structure: The shore section was stationary, and the outer part was a pontoon construction, which could be removed in the winter to avoid being destroyed by storms. The roof of the summer house had the word WILDWOOD painted in large letters so that the ferryboat could see it in inclement weather.

In 1929 the trolley line made the last run due to the increased popularity of the private automobile. The ability to move on your own, when you wanted to and where you wanted to, made this such a newfound freedom of this era. Any Wildwood land not already privately owned was bought by Philip F. Chapman in 1923. He and his wife made the Wildwood Inn their private home, so that attraction ceased to exist. Lots in the park began to sell quickly, owners converted their cottages to permanent houses, and the area became a year-round suburban area. The Wildwood Park Association came to be in 1934; members paid dues, and had many rules by which to abide.

World War II saw a great decline in conditions in the park, but after the war, in 1945, Mr. Chapman was approached by other residents to resume the Association and improve conditions. The war also caused the blacking out of streetlights there, so in 1948, the Wildwood people petitioned for lights. Legal proceedings to become a charitable corporation began in 1956, and became effective in 1960, after the Association was disbanded in 1960. This being done, Wildwood could legally raise funds to keep the park in good condition.

Because of the drought and fires of 1947, Wildwood residents created the Wildwood Park Fire Department, which consisted of a portable fire hose that was located on a trailer and hand-carried to fires. Women of the area were the daytime fire watchers, and the men took over at night. They diligently kept an eye out for sparks, cigarette butts, or any other potential fire danger. This constant gathering and watching became "a good excuse for a penny-ante poker game." Today, on the Fourth of July, the residents have their biggest community event of the year. Residents plan and organize a celebration for everyone in the park, Engine #3 of the Cumberland Fire Department leads a parade down Wildwood Boulevard, there are games and contests on the reserve and a cookout and picnic in the evening, finished off by a gun salute and "Taps."

Wildwood Park Association became Wildwood Park Associates in 1963, and the residents in the sixty-seven homes in the park today relish the beauty and the natural state of the area. The neighborhood here is much like a gated community in larger cities, with a great diversity in styles and sizes of homes. Wildwood residents are very protective of their beach and water access, and have adamantly discouraged town efforts to make them public, even to the point of talk of secession from the Town of Cumberland. That has not had to occur, and the park property remains the park property.

The traditions and community of Wildwood Park remain much the same as it has all along, even though the faces and/or names may not all be the same as they were in 1909.

Sources:

1. "The Lure of the Sea & Forest," Concord Realty Co., 1913.
2. Wendy L. Joy, "Wildwood Beach and Park."
3. Wendy L. Joy, Bill Dill, Betts Gorsky, and Betty Quinlan, "Wildwood: The Story of a Neighborhood."

Appendix I

Early Roads

By Harlan H. Sweetser

The record of the layout of a portion of the first range road, northeasterly of the Falmouth line, and called the Sanborn Road, was found under the date of 1762. The section beginning at the "King's Highway," now the Middle Road, and extending northwesterly beyond the Harris Road, was discontinued many years ago, and the one remaining house that was serviced by this road is now accommodated by another road. However, it must have had considerable use in the early days, as there are at least five abandoned cellar holes in this section.

In 1769, the Court of General Sessions was petitioned to lay out a through, or county road, from Falmouth, now Portland, to Bakerstown Plantation, now the vicinity of Auburn and Minot. This road would pass through the northwesterly part of the town of North Yarmouth. It was laid out in 1771 and was known as the Old Gray Road. In Falmouth it originally passed over the top of Blackstrap Hill, and is known today in that town as the Blackstrap Road. In the early days it had considerable traffic, and many taverns were located along the route for overnight accommodations. The heavily loaded freight wagons averaged only seven to ten miles a day, due to the poor road conditions, and the fact that they were mostly drawn by oxen. A large house formerly on Route 100, opposite its intersection with the Old Gray Road, was the Leighton Tavern. It was patronized extensively in the early days. This old tavern, now owned by Lee and Holly Thibodeau, was moved to a new location in Schooner Rocks in 1970.

The second range, or town, road, in what is now Cumberland and known as the Tuttle Road, began to be opened up at the same time as the first range road, or Sanborn Road, and lots were partly cleared and homes built some distance inland from the coast. Meanwhile, four or five settlers had gone to the northwesterly part of the town and cleared land and built homes on their lots. They called on the town to "way them out." There were three possible plans to accomplish this: first, to extend the first range road, or Sanborn Road; a second, to gain access to the newly laid out "county road" between Falmouth and Bakerstown, which went through the northwesterly part of the town; and third, to provide access from Tuttle Road. The town of North Yarmouth referred this to the Court of General Sessions in 1779, and the latter decided on access from Tuttle Road. The plan was to leave Tuttle Road as the dividing line between lots 47 and 48, which is the southeasterly boundary of the Drowne farm today, and then go southwesterly on the dividing line the depth of the lots, or one-half mile. From there the road would go northwesterly, along the back end of the lots, to the southeasterly boundary of lots 33 and 59, which would be about opposite the point where the Mill Brook crosses Blanchard Road. There were at least four houses served by this road. The Shaw house, later owned by Neal Dow, is the only one in existence today. It is now accommodated by the Range or Sanborn Road. In the layout of this road some thought was given to the terrain it went over, and it did not always follow the dividing lines between the lots, but took advantage of the best possible route. It probably was not much more than a bridle path as it was laid out during the Revolutionary War.

When the War came to a close there was much activity in road layout everywhere. The Sanborn Road was extended, and also Tuttle Road by what is now known as Blanchard Road. These were carried through to the western part of the town. And the section of the road, midway between them, laid out by the Court of General Sessions, was discontinued as a public way. Only near its northwesterly end is there any trace today of this discontinued section.

The alteration of Blanchard Road, above the fairgrounds, where it no longer follows the range line, took place in 1796.

Greely Road, the third range or town road, began to be opened up shortly after the beginnings on the Sanborn and Tuttle Roads. Because part of the way it followed the southwesterly boundary of the ancient Gedney Claim, its distance from Tuttle Road is now only a little over one-half mile where it intersects the Middle Road. The bend in it, from the same cause, has been mentioned previously. A section of this road, in the northwesterly part of the town, now known as Greely Road Extension, passed over some difficult terrain, and has not been developed as has the remainder of the road. In 1796, a road was laid out from the point where the "King's Highway" intersected Tuttle Road, as an extension of the former. This formed a part of the Middle Road in present Cumberland; then it went over present Portland Street in Yarmouth, to its intersection with Main Street, turning southeasterly down Main Street to the "Wood Landing" at tidewater. When Cumberland separated from North Yarmouth, this became a county or through road.

In the same year a county, or through, road was laid out from the New Gloucester Road at Walnut Hill in North Yarmouth to the lower falls of the Presumpscot River in Falmouth. This formed present Main Street and the section of the Winn Road that is in Cumberland. Another road, laid out jointly, in 1780, by the towns of North Yarmouth and Falmouth, in their respective towns, extended from the "King's Highway" near the Falmouth Corner to the point where the present Winn Road and lower Main Street intersect, making the present Longwoods Road, which is now a part of Route 9.

In 1948 US Route 1 was relocated from a point one-tenth of a mile southwesterly of the entrance to the Portland Country Club in Falmouth to a point one mile northeasterly from its original intersection with Route 115 in Yarmouth. Thus, Route 1 through Cumberland is on a new location farther from Casco Bay and the bypassed section, old Route 1 in Falmouth, Cumberland, and Yarmouth, is now known as Route 88. Relocated US Route 1, which borders Interstate Route 95 part of the way in Cumberland and Yarmouth, intersects Tuttle Road in Cumberland at 59.3. From this point it is 3.5 miles west to Cumberland Center.

Appendix II

Cumberland Center, 1830

This photo is of a wooden model of Cumberland Center as it was in 1830, made by Silas M. Rideout. Note church at four corners. Buildings are one to three inches in size. Notation with model says that the only shade trees were two elms in front of present Prince Memorial Library and four Balm of Gilead trees on south corner where Main Street and Tuttle Road meet.

Courtesy of Wayne Merrill

Appendix III

Superintendents of Cumberland Schools

Names and dates taken from Town Reports are as follows:

Benjamin F. Doughty, 1852–53

Rev. G. B. Richardson, 1874

Lyman P. Sturdivant, 1875, '76, '79, '82, '83

alternating with

Ezra K. Sweetser in 1878 and 1881

Horace E. Sawyer, 1884

Edmund D. Merrill, 1885

From 1886–91, a committee consisting of N. H. McCollister, E. K. Sweetser, and A. R. Littlefield

From 1892–94, a committee consisting of A. R. Littlefield, M. H. Moulton, and E. K. Sweetser

Oscar R. Sturdivant, 1895, '96, '97, '99

Frank H. Chase, 1898

Oscar R. Sturdivant, 1899–1905

C. W. Pierce, 1906–07

H. M. Moore, 1908–10

Daniel W. Lunt, 1911–26

Sherman I. Graves, 1927–28

John T. Gyger, 1929–39

H. Norman Cole, 1940–42

Rolf B. Motz, 1942–49

William H. Soule, 1949–56

Henry G. Perkins, 1957–63

Vaughn A. Lacombe, July 1963–June 1968

Morton E. Hamlin, July 1, 1968–87

John Nye, 1987–91

Franklin Harrison (interim), 1991–92

Dr. Robert Hasson Jr., 1992–2013

Sally Loughlin (interim), 2013–2014

Jeff Porter, 2014–present

Appendix IV

Pastors and Ministers

Cumberland Congregational Church (1794–2014)

By Phyllis Sweetser

Rufus Anderson (1794–1804)

Amasa Smith (1806–20)

Samuel Stone (1821–29)

Isaac Weston (1830–40)

Joseph Blake (1841–59)

Ebenezer S. Jordan (1859–70)

Uriah W. Small (1870–71)

Gilbert B. Richardson (1871–74)

Truman S. Perry (1874–86)

Ebenezer S. Jordan (1886–87)

Daniel Greene (1888–92)

Frank W. Davis (1892–99)

Paris E. Miller (1899–1909)

Talmage M. Patterson (1910–12)

Arthur C. Townsend (1912–16)

Austin I. Davis (1916–19)

Charles H. Meeker (1919–21)

John A. Wiggin (1922–24)

Burton A. Lucas (1924–33)

Andrew K. Craig (1933–37)

Harold G. Booth (1937–42)

Curtis Cady Busby (1942–46)

Lloyd Yeagle (1946–49)

Howard O. Hough (Interim)

Harding Gaylord (1950–53)

Valton V. Morse (1953–68)

Richard S. Merrill (1969–77)

Eric W. Kelley (1977–86)

Timothy Ensworth, Assoc. (1985–86)

Timothy Ensworth (1986–91)

John Fillmore-Patrick, Assoc. (1987–93)

William Dalke (Interim) (1992–93)

Carol Kerr (Interim) (1993–94)

Dana W. Douglass (1994–98)

Jennifer G. Bergen, co-pastor (1995–98)

Diane E. Bennekamper, co-pastor (1998–2005)

John N. Bixby Jr., co-pastor (1998–2005)

Diane E. Bennekamper (2005–present)

Methodist Ministers

By Emilie Chase Cram

Cumberland and Falmouth Circuit:

Joshua Taylor (1826–40)

Cumberland and Falmouth Methodist Church on the Town Line (before 1900):

Joshua Taylor (1831–1840)
Asahel Moore (1840)
Joshua Taylor (1841)
Phineas Higgens (1842)
H. J. Webster (1843)
Joseph Hawkes Jr. (1844)
Paul C. Richmond (1845)
Benjamin Burnham (1846)
Daniel Copeland (1847)
John Lord (1848)
Silas M. Emerson (1849)
Charles Munger (1850)
Supplied (1851–52)
Uriel Rideout (1853)
S. Wanton Ranks (1854)
Ezekiel Smith (1855)
Jesse Stone (1856–57)
John Rice (1858–59)
Charles W. Blackman (1860–61)
John Cobb (1862–63)
S. Wanton Ranks (1864)
Alvah Cook (1865–66)
Alpha Turner (1867–68)
O. H. Stevens (1869)
Ezra Sanborn (1870–71)
F. A. Patterson (1872)
O. H. Stevens (1873–74)
Benjamin F. Pease (1875–76)
Charles Andrews (1877)
E. R. Colby (1878–79)
Eliazar Hutchinson (1880–82)
Benjamin Freeman (1883)
Woodbury P. Merrill (1884–86)
O. S. Pillsbury (1887)
A. R. Sylvester (1888–89)
C. F. Parsons (1890)
A. C. Trafton (1891)
D. R. Ford (1892–93)
W. T. Chapman (1894)
M. B. Greenhalgh (1895–96)
John B. Howard (1897–99)

Cumberland and Falmouth Methodist Church on the Town Line (after 1900):

E. W. Kennison (1900–01)

F. K. Beem (1902–04)

B. F. Fickett (1905–07)

George R. Palmer (1908–15)

Woodbury P. Merrill (1916–24)

Charles Sinden (1924–27)

Merle Conant (1927–35)

Leslie W. Grundy (1935–36)

F. Jefferson Neal (Supply) (1936–37)

John Dunstan (1937–40)

Ralph Winn (1940–42)

Frank Oldridge (1942–44)

Dean Everett Lord (1945–55)

A. B. Clarke (1955–56)

Donald Jennings (1960–65)

George Dillon (1966–71)

Peter Mercer (1971–75)

Rev. Dr. Donald Hodgson (1976–87)

Rev. Dr. Paul Shupe (1987–2009)

Janet Dorman (2009–present)

The West Cumberland United Methodist Church

By Kenneth R. Dorr
Updated by Nancy Latham

1844–1900:

J. S. Rice (1844)
J. Clough (1845–46)
David Copeland (1847)
J. Lord (1848–49)
S. S. Cummings (1850–51)
S. Ambrose (1852)
L. B. Knight (1853)
M. Hobert (1854)
Jesse Stone (1855–56)
M. O. Centre (1857–58)
Asa Green (1859)
W. C. Stevens (1861)
I. E. Baxter (1863)
R. C. Bailey (1864)
S. V. Gerry (1866–68)
J. W. Howes (1869)
John Sanborn (1870–71)
E. Sanborn (1873)
J. Sidstone (1874)
E. Sanborn (1875)
C. S. Mann (1876)
M. Harriman (1877)
E. Gerry Jr. (1878)
G. W. Barber (1879–80)
J. E. Buddin (1881–82)
No appointment
A. O. Graffam (1889)
F. C. Potter (1890–91)
A. B. Clark (1892–93)
Wm. Bragg (1894–95)

After 1900:

W. H. Congdon (1903)
Howard Clifford (1915)
W. H. Varney (1917)
Louis S. Staples (1918)
Ordell Bryant (1919)
Frank C. Potter (1920)
A. R. Griffin (1921)
Auburn J. Carr (1924)
Walter Ourost (1925)
Elbert S. Emery (1926)
Walter Ourost (1928)
Roy C.Bennett (1928)
C. A. Quigley, OD (1929)
A. F. Leigh (1930)
George Holgate (1934)
S. D. Moores (1943)
Merle C. Conant (1947)
W. E. Conklin (1950)
Nelson Canfield (1953)
B. F. Wentworth (1956)

C. J. Wood (1961)

Ralph L. Miller (1962–65)

Perley C. O'Dell (1965–67)

Kingsley L. Strout (June 1967–October 1970)

Richard Arnold (October 1970–January 1971)

Kingsley L. Strout (January 1971–June 1974)

Russell Ingalls (June 1974–September 1974)

James H. Nason (September 1974–1977)

Robert H. Burton (June 1977–July 1988)

George W. Tripp (July 1988–June 1990)

Eva D. Cutler (June 1990–June 1992)

Donald P. Waye (July 1992–January 1994)

Casey Collins (February 1994–1997)

S. Peter Donatelli (July 1997–June 1999)

After 2000:

George W. Tripp (July 1999–June 2002)

Betty Westhoven (July 2002–February 2003)

Mervin Chadbourne (March 2003–June 2003)

Thomas Frey (July 2003–June 2005)

Lilian Warner (July 2005–October 2005)

Ruth Williamson (November 2005–June 2006)

Gayle Holden (July 2006–2010)

Geoffrey Gross (2010–present)

Tuttle Road United Methodist Church

Eliazar Hutchinson (1882)
Benjamin Freeman (1883)
W. P. Merrill (1884–86)
O. S. Pillsbury (1887)
A. R. Sylvester (1888–89)
C. F. Parsons (1890)
A. C. Trafton (1891)
Daniel R. Ford (1892–93)
W. T. Chapman (1894)
M. B. Greenhalgh (1895–96)
John B. Howard (1897–99)
E. W. Kennison (1900–01)
Franklin K. Beem (1902–04)
B. F. Fickett (1905–07)
George R. Palmer (1908–14)
Benjamin C. Wentworth (1915–18)
I. T. Johnson (1919–20)
H. C. Glidden (1921–23)
George A. Rideout (1924)
E. Lincoln Bigelow (1925)
John G. P. Sherburne (1926–27)
Merle S. Conant (1927–35)
Leslie W. Grundy (1935–36)
F. Jefferson Neal (1936)
John Dunstan (1937–40)
Ralph H. Winn (1940–42)
Frank Oldridge (1942–44)
Supplied (1943–45)
H. Travers Smith (1945–48)
Lawrence Porter (1949–52)
Elwin Parkhurst (1953–56)
Kenneth Cook (1957–63)
Norman Langmaid (1964–65)
Alice T. Hart (1965–70)
Richard Arnold (1971–74)
Mervin Chadbourne (1974–78)
Jody Stiles (1979–81)
Michael E. Davis (1981–87)
John W. Neff (1988–93)
Mark Monson Alley (1993–2005)
Meg Queior (2005–2014)
Linda Brewster (2014–present)

Appendix V

Military Lists

By Donna L. Miller and Antoinette N. Packard

The following is a list of all Civil War Veterans, who were born, lived, or are buried in Cumberland. Also included are the twenty-two men who served as substitutes for residents of Cumberland. They are designated by a #.

Civil War Veterans

1862		Adkins (Adkinson), Moses: Served in Company B., 25th Infantry.
1864–65		Aiken, Henry P.: #
1861		Allen, Daniel A.: Of Falmouth, Maine, enlisted in Company C. 12th Infantry, as a private: reenlisted as a veteran volunteer in 1864; transferred to Company C., 12th Battalion, 12/22/1864. Deserted 10/30/65 at Savannah, Georgia.
		Annis, Hiram
1862	*	Baston, Jeremiah R.: Served as a private in Company E. 17th Infantry; reported missing in action 5/12/1864 near Spottsylvania, Virginia.
1864–65		Bates, John: #
		Bean, A. S.
1864–65		Becker, John: #
1864–65		Berle, William: #
1864–65		Berry, James H.: Officer in the United States Navy.
1862		Bishop, Benjamin: Of Chebeague Island, served in Company E, 25th Infantry.
1861		Blanchard, Addison: Chaplain and lieutenant of Colored Troops.
1861		Blanchard, Brainard P.: 13th Massachusetts Regiment, Infantry Division.
1862		Blanchard, Charles A.: Joined the United States Navy; served as acting ensign on USS *Jasmine*, also the USS *Commodore Morris*, USS

Althea, and USS *Jonathan*.

1861 Blanchard, David L.: Played in the Regimental Band of the 10th Infantry as 3rd class musician. Enlisted as a seaman in the navy in 1863.

1861 Blanchard, Ferdinand Clinton: 1st Missouri Light Infantry (Union).

1864 Blanchard, Frank W.: US Navy paymaster/steward on board steamer *Yankee*.

1862 * Blanchard, Homer E.: Served in Company E, 17th Infantry; died of disease at Falmouth, Virginia, 12/1/62.

1862 Blanchard, Horatio S.: US Navy, acting master on USS *Quaker City*.

1862 * Blanchard, Joseph H.: Served in Company B, 25th Infantry; died at Arlington Heights, Virginia, 12/7/1862.

1862 Blanchard, Solomon L.: Served in Company E, 17th Infantry; transferred to the Invalid Corps, 1864.

1861 Blanchard, William F.: Served in 13th Massachusetts Regimentary Infantry, and as lieutenant of Colored Troops.

1862 Brown, Albion H.: US Navy sloop of war, *Powhatan*.

1864–65 Brown, James: #

1862 Bruce, Frederick: US Navy seaman.

1862 Bryan, William J.: Of Chebeague Island, served in Company E, 25th Infantry.

1863 * Chase, Heber: Of Boston, was a teacher before he enlisted in the 11th Massachusetts Infantry; a prisoner of war 10/27/1864 at Hatchers Run, Virginia. Died in prison, 11/27/64, in Salisbury, North Carolina.

1862 Clough, Simon L.: Served in Company B., 25th Infantry.

1862 Coffin, Rufus: Served in Company G, 13th Infantry, promoted to corporal.

1861 Copp, John F.: Of Portland, enlisted in Company A, 1st Infantry; later reenlisted, serving in the 25th Regiment.

1862 Davis, Calvin: Served in 20th Maine Regiment.

1862 Doughty, George H.: First served in Company B, 25th Infantry, reenlisted as corporal in Company F, 30th Infantry.

1862 Eaton, Cyrus H.: Served in Company B, 25th Infantry.

1862 Emery, William R.: Served in 27th Maine Regiment.

1862 * Long: Engineer, US Navy, lost at sea on the *Monitor* off Cape Hatteras.

1862 Farwell, Francis O.: Mustered into Company B, 25th Infantry.

1861 Farwell, Frederick S.: Served in 6th Massachusetts Infantry.

1862 Farwell, Horace A.: Of North Yarmouth, served in Company B, 25th

Infantry.
1862 Farwell, Simeon L.: Mustered in Company B, 25th Infantry.
1862 Field, Amos L.: 25th Maine Regiment.
1862 Flint, Leonard: Of Bath, Maine; Company C, 21st Infantry.
1862 Graham, William, Jr.: Of Westbrook; Field and Staff, 25th Infantry, discharged as commissary sergeant.
1864–65 * Graham, William N.: # (May have been same as above). Died in service.
Gales, John: US Navy Gulf Squadron.
1861 Gould, Samuel: Company G, 2nd Infantry.
1862 Greely, Charles H.: Company E, 17th Infantry; wounded May 5, 1864.
1862 Greely, Edward Nelson: Captain, 1st Maine Regiment, transferred to 25th Maine Regiment.
1861 Greely, Eliphalet: 47th Massachusetts Infantry.
1862 Greely, Horace B.: Sergeant, Company G, 13th Infantry.
1862 Greely, Horatio: Corporal, Company B, 25th Infantry.
1861 Greely, Rensalear: 1st Maine Infantry.
1861 Hall, George W.: Company B, 10th Infantry.
1864–65 Hall, John: #
1862 Hall, William J.: Company B, 25th Infantry.
1862 Hamilton, Reul D.: Company E, 25th Infantry.
1862 Hamilton, Sylvanus: Company E, 25th Infantry.
1863 Hanby, Thomas: Sergeant, Company E, 29th Infantry.
1861 Hanley Thomas: First man living in Cumberland to enlist in the Union Army, May 3, 1861. He was born in England and moved to Cumberland as a child.
1864–65 Harrington, Patrick: #
1865 Heron, Daniel: Company A, 20th Infantry.
1862 Hersey, Albion: Captain while serving in Company B, 17th Infantry.
Hiles, Oliver

Photo from collection of Phyllis Sweetser

Daguerreotype of Thomas Hanley, first enlisted soldier from Cumberland in the Civil War.

1864–65 * Hill, Henry L.: # Company E, 15th Infantry; died of congestive chills, October 16, 1865, Georgetta, South Carolina.
1862 Hill, Samuel L.: Of Kennebunk; Company I, 27th Infantry.
1864–65 Hughes, John: #
1862 Jenkins, Harrison: 1st Massachusetts Heavy Artillery.
Johnson, John: US Navy Gulf Squadron
1864–65 Johnson, William: #
Kenton, Robert H.: US Navy.
1862 Latham, James F.: Sergeant, Company B, 25th Infantry, Volunteers
1862 Latham, Seward H.: Corporal, Company G, 5th Infantry; transferred to Company A, 1st Veteran Infantry.
1864–65 Leighton, Charles H.: #
1862 Leighton, Elias F.: Company B, 25th Infantry.
1861 Leighton, Henry H.: Company, 6th Infantry, discharged with disability.
1862 Leighton, Moses W.: Company B, 25th Infantry.
1862 Leighton, Patrick H.: Company B, 25th Infantry.
1862 Mansfield, James: Of Chebeague Island; Company B, 25th Infantry.
1862 Mansfield, John: Company B, 25th Infantry.
1861 Means, John T.: 12th Maine Regiment.
1862 Merrill, Josiah: Company B, 25th Infantry.
1864 Merrill, Louville H.: US Navy, acting assistant paymaster on steamer *Yankee*.
1862 Merrill, William: Master's mate on ship *South Carolina*.
1862 Merrill, William H. C.: Company B, 25th Infantry.
1863 Meserve, Vincent: Company E, 17th Infantry.
Morrill, Josiah Jr.
1864–65 Morris, John: #
1861 Morrison, John T.: Company C., 12th Infantry.
* Morton, Henry B.: US Navy Revenue Cutter.
1862 Mountfort, Daniel H.: Company B, 25th Infantry.
1862 Mountfort, Hollis R.: Sergeant, Company B, 25th Infantry.
1862 Mountfort, James W.: Company B, 25th Infantry.
1862 Mountfort, Otis A.: Company B, 25th Infantry.
1864–65 Mulligan, Francis: #
1864–65 Neagle, James H.: #
1864–65 Nicholas, William: #
1862 Peterson, David: Seaman in the US Navy.
1862 Pettingill, Edward: US Navy.

1865 Phalon, William: Company A, 20th Infantry.
1862 Pote, Othernial M.: US Navy, frigate *St. Lawrence*.
1862 Pride, Charles A.: Of North Yarmouth; Company G, 25th Infantry.
1862 * Pride, Frederick M.: Company E, 17th Infantry.
1862 Prince, Albert F.: Of North Yarmouth, Company G, 25th Infantry; reenlisted 1/25/1864 in Company L, DC Cavalry, then transferred to Company B, 1st Cavalry as corporal.
1862 Prince, Albion C.: US Navy, acting ensign on board the USS *Nipsis*.
1863 Prince, Frederick C.: 1st Sergeant, Company C, 2nd Cavalry.
1862 Prince, Howard I.: Company A, 20th Infantry; joined as captain, wounded 5/8/1864.
1864 * Prince, William B.: Company B, 1st Cavalry; also Company L, 1st Cavalry; killed in action at age seventeen, 1864.
1861 Ramsdell, Seth A.: Of Gray, Maine, Company H, 11th Infantry; reenlisted as veteran volunteer, promoted to corporal, sergeant, and 1st sergeant.
1862 * Rideout, Joseph M.: Company B, 17th Infantry; wounded on 5/5/1864 during the Battle of the Wilderness. Died of wounds at Andersonville, Georgia.
Rideout, Renfrue; ?
1862 * Rideout, Reuben: Company B, 17th Infantry; died of disease in Washington, DC, 10/27/1862.
1862 Rideout, Royal T.: Company E, 17th Infantry; discharge for disability.
Rines, Charles H.: Company E, 25th Maine Infantry.
1864–65 Rogan, James: #
1862 Ross, William H.: Of Chebeague Island; Company E, 25th Infantry.
1863 * Rowe, A. N.: Of North Yarmouth, 25th and 30th Infantries; died in Winchester, Virginia, 1864.
1862 Sanborn, James: Company B, 25th Infantry.
1862 Sanborn, Josiah: Company B, 25th Infantry.
Shaw, Bryant
1862 Shaw, Elias: Company B, 25th Infantry.
1862 Skillings, William H.: US Navy, *Monongahela*.
1864 Small, Benjamin: Of Augusta, Company K, 32nd Infantry.
1865 Smith, William: Company A, 20th Infantry.
Soule, William S.: 13th Massachusetts Infantry.
1862 Sparks, James E.: Of Yarmouth, Company E, 17th Infantry, transferred to Veteran Volunteer Corps; wounded in action.

		Stubbs, D. N.
1861		Stubbs, Daniel: 5th Mounted Artillery.
1861		Sweetser, Francis E.: Of Westbrook, Company G, 25th Maine Militia.
1862		Sweetser, Henry: US Navy.
1862		Taylor, Warren: Company G, 25th Infantry.
		Thayer, S.B.
1862		Thompson, George L.: Company B, 25th Infantry.
1861	*	Trowbridge, John: Of Portland; Company B, 1st Infantry, reenlisted Company B, 10th Infantry. Killed at Antietam Creek, 9/17/1862.
1862		True, Hollis: Company E, 17th Infantry; wounded in action.
1862		Vannah, Ambrose: Of Boston, Company E, 3rd Regiment, Massachusetts Cavalry.
1865		Warren, George: #
		Webster, William
1861		Wilson, Edward H.: sergeant, major, 2nd lieutenant, 1st lieutenant, adjutant, transferred to Field and Staff, Company G, 13th Infantry.
1864–65		Wilson, John: #
1862		Wilson, Nathaniel B.: Of Falmouth; Company B, 25th Infantry musician.
		Winslow, E. H.
		Wixon, John
1861		Wyman, Charles W.: Company F, 1st Cavalry.

* *Died in service.*

Source:

From Maine Historical Society Records.

Added names (without dates) found in *Cumberland and North Yarmouth 1904 Register*, compiled by Mitchell, Russell, and Strout.

World War I (1917–1918)

By Harold M. Ross

Cumberland Mainland:

Fred O. Adams
Paul E. Alden
Antonio Battista
Albert T. Bjorn
Morris W. Blanchard
Ralph L. Blanchard
Robert G. Blanchard
Roy M. Blanchard
Ralph M. Bragdon
Edward E. Bragg
Victor Burnell
William H. Chambers
William M. Christensen
Francis H. Cloudman
Clifton H. Copp
John Cummings
Glendon B. Doane
Ralph W. Doble
Leslie L. Edwards
Joseph L. Ennis
John W. Hall
John Hansen
Otto C. Hanson
Grol Hawkes
Everett L. Hill
Albert Kay
Ernest A. Leighton
Carl B. Lufkin
Floyd W. Norton
John H. Peterson
Mads F. Peterson
Benjamin F. Porter
Charles B. Porter
Earle R. Porter
Ernest A. Rand
William P. Randall
Harold M. Ross
Robert A. Ross
Vernon B. Russell
Harvey D. Sederquist
Elsie A. Smith
Roy Vaughn P. Sprague
Ernest Osgood Sweetser
Marston O. Sweetser
Walter M. Thurston
Royal P. Webber
Willis E. Wilson

List prepared with help from Victor Burnell and Halvor S. Merrill.

World War I

By Donna L. Miller

Chebeague:

George A. Cleaves
George Stanley Doughty
* Gerald C. Doughty
Charles A. Grannell
Ernest W. Hamilton
Ervin O. Hamilton
* Louis F. Hamilton
Paul J. Hamilton
Sidney W. Hamilton
Theodore P. Hill
Captain James L. Long
Harry L. Mansfield
Walter H. Mansfield
Carlyle A. MacDonald
Perley J. MacDonald
Carlos A. Newcomb
* Robert L. Ricker
Clifton E. Ross
James W. Ross
Everett L. Soule
Joseph C. Thompson
Captain Thomas D. Turner
Harlan B. Webber
Roland I. Webber

World War II (1941–1945)

From *Cumberland Town Report* for 1945 and Halvor S. Merrill.

Cumberland Mainland:

William H. Akerley
Harold G. Ashley
Louis N. Baker
Robert C. Baker
William M. Baker
Colby L. Berry
Lewis F. Berry
George M. Blake
Bradford Bonney
Lee F. Brackett
Robert A. Irish
George P. Jacobs
Franklin C. Jeffery
Ernest L. Larson
* Carroll A. Leavitt
Forrest G. Legge
John E. Leighton
Norman E. Leighton
W. Edward Leland
Elmer R. Little

Arthur S. Brown
Frank M. Brown Jr.
John A. Brown
Millard K. Brown
Ralph Brown
Warren H. Buxton
Richard C. Cashman
Dana B. Chase
Philip A. Chase
Norman C. Christensen
Michael A. Ciampi
Richard S. Clement
Eugene Collins
Milton Copp
Eugene W. Corcoran
Francis E. Corcoran
Horace D. Corcoran
Norman D. Corcoran
Robert Cram
* Harold E. Crocker
Lloyd B. Daley
John W. Daniels
Leland H. Davis
Arthur W. Dean
Kenneth W. Dorr
* George R. Dunn
* James L. Dunn II
Robert R. Feeney
Norman A. Fickett
Richard E. Fickett
R. Alton Fields
Charles R. Finks

Elton S. Little
James A. Logan
Joseph R. Malone
Harold C. Mayberry
Donald B. Mayo
John H. Mayo
John M. McGorrill
Frank D. Merrill
Halvor S. Merrill
Norman F. Moore Jr.
Ralph O. Morgaridge
John C. Mosher
Kenneth W. Olson
Delbert D. Pearce
Howard S. Pearce
Alvah N. Prince
Donald Rawson
Gordon Rawson
Merton E. Rawson Jr.
Walter P. Reed
George A. Robinson
Henry Royce
Arnold M. Sanborn
Elmer A. Scott
Kenneth K. Scribner
Donald P. Searles
Elisha R. Searles Jr.
Wesley H. Shaw
Arthur A. Sloat
Harold K. Sloat
Waldo P. Strahan
* Chester O. Strout

Theodore W. Fisk
Albert R. Foster
Herbert Foster Jr.
Roland Genthner
William M. Gower
Alta S. Gray
Clifford E. Grover
James N. Grover
* William A. Grover
John T. Gyger Jr.
Earl C. Hale
Earl G. Ham
Arthur C. Hansen
Glen R. Hansen
Philip H. Hansen Jr.
Clayton D. Hersey
Perley L. Hutchins
Charles T. Ireland Jr.
Philip S. Sweetser
Richard W. Sweetser
Paul W. Thompson
Dwight C. Verrill
Randall B. Verrill
Richard H. Verrill
* David Warren
Earl O. Watson
H. David Watson
Leroy M. Watson
Medley A. Watson Jr.
Calvin H. Whitney
Helen Winslow
Raimond L. Winslow
Philip C. Young
Robert E. Young
Roger M. Young

World War II

By Donna L. Miller

Chebeague:

Albert R. Bryan
Alger F. Burgess
Norris Burns
Chesley A. Calder
John H. Calder
Norman D. Calder
Harold Cleaves
Willis E. Cleaves
Ashley C. Johnson
Charles M. MacIntosh
Edward W. McCormack
Richard A. McCormack
Donald M. McKee
Ellsworth D. Miller
Lewis S. Moynihan
Alvin L. Newcomb

Charles L. Doughty
Earle E. Doughty
Sanford E. Doughty
Carroll A. Dyer
James E. Grindle
Gerald C. Goodwin
Neville W. Goodwin
Albert R. Hamilton
Charles R. Hamilton
Floyd C. Hamilton
Kenneth H. Hamilton
William M. Hamilton
Charles F. Newcomb
Donald G. Parr
Walter F. Rines
Bernard T. Robinson
Donald W. Ross
Emery R. Ross
Lewis C. Ross
* Richard H. Seabury
Clifton H. Thompson
Robert L. Wheldon
Raymond L. White

* *Died in service.*

Vietnam (1964–1973)

Chebeague:

Herbert P. Bennett Jr.
Bruce R. Bowman
Peter Bowman
Kenneth Campbell
Lawson Doughty
Robert A. Dyer Jr.
Wayne C. Dyer
Helen Wheldon Green
Leland M. Hamilton
Leon A. Hamilton
Sherman E. Hamilton
Stephen Hamilton
Stephen Johnson
James Komlosy
Jeffery LeClair
Stephen O'Neil
Robert Parker
Everett E. Robinson
Stephen Slowick
Linden Smith
Daniel Todd
Stephen Walker
Gunnar Wood

No records available for Cumberland mainland, except for:

Bill Brown

John Brown

Clarence Cook

Kenneth Moore

Vincent A. Moore

Linwood N. Packard

George B. Small

Robert E. Woodbury

Korean War

Theodore W. Moore

Nelson Haynes

Appendix VI

Postmasters

Cumberland, Cumberland County, Maine
Established as Cumberland East on June 2, 1821
Name changed to Cumberland on August 23, 1821
Discontinued on March 30, 1918 (mail to Portland)

Postmasters	Appointment Dates through March 30, 1918
James Prince	June 2, 1821
William Buxton	August 23, 1821
Charles Poland	December 22, 1842
Jacob Merrill	June 19, 1849
Charles Poland	January 7, 1853
David Gray	January 20, 1853
John N. Dunn	July 7, 1870
Edward H. Trickey	November 18, 1895
Alfred W. Doughty	September 16, 1904

Cumberland Center, Cumberland County, Maine
Established as Cumberland Centre on May 16, 1826

Postmasters	Appointment Dates through September 30, 1972
William Bird	May 16, 1826
Howard Willis	March 30, 1827
Reuben Rideout	April 7, 1828
Joseph Waterhouse	March 18, 1839
Joel Prince Jr.	June 29, 1841
Willard Clough	December 3, 1845
Samuel True	May 3, 1849

Everett L. Blanchard	December 2, 1878
Nellie H. McCollister	February 12, 1886
Benjamin Whitney	August 2, 1888
James L. Dunn	October 11, 1892
George W. Jordan	April 26, 1923
Mrs. Nellie B. Jordan	August 26, 1930
Norman Hulit	July 15, 1936 (assumed charge)
	August 3, 1937 (confirmed)
Mrs. Frances M. Nelson	April 3 1971 (assumed charge)
Mrs. Rena M. Lamson	September 16, 1972
Mary Hodgetts	1980–1982
Jean Seeley	1982–1985
Donald Haskell	1985–1992
Doris D. Clark (officer-in-charge)	1992–1993
Ellen N. Call	1993–2002
Elaine P. Edwards	2002–2012
Lori-Anne Grassi	2012–2016
Supplied	2016

West Cumberland, Cumberland County, Maine
Established on January 28, 1846
Discontinued on December 20, 1900 (mail to Portland)

Postmasters	**Appointment Dates through December 20, 1900**
Greenleaf Mountfort	January 28, 1846
Mrs. Hannah T. Mountfort	March 3, 1873
James W. Mountfort	June 29, 1875
Lorenzo H. Wilson	September 27, 1878
Alnah L. Wilson	December 31, 1883

Appendix VII

Cumberland Fire and Police

Fire Department Charter Members, December 11–17, 1928

George Blanchard
The Garsoe Brothers
Frank Little
Arthur N. Blanchard
Arno S. Chase
M. O. Sweetser
Carl Doughty
A. B. Wyman
W. C. Campbell
B. F. Doughty
F. M. Doughty
C. W. Small
Walter Nelson
K. W. Chase
H. C. Blanchard
H. P. Sweetser
H. M. Bragg
E. E. Bragg
Gilbert L. Strout

Cumberland Fire Chiefs

Lester B. Bragg
Gilbert L. Strout
Edward E. Bragg
Carroll Lewis
Kenneth W. Chase
Harold M. "Cap" Bragg
Philip Chase
Maurice Small
Ralph Brown
Kenneth Wagner
George Small
William Fischer
Daniel Small

Chebeague Captains

Leroy Hill
Albert S. Bennett
Clyde Bowen
Richard L. Calder
Linden Smith

Police Chiefs

Earle A. Woodbury	1954–1965
Richard J. C. Andersen	1965–1974
King W. Carter Jr.	1974–1976
Leon H. Planche	1976–1992
Joseph J Charron and Mark Austin (interim)	1992–1993
Acting Chief Jeseph J. Charon	1993–1995
Joseph J. Charron	1995–2016
Lt. Milt Calder	April 1,2016–June 2, 2016
Charles Rumsey	June 2, 2016–present

Appendix VIII

Selectmen and Town Council

By Grace Hutchinson

David Prince, 1821–1824

William Buxton, 1821–1831, 1855

Beza Blanchard, 1821–1823

William Rideout Jr., 1823–1824

Nicholas Rideout Jr. 1823–1833, 1837

James Prince, 1824–1837

Tristan Sanborn, 1830–1834, 1837–1839

Ephraim Sturdivant, 1833–1834

Moses Leighton, 1834–1839, 1849–1861

Andrews Blanchard, 1834–1835

Revel Drinkwater, 1836–1837, 1840

Reuben Blanchard, 1837–1840

Joseph Smith, 1839

William Reed, 1840

Sewell Blanchard, 1847, 1862, 1864

Matthias Morton, 1847–1848, 1849

J. M. Rideout, 1847–1849, 1856–1868

Alvan Sturdivant, 1848–1852, 1855

Asa Greely, 1851, 1873

Ebenezer Hill, 1852–1854, 1866

Stephen Orr, 1855–1856, 1859

N. L. Humphrey, 1858

Samuel Ross Jr., 1856–1858, 1865

Elijah Soule, 1858

William L. Prince, 1859

Robert Dyer, 1861–1863

Daniel Stowell, 1863–1864

Willard Clough, 1864–1866

Charles Wyman, 1866–1867

William Russell, 1867–1870

Robert H. Rogers, 1868–1870

Donald M. Smith, 1868–1870

N. L. Humphrey, 1870–1873

F. C. Blanchard, 1870–1873

Robert Hamilton Jr., 1870–1873

Charles E. Herrick, 1874–1876

William S. Blanchard, 1874–1877

Asa Sawyer, 1874–1877

Ammi R. Littlefield, 1876–1879

Daniel R. Alien, 1877–1879

Nelson M. Shaw, 1877, 1890–1892

Hollis Doughty, 1879–1881

Joseph Harris, 1881–1883

Clinton M. Hamilton, 1883, 1890–1891, 1915–1917

E. D. Merrill, 1884, 1893

Joseph Starling, 1885–1886

Edward W. Ross, 1885–1890, 1903

D. L. Blanchard, 1886–1887, 1894–1903

Otis A. Mountfort, 1887–1890

P. M. Leighton, 1890–1892

Edward H. Trickey, 1891–1908

S. F. Hamilton, 1892–1903

F. L. Haskell, 1893–1894

R. E. Littlefield, 1894

William H. Rowe, 1903–1907

George E. Beals, 1906–1909

Frank H. Jones, 1907–1910

Albert C. Robbins, 1909–1914

Fred E. Burnell, 1909–1912

Arthur W. Stanley, 1910–1914

Willard Wilson, 1912–1914

Eugene H. Strout, 1914–1917

Alphonzo J. Davis, 1914–1915

Alfred E. Hamilton, 1914–1915, 1918–1922

Dennis B. Hamilton, 1915–1923, 1925

Philip L. Blanchard, 1917–1921, 1924–1925

Osro L. Huston, 1921–1928

Frank W. Rines, 1922–1947

Fred R. Sweetser, 1923–1924

Howard L. Winslow, 1928–1929

Sumner S. Lowe, 1928–1936, 1947

Theodore R. Jordan, 1929–1932

Ernest A. Rand, 1932–1947

Herbert L. Marrinor, 1936–1939

Fred L. Robinson, 1939–1942, 1961–1967

Glendon B. Doane, 1942–1952

Philip A. Seabury, 1947–1949

Earle A. Woodbury, 1949–1961, 1967–1972

Leroy H. Hill, 1949–1964

Stanwood R. Cook, 1949–1955

Noel C. Phelps, 1952–1957

Robert L. Cram, 1953–1956

Maurice W. Small, 1955–1958, 1961–1967

Henry Steinfeld, 1956–1962

Robert G. Dillenback, 1957–1969

William J. Garsoe, 1958–1961

John A. Mitchell, 1962–1963, 1968–1971

Robert C. Robinson, 1963–1968

Harold J. Todd, 1964–1967

Richard F. Blanchard, 1967

J. Gordon Dodge, 1968–1970

L. Robert Porteous Jr., 1971

Harold M. Bragg, 1969–1972

Earle E. Doughty, 1967–1972

Harland E. Storey, 1969–1977, 1979–1981, 1991–2005

Mary Louise Smith, 1972–1975, 1977–1979

David R. Higgins Jr., 1972–1977

Dr. Kenneth Partyka, 1973–1981

Richard F. Blanchard, 1973–1977

Richard L. Walker, 1973–1976

Kenneth M. Hamilton, 1973–1979

E. Stephen Murray, 1976–1981, 1988–1993

Charles E. Googins, 1978–1979

William C. Stiles, 1978–1982

Robert C. Allen, 1978–1981

Wayne R. Webster, 1980–1981

Donna M. Damon, 1980–1982, 2002–2006

Alvin K. Ahlers, 1982–1984, 1987–1989

Robert B. Humphreys, 1982–1985, 1988–1993

Richard J. C. Andersen, 1982

Robert L. Cram, 1982–1987

Michael D. Cooper, 1982

Beverly S. Johnson, 1983–1985

Daniel W. Bates, 1983–1986

Richard G. Moon, 1983–1986

Daphne G. Warren, 1983–1987

Jeff Butland, 1985–1987

William Putnam, 1986–1988

David Williams, 1986–1991

Stephen Moriarty, 1987–1992, 1998–2012

Robert Harmon, 1988–1990

Gary Varney, 1989–1994

Susan McGinty, 1990–1994

George Small, 1992–1994

Philip Gleason, 1993–1998

Philip Allen, 1994–1997

John Lambert, 1994–2001

Peter Bingham, 1995–2002

Josiah Drummond, 1995–1997

James Phipps, 1995–2001

Mark Kuntz, 1998–2005

Jeffrey Porter, 1999–2011

Bill Stiles, 2002–2015

Michael Savasuk, 2003–2005

George Turner, 2006–2015

Shirley Storey-King, 2006–2015

Ronald Copp Jr., 2006–2015

Michael Perfetti, 2005–2013

Jon Jennings, 2012–2013

Thomas Gruber, 2011–2015

Mike Edes, 2013–2015

Peter Bingham Sr., 2013–2015

Index

Note: Page number(s) directly following "illus." indicate that a photograph or illustration is found on this page.

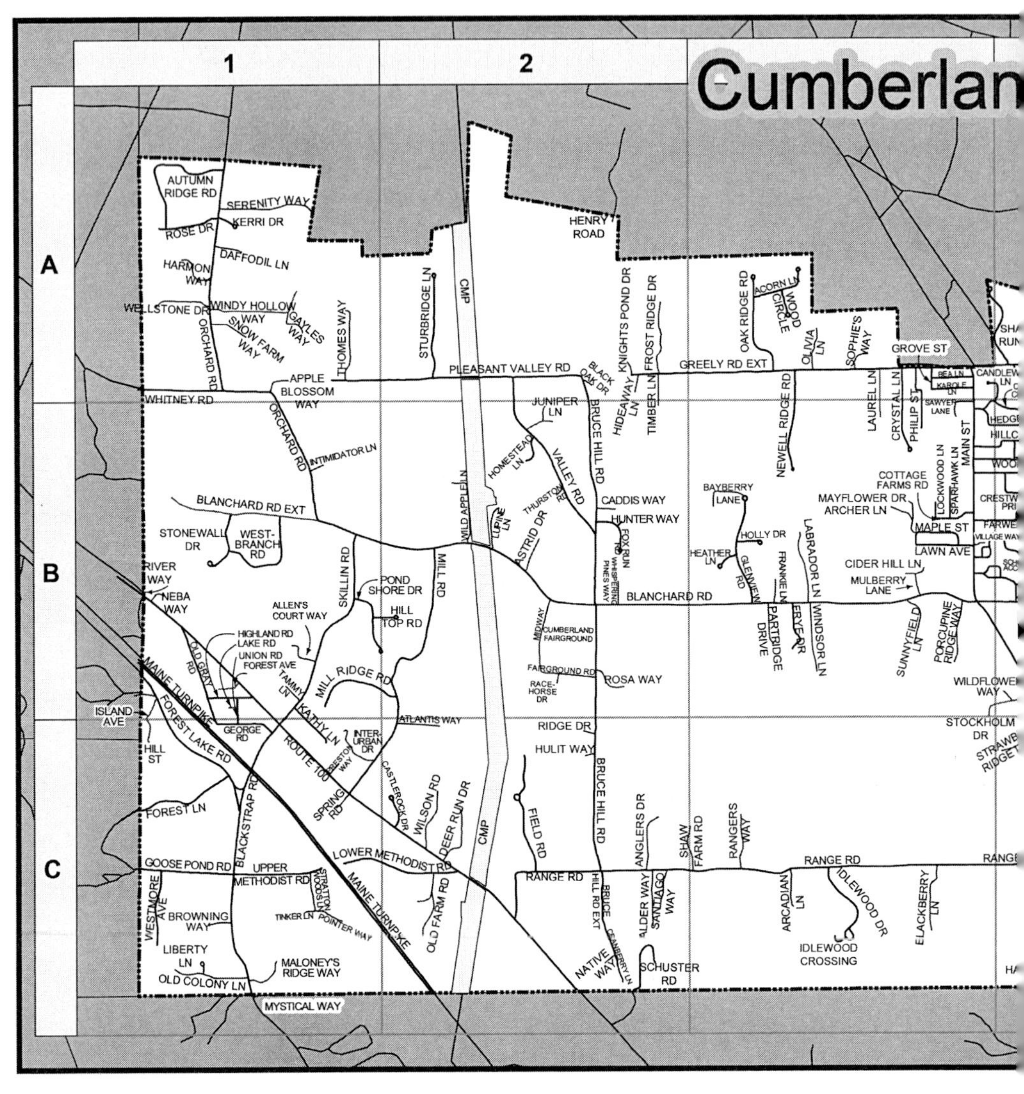

A
ACORN LN: A3
ALDER WAY: C2
ALLEN'S COURT WAY: B1
AMANDA'S WAY: B4
AMY LN: C6
ANDREA WAY: C5
ANGLERS DR: C2
APPLE BLOSSOM WAY: A1
ARCADIAN LN: C3
ARCHER LN: B3
ASPEN CREST RD: A4
ASTRID DR: B2
ATLANTIS WAY: C2
AUTUMN RIDGE RD: A1

B
BALSAM DR: B4
BAYBERRY LN: B3
BEA LN: A3
BIRCH LN: B6
BIRKDALE RD: C4
BITTERSWEET LN: B5
BLACK OAK DR: A2
BLACKBERRY LN: C3
BLACKSTRAP RD: C1
BLANCHARD RD: B1, B2, B3
BLUE HERON LN: B6
BRENTWOOD DR: A6
BROAD COVE WAY: A6
BROADMOOR DR: B4
BROOK RD: B5, C5
BROOKSIDE DR: A4, B4
BROWNING WAY: C1
BRUCE HILL RD: A2, B2, C2
BRUCE HILL RD EXT: C2
BUTTERWORTH FARM RD: B6

C
CADDIS WAY: B2
CANDLEWICK LN: A3, A4, B4
CARILLON RIDGE RD: B6
CAROL ST: B4
CARRIAGE RD: B6, C6
CASTLEROCK DR: C2
CATALPA LN: B4
CHANNEL ROCK LN: A6
CHESTNUT WAY: C6
CHETS WAY: B5
CIDER HILL LN: B3
CONCORD CIR: B6
CONIFER LEDGES: C7
CONIFER RIDGE RD: C6
COREY RD: C4
COTTAGE FARMS RD: B3
COUNTRY CHARM RD: B3, B4
COVESIDE DR: B6, C6
CRANBERRY LN: C2
CRESTWOOD RD: B4
CROSS RD: C4
CROSSING BROOK RD: B4
CRYSTAL LN: A3, B3
CUMBERLAND COMMON: B4
CUMBERLAND FAIRGROUND: B2
CUTTER WAY: C6

D
DAFFODIL LN: A1
DEANS WAY: C7
DEER RUN DR: C2
DOUGHTY RD: A4
DROWNE RD: B4

E
EAGLES WAY: C6
EBB TIDE DR: A6
EDES RD: B5
EVERGREEN LN: C6

F
FAIRGROUND RD: B2
FAIRWIND LN: A6
FALCON DR: C6
FARMS EDGE WAY: B5
FARWELL AVE: B3, B4
FERNE LN: A6
FIELD RD: C2
FLINTLOCK DR: B5
FORESIDE RD: A6, B6, C6, C7
FOREST LAKE RD: B1, C1
FOREST LN: C1
FOX RUN RD: B2
FRANKIE LN: B3
FRIAR LN: B6
FROST RIDGE DR: A2
FRYE DR: B3

G
GAYLES WAY: A1
GEORGE RD: C1
GLENVIEW RD: B3
GOOSE LEDGE RD: B6
GOOSE POND RD: C1
GRANITE RIDGE RD: C6
GREELY RD EXT: A2, A3
GREELY RD: A3, A4, A5, B5, B6
GROVE ST: A3

H
HALLMARK RD: B6
HARMON WAY: A1
HARRIS RD: B5, C5
HARVEST RIDGE RD: C4,C5
HAWTHORNE CT: B4
HAZELTINE DR: C4
HEATHER LN: B3
HEDGEROW DR: B3, B4
HEMLOCK DR: B4
HENRY RD: A2
HERITAGE LN: B6
HERON LN: C6
HIDEAWAY LN: A2
HIGHLAND RD: B1
HILL ST: B1
HILL TOP RD: B1, B2
HILLCREST DR: B3, B4
HILLSIDE AVE: A5, B5
HOLLY DR: B3
HOMESTEAD LN: B2
HOPES WAY: B5
HULIT WAY: C2
HUNTER WAY: B2

I
I295: A6, B6, C6
IDLEWOOD CROSSING: C3
IDLEWOOD DR: C3
INTERURBAN DR: C1
INTIMIDATOR LN: B1
ISLAND AVE: B1, C1
ISLAND POND RD: C6
ISLAND VIEW DR: A6

J
JAMES WAY: A4, B4
JESSIE'S LN: B6
JUNIPER LN: B2
JUSAM WAY: C4

K
KAROLE LN: A3
KATHY LN: B1, C1
KERRI DR: A1
KINGS HIGHWAY: B6
KNIGHTS POND DR: A2

L
LABRADOR LN: B3
LAKE RD: B1
LANEWOOD RD: C6, C7
LANTERN LN: C7
LAUREL LN: A3, B3
LAWN AVE: B3
LEDGE RD: B6
LIBERTY LN: C1
LINDA ST: B4
LINDEN CT: B4
LOCKWOOD LN: B3
LONG MEADOWS RD: C7
LONGVIEW ST: B4
LONGWOODS RD: C4, C5
LOWER METHODIST RD: C1, C2
LUPINE LN: B2

M
MACKWORTH LN: A6, B6
MAEVES WAY: C7
MAIN ST: A3, B3, B4, C4
MAINE TURNPIKE: B1, C1, C2
MALONEY'S RIDGE WAY: C1
MAPLE ST: B3
MARION CIR: B4
MARY LN: C7
MAURICE WAY: B4
MAYFLOWER DR: B3
MEADOW LN: B4
MEADOW WAY: B4
MEADOWVIEW RD: B4
MERE WIND DR: A4
MERION WAY: C4
MIDDLE RD: A6, B6, C6
MIDWAY: B2
MILL RD: B2, C1, C2
MILL RIDGE RD: B1, B2